Bibliography of

New Religious Movements

in Primal Societies

Volume 5

Latin America

Other Volumes

Bibliography of

New Religious Movements

in Primal Societies

Volume 5

Latin America

HAROLD W. TURNER

G.K. Hall & Co.

70 Lincoln Street • Boston, Mass.

First published 1991
by G.K. Hall & Co.
70 Lincoln Street
Boston, Massachusetts 02111

10 9 8 7 6 5 4 3 2 1

Library of Congress Cataloging-in-Publication Data

(Revised for vol. 5)
Turner, Harold W.
    Bibliography of new religious movements in primal societies.

    (v. 1: Bibliographies and guides in African Studies)
    Includes indexes.
    Contents: v. 1. Black Africa. – v. 2. North America – [etc.] –
    v. 5. Latin America.
    1. Religion – Bibliography. 2. Religion,
    Primitive – Bibliography.
    I. Bibliographies and guides in African Studies.
    Z7835.C86T87 1977 [BP603]   016.2   77-4732
    ISBN 0-8161-7929-8 (v. 5)   CIP

The paper used in this publication meets the minimum requirements of
American National Standard for Information Sciences – Permanence of
Paper for Printed Library Materials, ANSI Z39.48-1984. $\otimes^{tm}$

MANUFACTURED IN THE UNITED STATES OF AMERICA

For our youngest daughter, Carolyn,
in acknowledgment of her help in bringing
this series to a conclusion.

Contents

Contents

PARTICULAR MOVEMENTS

Preface

This fifth volume in the series has been the most difficult to compile because it lies less than any of the others within the expertise of the compiler. Special thanks are therefore offered to two members of the staff of the Centre for New Religious Movements at the Selly Oak Colleges who made the volume possible. First James Glick, with Mennonite industry and fluency in Spanish applied to the Latin American resources of the Library of Congress, enabled us to proceed with more confidence. Then his successor, Ralph Woodhall, S.J., enlarged his many language skills by adding Brazilian Portuguese to them especially for the work of the Centre and so made it possible to complete the volume.

Since many of the special names of movements and religious forms in Latin America are largely unfamiliar to anglophone readers, we have listed the more common of these terms in a special glossary before the indexes. In the annotations (but not, of course, in the original titles) we have anglicized them and omitted accents. We have also treated them all as proper nouns in the annotations, and therefore with initial capital letters; thus we show Santeria, Vodou, Candomble, etc.

Introduction

The Geographical-Cultural Area and Its Main Divisions

In this, Volume 5 of the series on New Religious Movements in Primal Societies, the term *Latin America* excludes the island world of the West Indies and those littoral countries with which this world is usually associated – Venezuela, Guyana, Surinam, and French Guiana. This area is only in part "Latin," both culturally and historically, and is usually given its own identity as "The Caribbean," to which the final volume of the series will be devoted. At the same time this division has to be modified by the development of a nongeographic category of "Afro-American" for items that refer in a more general way to movements among the black population in any part of this whole region, and for items that span the two areas, the Caribbean and Latin America. Otherwise the latter area is regarded in the usual way as commencing with central Mexico (northern Mexico is included in Volume 2, North America) and covering the rest of Central America, and South America apart from the northeast littoral described above.

The main divisions of this volume are therefore Afro-American, Central America, and South America, followed by Particular Movements, under which there is one section, on Umbanda in and from Brazil.

A Variety of Populations and Their Movements

The whole region differs from other parts of the world in the complexity of the populations and movements to which the term "primal" may in some sense be applied. There are at least three foci, and the boundaries associated with them are difficult to determine. There is first the Amerindian population, the smallest in number and the most like the tribal populations involved elsewhere in this world field. Estimates suggest they comprise perhaps 11 percent of the population, or less than 30 million people. They are unevenly distributed, being rare at the southern end of the continent and only a small minority in Brazil (perhaps only 0.1%) but forming a majority of the population in Guatemala and Bolivia and nearly one half in Peru and Ecuador. But the term *Indian* varies according to whether the definition is based on racial origin, on contemporary culture, or on social class, and again on whether the group concerned maintains a self-sufficient tribal style of life (perhaps about 5 million in some 600 tribes), consists of peasant agriculturalists (the great majority), or has migrated to the large cities. No attempt is made to apply these possible distinctions here, and so the term is used in a wide sense.

The largest group consists of people of African descent, the Afro-Americans, whose ancestors were forcibly taken as slaves to the New World. They are therefore removed from their original primal religious milieu and their religious developments have been shaped by the traumatic experiences of transportation and slavery, and by interaction in various measures with the Indian and white populations. Their religious movements will be documented chiefly in the sections on Afro-American, and especially on Brazil where "Afro-Brazilian" movements have long flourished; but there will be some examples in various other countries.

The boundaries for our materials are complicated by the existence of mixed groups: European-Amerindian variously known as *mestizos* (South American) or *ladinos* (Central America), and European-Negro or *mulattos*, together with others combining Amerindian-Negro or all three sources. These blendings may be biological and/or cultural, and some of their religious movements are included here as forms of folk-syncretisms which include influences from the primal African or Amerindian religions. Some elements may derive from European folk Catholicism which has its own affinities with primal religions. Then again there is the increasing category of "spiritist" movements which add to the above three strands further influences from European Spiritualism, and which are found especially in Brazil as Umbanda, etc.

Folk Catholicism, or Christo-paganism as it has been called in Central America, is not as such within our agenda. It is, however, impossible to draw a boundary between popular Catholicism and movements such as the Afro-Brazilian and spiritist cults when each influences the other and the same people may participate in both Catholic and other practices. Similarly it is hard to distinguish the religious from the folklorish in the area of legends, rites, dances, songs and festivals. We have therefore included a few items on festivals and cults of saints, especially if there seems to be an Indian or African influence, by regarding them loosely as independent religious movements; see the item by J. Liscano (entry 31, in Latin America: General) on these festivals, and especially on their syncretistic forms.

Consequent upon the rapid spread of Pentecostal forms of Christianity since the mid-century there is now emerging what might be called a Folk Pentecostalism that links in to the primal religious traditions. While Pentecostalism as such is not our concern some of the popular forms it takes are included, and an item by L. Margolies (entry 34) is included in Latin America: General as an introduction to this field.

The harsh treatment meted out to both Indians and Africans produced slave insurrections and Indian political and military revolts that usually had some religious dimension. The extensive literature on this subject usually focuses on the political and military aspects, and the religious features are dealt with only briefly. As introductory items see A. Q. Obregón (entry 38) and N. Wachtel (entry 46, with English translation), both in Latin America: General. The literature on the movements that have been studied as primarily religious will be readily identified in the various countries.

One special form of movement is the religious fraternity or "cofradia" found among both Indians and blacks from an early stage. They were similar to the brotherhoods or "hermandades" among the ladinos, as in Spain today, and also akin to the popular "pious associations" among African Catholics. These were semi-independent of the Church system, gave an identity and stability to the group concerned, and often involved a degree of syncretism between the Christian and the primal religious elements. See G. M. Foster (entry 25) and J. Swetnam (entry 45) in Latin America: General, and S. L. Orellana (entry 173) in Guatemala.

Millennial or messianic movements have occurred among the Indians, with notable examples among the Guarani people from precontact times, but not among the black population. The most famous messianic movements have appeared within the last century among the mestizo or near-white rural Catholic populations, especially of the poor and arid regions of northeast Brazil, and are not within our agenda. But see further in the introductory note to the next section, Latin America: Theory.

Latin America: Theory

This section includes items of a more theoretical nature concerning Latin America (from central Mexico to Argentina) but not the Caribbean as such. The items often refer to particular movements or areas for illustration, as with R. Bastide and the Afro-Brazilian movements in which he has specialized. See Bastide (entry 4), and F. Morin (entry 35) for a discussion of Bastide's methodology and its new conception of the anthropology of religion.

For introductory study the following may be suggested: R. Bastide (entry 4), R. Benedict (entry 5), G. M. Foster (entry 9) and M. I. Pereira de Queiroz (entry 308). For special themes see M. Posern-Zielinska and A. Posern-Zielinski's discussion of charismatic leaders across both North and South American movements (entry 12). On messianism see M. I. Pereira de Queiroz, (entry 13); her large work, *O Messianismo – no Brasil e no mundo* has more theoretical sections on messianism among the "primitivos" but not on Latin America as such – it concentrates on Brazil (where we deal with it). On messianism, see in Latin America: General, R. Bastide (entry 20) and A. Q. Obregón (entry 38). On syncretism see R. Bastide (entry 21). On Pentecostalism see L. Margolies (entry 34).

Other relevant items will be found in the South America: Theory section, and especially there in B. Ertle (entry 291). See also G. E. Simpson (entry 15). Further relevant items will be found in the Theory sections that introduce each of the other continents or major regions. There is, of course, much theoretical material attached to many particular local or individual movement studies. The items placed in this Theory section are primarily theoretical, but they may also contain more concrete studies.

1 Bastide, Roger. "Mémoire collective et sociologie du bricolage." *L'Année Sociologique*, 3d ser. 21 (1970): 65-108.

Provides a theoretical analysis as a background to Afro-Brazilian cults; see exposition by R. Ortiz (entry 1365), pp. 92-94.

2 Bastide, Roger. *Le prochain et le lointain*. Collection Genèse. Paris: Éditions Cujas, 1970, 302 pp.
A collection of articles and unpublished papers on race relations, acculturation, messianism, etc.; most are included elsewhere in this bibliography.

3 Bastide, Roger. "Réflexions sans titre autour d'une des formes de la spiritualité africaine." *Présence Africaine* 17-18 [i.e., 18-19], February-March 1958: 9-16.
African religious mysticism, as in Brazilian cults, is a major form and not inferior to Hindu, Christian, or Islamic forms.

4 Bastide, Roger. "Le sacré sauvage." In *Le besoin religieux: Rencontres internationales de Genève, 1973*. Neuchâtel: La Baconnière, 1974, pp. 123-71 (texts and discussions). Reprinted in *Le sacré sauvage et autres essais*. Paris: Payot, 1975, pp. 214-36.
A theoretical discussion of trance and possession and the various controls usually operative; pp. 219-25, illustrative reference to Afro-Brazilian cults, Macumba and Umbanda.

5 Benedict, Ruth. "Two patterns of Indian acculturation." *American Anthropologist* 45, no. 2 (1943): 207-12.
The two kinds of response are associated with "high cultures" (which accepted the new masters, as in Mexico and Peru, where the number of Indians remains high and they became peons, etc.) and with simpler societies (which were wiped out as useless, or retreated to Amazonia, etc.), so that Argentina, Uruguay, and Costa Rica are almost all white now, and Brazil has few Indians. Explanation in terms of degrees of technology is replaced by the kind of social and political system. High cultures were *used* to masters, centralization, professional armies, public labor (as the simpler cultures were not), and could replace their own ruling class with the Spaniards, instead of rebelling en bloc, as in simpler societies.

6 Brintnall, Douglas Edgar. "Revolt against the dead: Religious change in the western highlands of Guatemala." Ph.D. dissertation (anthropology), Columbia University, 1974, 299 pp.
The breakdown of a cult of the dead and its associated political system, and replacement by Catholic or Protestant affiliation – religious change as rooted in the modernization process.

7 Crumrine, N. Ross. "Folk drama in Latin America: A ritual type characterized by social group unification and cultural fusion." *Canadian Journal of Latin American Studies*, n.s. 6, no. 12 (1981): 103-25.

Based on the Mayo Easter ceremony (N.W. Mexico), the Catacos Holy Week drama (northern Peru), and Holy Week in Marinduque (a Philippines island province).

8 Dussel, Enrique. "Volksreligiosität in Lateinamerika, grundlegende hypothesen." *Neue Zeitschrift für Missionswissenschaft* 42, no. 1 (1986): 1-12.

9 Foster, George McClelland. *Culture and conquest: America's Spanish heritage.* Viking Fund Publications in Anthropology, no. 27. Chicago: Quadrangle Books, 1960, 272 pp.

Especially chaps. 1, 2, 17, on theory of acculturation.

10 Laplantine, François. *Les trois voix de l'imaginaire: Le messianisme, la possession, et l'utopie. Étude psychiatrique.* Collection "JE." Paris: Éditions Universitaires, 1974, 256 pp.

The imagination treated as an important factor in the causes of millennialism; chap. 6 (pp. 109-48), on messianism in general, is the section most relevant to Latin America.

11 Padilla, Raúl N. "El sincretismo religioso en hispanoamerica." *Certeza* (Buenos Aires), no. 74 [19] (July-September 1979): 46-49, illus.

The features of Spanish Catholicism readily amenable to "Christo-paganism," and "popular religiosity," including spiritual healers, with Gregorio Hernandez of Venezuela as example leading to a new cult.

12 Posern-Zielinska, Miroslawa, and Posern-Zielinski, Aleksander. "Charismatic leader in American Indian socio-religious movements." *Etnologia Polona* 2 (1976): 63-85.

Covers North and Latin American Indian leaders.

13 Queiroz, Maria Isaura Pereira de. "Aspectos gerais do messianismo." *Revista de Antropologia* (São Paulo) 8, no. 1 (1960): 63-76.

A general account of messianism, prophets, etc., with special reference to Vittorio Lanternari's, "Fermenti religiosi e profezie di libertà dei popoli coloniali. *Nuovi Argomenti* (Rome) 37 (1959): 54-92.

14 Queiroz, M[aria] I[saura] Pereira de. "Principe de participation et principe de coupure: La contribution de Roger Bastide à leur

définition sociologique." *Archives de Sciences Sociales des Religions*, no. 47 [1] (January-March 1979): 147-57.

15 Simpson, G[eorge] E[aton]. "The psychological factor in Caribbean cults." In *Black religions in the New World*. New York: Columbia University Press, 1978, pp. 130-40, and notes pp. 342-45.
   Spirit possession and healing.

16 Steward, Julian H. "Acculturation studies in Latin America: Some needs and problems." *American Anthropologist* 45, no. 2 (1943): 198-204; pp. 204-206, discussion by Frank Tannenbaum.

17 Wachtel, Nathan. "La vision des vaincus: La conquête espagnole dans le folklore indigène." *Annales: Economies, Sociétés, Civilisations* (Paris) 22, no. 3 (1967): 554-85.
   Memories of the Spanish invasion have survived more vividly in the Andes than in Mesoamerica, and this corresponds with "messianic" movements present in the former, but rarer in the latter area.

Latin America: General

The region is so vast and so varied in the relevant populations and movements that there is almost no literature of any substance that is really comprehensive. World surveys such as those of V. Lanternari, *The religions of the oppressed* (London: MacGibbon & Kee, 1963), G. Guariglia, *Prophetismus und Heilserwartungs-Bewegungen....* (Vienna: F. Berger, 1959), or B. R. Wilson, *Magic and the millennium* (London: Heinemann Educational Books; New York: Harper & Row, 1973) do not offer comprehensive surveys but deal with particular areas or movements. The following, however, may provide a more general introduction: J. J. Considine (entry 23), E. Willems (entry 47) and B. Kloppenburg (entry 28).

This section of course has to include those items that span more than one country when these countries do not both lie within either Central or South America – see D. Gow (entry 26) on Peru and Mexico. General surveys covering either Central or South America, which are more feasible, will be found in those sections below, and general treatment of the black dimension will be found in the section on Afro-American movements.

A reminder may be given that the themes of messianism, syncretism, Pentecostalism, and folk religion have already been referred to in the general introductory notes to this whole region and in the notes to the Latin America: Theory section.

18 Barabas, Alicia M[abel]. "Secular and religious ethnic movements in Latin America: An approach towards the creation of an Indian utopia." *América Indígena* (Mexico) 46, no. 21 (1986): 495-529.

19 Bastián, Jean Pierre, ed. "Sectas y nuevos movimientos religioses." *Cristianismo y Sociedad* (Buenos Aires) 25, no. 3 (1987): 9-114.

20 Bastide, Roger. "Les mythes politiques nationaux de l'Amérique latine." *Cahiers Internationaux de Sociologie*, n.s., no. 33 [9, no. 2] (1962): 75-84. Reprint. "Messianisme et nationalisme (en Amérique latine)." In *Le prochain et le lointain*. Paris: Cujas, 1970, pp. 287-96.

Messianism as precursor of nationalism, with differences in Portuguese and Spanish forms; messianism found among the white colonial class rather than among Africans or Indians.

21 Bastide, Roger. "Le syncrétisme mystique en Amérique latine." *Bulletin Saint Jean-Baptiste* 5, no. 4 (1965). Reprinted in *Le prochain et le lointain*. Paris: Cujas, 1970, pp. 237-41.

22 Campbell, Leon G. "Native rebellions in colonial Spanish America." In *Past and present in the Americas*, edited by J. Lynch. Proceedings, 44th International Congress of Americanists. Manchester: Manchester University Press, 1984, pp. 45-47.

On the five papers relevant to this subject.

23 Considine, John J[oseph], ed. *The religious dimension in the new Latin America*. Notre Dame, Ind.: Fides Publishers, 1966, 238 pp.

See also W. Jiménez-Moreno, "Popular religious expression in Latin America" (entry 220), W. J. Price, "The Costumbre . . ." (entry 249), and B. Kloppenburg, "The prevalence of spiritism in Brazil" (entry 714).

24 Crapanzano, Vincent, and Garrison, Vivian, eds. *Case studies in spirit possession*. New York and London: John Wiley & Sons, 1977, xvi + 457 pp., illus.

See E. Pressel, "Negative spirit possession . . ." (entry 1372), and J. D. Koss, "Spirits as socializing agents . . ." and V. Garrison, "The 'Puerto Rican syndrome' in psychiatry and *Espiritismo*" under Puerto Rico in vol. 6 of this series, *The Caribbean*.

25 Foster, George M[cClelland]. "Cofradía and compadrazgo in Spain and South America." *Southwestern Journal of Anthropology* 9, no. 1 (1953): 1-28.

Compares religious brotherhoods in Spain and Latin America—their functions as suited to their situations.

26 Gow, David D[rummond]. "Simbolo y protesta: Movimientos redentores en Chiapas y en los Andes peruanos." *América Indígena* 39, no. 1 (1979): 47-80.

Mexican revolts: Tzeltal, 1712, and Tzotzil, 1868-70; Peruvian movements: Taqui Onqoy, 1565, and St. John, 1811 – analysis and comparison in relation to the history and culture of each area.

27 Hurtado-Lopez, Juan Manuel. "Profetismo en America latina." *Servir*, no. 107 [20] (1984): 361-74.

28 Kloppenburg, Boaventura. "Die Nicht-Katholiken in Latein-amerika." *Ordensnachrichten* (Vienna) 20, no. 5 (1981): 348-67.
Background survey from a sympathetic Catholic viewpoint; includes Christian "sects," Muslims, Jews, and Spiritism.

29 LaBarre, Weston. *Ghost Dance: Origins of religion*. Garden City, N.Y.: Doubleday & Co., 1970, 677 pp.
See vol. 2 in this series, *North America*, entry no. 54, for general comments. On specific movements see index "cult leaders" and especially pp. 202-3, the Tupi; pp. 261-62, Talking Cross; pp. 261-62, etc., Maria Candelaria; pp. 261, 265, 275, 281, Ras Tafari.

30 Lembke, Ingo. *Christentum unter den Bedingungen Lateinamerika: Die Katholische Kirche vor den Problemen der Abhängigkeit und Unterentwicklung*. Bern and Frankfurt am Main: Herbert Lang & Peter Lang, 1975, 281 pp.
Pp. 61-64, Spiritism.

31 Liscano, Juan. "The feast of St. John." *Américas* (Washington, D.C.) 8, no. 5 (1956): 14-19.
Discusses the festival in Latin America, but especially in its Afro-Catholic syncretic forms, as in Haiti.

32 Mackay, John A. *The other Spanish Christ: A study in the spiritual history of Spain and South America*. London: Student Christian Movement Press, 1932, 288 pp.
Pp. 177-80, Spiritism.

33 Mahn-Lot, Marianne. "Millénarisme et mission au Nouveau Monde: À propos d'un livre récent." *Revue Historique*, no. 504 [248] (1972): 323-32.
A review article on *The millennial kingdom of the Franciscans in the New World*, by J. L. Phelan, 2d ed. (Berkeley: University of California Press, 1970), 179 pp.

34 Margolies, Luise. "The paradoxical growth of Pentecostalism." In *Perspectives on Pentecostalism*, edited by S. D. Glazier. Washington, D.C.: University Press of America, 1980, pp. 1-5.
On the volume and the variety of interpretations of this new phenomenon in relation to social change and modernization.

35 Morin, Françoise. "Roger Bastide ou l'anthropologie des gouffres." *Archives de Sciences Sociales des Religions*, no. 40 [20, no. 2] (1975): 99-106.
Bastide's personal history in relation to the development of a methodology appropriate to the understanding of Afro-Brazilian cults, which led him beyond the common explanations in terms of "survivals" and "syncretisms," and finally to a new conception of anthropology of religion.

36 Nida, Eugene A. *Understanding Latin Americans with special reference to religious values and movements*. South Pasadena, Calif.: William Carey Library, 1974, 163 pp.
Pp. 137-48, indigenous churches in Latin America.

37 Nodal, Roberto A. "El sincretismo afrocatólico en Cuba y Brasil." *Anuario Científico* (San Pedro de Macoris, Dominican Republic, Universidade Central del Este) 3, no. 3 (1978): 207-22. Reprinted in *Estudos Ibero-Americanos* (Pôrto Alegre) 5, no. 2 (1979): 207-18.
Includes discussion of Santeria and Candomble.

38 Obregón, Aníbal Quijano. "Los movimientos campesinos contemporáneos en Latinoamérica." *Revista Mexicana de Sociología* 28, no. 3 (1966): 603-63.
Pp. 606-9 (and notes p. 660), movements with millennial or messianic aspects.

39 Prien, Hans-Jürgen. "Volksfrömmigkeit in Lateinamerika: Uberlegungen von der Kirchengeschichte her." *Neue Zeitschrift für Missionswissenschaft* 42, no. 1 (1986): 28-43.

40 Promper, Werner. *Priesternot in Lateinamerika*. Louvain, Belgium: Latein-Amerika-Kolleg der Katholischen Universität, 1965, 317 pp.
Pp. 177-80, 214-16, Spiritism and syncretism.

41 Queiroz, Maria Isaura Pereira de. "Die Teilnahme des brasilienischen Negers an messianischen Bewegungen und das Problem der Marginalisierung." In *Klassengesellschaft und Rassismus: Zur*

Marginalisierung der Afroamerikaner in Lateinamerika, edited by Jürgen Gräbener. Interdisziplinäre Studien, 4. Düsseldorf: Bertelsmann Universitäts-verlag, 1971, chap. 3.

42 Read, William R.; Monterroso, Victor M.; and Johnson, Harmon A[lden]. *Latin American Church growth*. Grand Rapids, Mich.: William B. Eerdmans, 1969, 421 pp.
Pp. 247-54, the growth of other religions.

43 Roman Catholic Church. Ecumenical Conference of CLAI, CCC, and the Ecuadoran Bishops' Conference. "New religious movements (Sects). Cuenca, Ecuador, 04-10.11-.1986." *Latinamerica Press*, no. 45 [18] (1986): 3ff., 8. Reprinted in *Theology in Context* 4, no. 2 (1987): 125-26.
Includes both older "sects" such as Mormons and Jehovah's Witnesses and newer ones such as Hare Krishna, Divine Light Mission, and Unification Church; therefore marginally relevant.

44 Stockwell, Eugene. "NRMs in Latin America and the Caribbean." *Ecumenical Press Service* 53, no. 37 (6-20 December 1986), item 86.12.35.

45 Swetnam, John. "Class-based and community-based ritual organization in Latin America." *Ethnology* 17, no. 4 (1978): 425-38.
Ladino religious fraternities (*hermandades*) as "class-based" as compared to Indian fraternities (*cofradías*) which are "community-based"; especially pp. 423, 434-37.

46 Wachtel, Nathan. *La vision des vaincus: Les Indiens du Pérou devant la conquête espagnole*. Paris: Gallimard, 1971, 395 pp., illus., maps, bib. English translation. *The vision of the vanquished: The Spanish conquest of Peru through Indian eyes, 1530-70*. Hassocks, Sussex: Harvester Press, 1977, 328 pp., illus.
Pp. 233-38, continuing *huaca* cults, and syncretisms; Part 3 (pp. 255-99), Revolts: pp. 255-63, 266, revolt of Manco Inca, and revival of Inca religion; pp. 269-76 (and index), Taqui Ongo, a nonviolent millennial movement against the Spanish presence (with archival references and extracts–a good account); pp. 278-82, Mixton revolt in Mexico of 1541-42 as a millennial movement adopting violence, and compared with Taqui Ongo; pp. 289-96, Araucan revolt in Chile, late sixteenth century, and supporting neo-primal religious development (p. 294).

47 Willems, Emílio. *Latin American culture: An anthropological synthesis*. New York: Harper & Row, 1975, 423 pp. (bib., pp. 395-410.)
  Pp. 370-75, religion–the influence of Spiritualism and African cults.

Afro-American

This category includes the more general discussion of the new religious movements among the black peoples of African descent in the Caribbean and Latin American regions as distinct from the more particular studies related to individual countries. It also contains discussions of these religious forms in more than one country, such as P. Verger (entries 147 and 148) and R. A. Nodal (entry 113) on Brazil and Cuba.

There is a problem in defining the boundaries of "Afro-American" for the purposes of this collection. In principle it includes the religions of the Negro, or black, peoples in the New World, and hence of black religion in the United States. This subject already has its own organized resources and in any case is too vast for inclusion here. In addition, the religious life of United States black peoples is a world of its own, the result of religious interaction under special historical and social conditions over a long period. Just as African independent churches are beginning to leave the category of new religious movements and to join the mainstream of ordinary Christian history, so also Negro religion in the United States may be regarded as better approached from this perspective. Even the "new religions" such as that of Father Devine should be seen in this context. There are, however, a few instances of deliberate revivals of traditional or primal African religions, and a Yoruba example has been included here; see C. M. Hunt (entry 101) on Oyotunji Village, and the review by T. O. Beidelman (entry 68); J. L. Truluck (entry 146); and J. G. Melton (entry 110), which also refers to Afro-American influences from the Caribbean among black peoples of the United States. On the other hand, much of the material in this Afro-American section is also relevant to the question of African influences and forms as found in Negro religion in the United States.

Other problems concerning the boundary of the Afro-American materials arise in connection with the communities that have arisen from

11

slave revolts or escapes such as the Maroons in eastern Jamaica and the Bush Negroes in Surinam. The religious dimensions of these communities doubtfully qualify as a "new religious movement" born from interaction with Christianity or any other faith, and yet such new influences are evident and it would be somewhat arbitrary to exclude them. They are therefore found below in their respective countries. A query might also be raised concerning Vodou, or the popular religion of Haiti, but again exclusion would be unfortunate, and the fact that it is included may help to dispel common derogatory attitudes towards a most important religious form; most Vodou materials will, of course, be found in the relevant country section, Haiti. Brazil also presents problems insofar as the African-related movements share in the rise and the content of Macumba and Umbanda and the various forms of Spiritism which also embrace large sections of the mestizo and the white populations. Of necessity the materials can only touch on these areas, but to ignore them would be arbitrary.

It should be remembered that many peoples of African descent have not lived in their own original tribal groups or cultures for several centuries; it is therefore dangerous to assume that the term "African" in the American context can be interpreted simply by reference to either earlier or contemporary Africa. Nor can the concept of colonialism be interpreted identically on the two sides of the Atlantic, and not only because it was interwoven with slavery in the New World. It has been suggested that the religious encounter in the latter occurred in a noncrisis situation, as compared with Africa: see J. Roback (p. 263, no. 27) in the Guyana section of volume 6, and in this section H.-A. Steger (entry 142, with English summary at the end) who discusses the nonrevolutionary religions as explanatory of the absence of messianism.

Attention may be drawn to the following items in this section as offering some general survey or introduction: H. Aguessy (entry 50) on survival by religious syntheses; W. R. Bascom (entry 54) on the wide influence of Yoruba cults; R. Bastide's book on the whole subject (entry 55, with English translation), and his encyclopaedia article (entry 56); J. Gräbener (entry 89); M. J. Herskovits (entry 90) on the transposition of African gods into Catholic saints; E. A. Nida (entry 112) for a simple account of African influence; D. Richards (entry 136) on African retentions; G. E. Simpson (entry 141) for extracts from the major book by a pioneer in this field; for a review of this book and also of the other general survey, R. Bastide, *The African religions of Brazil* (entry 431), see L. G. Desmangles (entry 79); I. Pereda Valdés (entry 119) on rituals, festivals and songs; M. Gonzalez-Wippler (entry 88) appears to be on Cuban Santeria but is a more general account.

S. S. Walker (entry 149) on possession as the basic religious act common to black religion in the United States, the Caribbean and Latin

America; D. Beckmann (entries 66 and 67) traces trance and possession in American Pentecostalism, both black and white, back to African origins; M. J. Herskovits (entry 99) discusses the mutual influence of whites and blacks in this matter.

How far the influence of Marcus Garvey, the Jamaican active in the United States in a Back-to-Africa movement, was religious, and therefore relevant to Rastafarianism and to other religious developments in the Caribbean and even among African independent churches, is examined in R. K. Burkett (entry 73); see also J. H. Clarke (entry 76).

For more theoretical material, N. E. Whitten and J. Szwed (entry 153) offer a critique of anthropological approaches since M. J. Herskovits, many of whose own items have a methodological concern. Similarly, T. O. Ranger (entry 135) discusses recent developments in African historiography and their relevance for Afro-American studies.

48 Acosta Saignes, Miguel. *Elementos indígenas y africanos en la formación de la cultura venezolana.* Caracas: Instituto de Filosofía, Facultad de Humanidades y Educación, Universidad Central de Venezuela, [1955?], 33 pp.

49 Acquaviva, Marcus Cláudio. *Vodu. Religião o magia negra no Haiti e no Brasil.* 2d ed. São Paulo: Aquarius Editora e Distribuidora de Livros, 1977, 90 pp., illus.

50 Aguessy, Honorat. "Les dimensions spirituelles: Religions traditionelles africaines." *Présence Africaine*, nos. 117-18 (1981), pp. 138-48.
On the strength and endurance of African primal religions in Cuba, Haiti, Venezuela, Martinique, Guadaloupe and Brazil, enabling the slave population to survive by synthesis of African and Christian resources.

51 Anderson, John Q. "The New Orleans Voodoo, ritual dance, and its twentieth century survivals." *Southern Folklore Quarterly* 24, no. 2 (1960): 135-43.

52 Bascom, William [Russell]. "Oba's ear: A Yoruba myth in Cuba and Brazil." In *African folklore in the new world*, edited by D. J. Crowley. Research in African Literature 8, no. 2. Austin: University of Texas Press, 1977, pp. 3-19.
A Yoruba myth preserved remarkably intact.

13

53 Bascom, William [Russell]. "La religion africaine au Nouveau Monde." In *Les religions africaines traditionelles*. Recontres Internationales de Bouaké, Ivory Coast, 1962. Paris: Éditions du Seuil, 1965, pp. 119-37.

54 Bascom, William R[ussell]. *Shango in the New World*. Occasional Publication. Austin: University of Texas African and Afro-American Research Institute, 1972, 23 pp., illus.
    The place of Shango in Candomble, Macumba, Batuque, and Umbanda, and in various Brazilian cities; also in relation to Lucumi and Santeria, and (p. 20) the latter's post-Castro spread to cities in U.S. and elsewhere in the Caribbean.

55 Bastide, Roger. *Les Amériques noires: Les civilisations africaines dans le Nouveau Monde*. Paris: Payot, 1967, 236 pp. Spanish translation. *Las Américas negras: Las civilizaciones africanes en el Nuevo Mundo*. Madrid: Aliazo Editorial, 1969, 225 pp. English translation. *African civilizations in the New World*. London: C. Hurst; New York: Harper & Row, 1971, 232 pp.
    The Negro minority communities in Latin American countries have remained largely unchanged despite urbanization, etc. Chap. 7 (pp. 152-70, English translation) on syncretism and amalgamation between religions.

56 Bastide, Roger. "Les cultes afro-américains." In *Histoire des Religions*, edited by H.-C. Puech. Encyclopédie de la Pléiade, vol. 3. Paris: Gallimard, 1976, pp. 1027-50.
    The sociology, history, transformations and common characteristics of Vodou, Santeria, Obeah-religion, Maroons' religion, Candomble, and Batuque.

57 Bastide, Roger. "Dans les Amériques noires: Afrique ou Europe?" *Annales: Economies, Sociétés, Civilisations* (Paris) 3, no. 4 (1948): 409-26.

58 Bastide, Roger. "La divination chez les Afro-Américains." In *La divination: Études recueillies par André Caquot et Marcel Leibovici*, edited by A. Caquot and M. Leibovici. Vol. 2. Paris: Presses Universitaires de France, 1968, pp. 393-427.
    Includes, pp. 396-403, the blacks of Surinam and French Guiana; p. 403, syncretist cults – Convince, Angel men, Bedwardites; dreams; pp. 404-8, Black Caribs; pp. 408-12, Afro-Cubans; pp. 413-15, Afro-Brazilians; pp. 451-17, Trinidad; pp. 417-20, Vodou (Haiti); pp. 420-21, New Orleans Vodou; pp. 421-24, other blacks; pp. 424-27, conclusions.

59 B[astide], R[oger]. "Négro-Américaines (Religions)." In *Encyclopaedia Universalis*. Vol. 11. Paris: Encyclopaedia Universalis France, 1971, pp. 644-45, bib.

60 Bastide, Roger. "The present status of Afro-American research in Latin America." *Daedalus* 103 (Spring 1974): 118-19.

61 Bastide, Roger. "Religiões africanas, estruturas da civilização." *Afro-Asia* (Salvador), nos. 6-7 (June-December 1968), pp. 5-16; English and French summaries.

62 Bastide, Roger. *Le rêve, la transe, et la folie*. Paris: Flammarion, 1972, 263 pp.
    Pp. 11-96, discipline and spontaneity in Afro-American possession cults (Vodou, Shango, etc.); pp. 157-82, mental illness among blacks in South America (with bib. pp. 180-82); pp. 183-219, introduction to some Afro-Brazilian complexes – concerning color, inferiority, etc.

63 Bastide, Roger. "Syncretism and amalgamation between religions." In *African civilizations in the New World*. London: C. Hurst, 1971, pp. 152-70.

64 Bastide, Roger. "La théorie de la réincarnation chez les Afro-Américains." In *Réincarnation et vie mystique en Afrique noire*, edited by D. Zahan. Paris: Presses Universitaires de France, 1965, pp. 9-29.

65 Becco, Horacio Jorge. "Lexicografía religiosa de los Afroamericanos." *Boletín de la Academia Argentina de Letras*, no. 77 [20] (July-September 1951): 305-38.

66 Beckmann, David M. "Black indigenous churches." *Afro-American Studies* 3 (1975): 245-53, bib.
    Independent black churches in Africa, the West Indies, and the U.S.; their history, forms, and theology.

67 Beckmann, David M. "Trance: From Africa to Pentecostalism." *Concordia Theological Monthly* 45, no. 1 (1974): 11-26.
    Trance, which originated in African religions, was given Christian legitimation in the Second Great Awakening in the U.S. (early nineteenth century) and later in the Azuza Street, Los Angeles, revival; then it was carried back to Africa by missionaries.

68 Beidelman, Thomas Owen. Review of *Oyotunji village: The Yoruba movement in America*, by C. M. Hunt (entry 101). *Anthropos* 77, nos. 1-2 (1982): 299-300.
A community in South Carolina, established in the 1960s, and influenced by Vodou and Santeria.

69 Beltran, Luis. "L'héritage dans les pays hispano-américains." *Revue Congolaise des Sciences Humaines*, 3 July 1971, pp. 39-50; English summary.
The African imprint as important in formation of national identity, especially through folklore, language and religion.

70 Bennett, Louise. "Jamaica traditions of African origins." *Caribe* 5, no. 2 (1981): 32-37, illus.

71 Betsch, Johnnetta. "The possession pattern in traditional West African and New World Negro cultures." M.A. thesis, Northwestern University (Evanston), [pre-1973].

72 Bourguignon, Erika. "Importante papel de las mujeres en los cultos afroamericanos." *Montalban* (Caracas, Universidad Catolica Andrés Bello), no. 4 (1975), pp. 423-38.

73 Burkett, Randall K[eith]. *Garveyism as a religious movement: The institutionalism of a black civil religion*. ATLA Monograph Series, no. 13. Metuchen, N.J.: Scarecrow Press; American Theological Library Association, 1978, 216 pp.
Introduction, pp. 1-14; pp. 71-110, "Sect or civil religion: the debate with George Alexander McGuire."

74 Campbell, Mavis. "African religion and resistance in the Caribbean under slavery." Paper, 44th International Congress of Americanists, Manchester, 1982. Digest in *Abstracts of the Congress*. Manchester, 1982, p. 393.

75 *Casa de las Américas* (Havana), nos. 36-37 [6] (May-August 1966).
Special theme: "Africa en América," with articles on Afroamerican themes, located in their appropriate areas in vols. 5 and 6 of this series; see entry 84.

76 Clarke, John Henrik, ed. *Marcus Garvey and the vision of Africa*. New York: Random House, Vintage Books, 1974, xxxii + 496 pp.

One of the important new studies of Garvey, but little on religion. Pp. 318-82, Garvey's belief in the God of Africa and the Black Race.

77 Contee, Clarence G. "Ethiopia and the Pan-African movement before 1945." *Black World* 21, no. 4 (February 1972).

78 D'Anna, Andrea. *Le religioni afroamericane.* Quaderni Nigrizia – Seconde Serie. Bologna: Editrice Nigrizia, 1972, 133 pp.
     Pp. 7-22, Umbanda; pp. 25-33, Bush Negroes of Surinam and Guiana; pp. 37-55, Vodou; pp. 59-62, Honduras Caribs; pp. 65-76, Cuba (Santeria, Mayombe, Nanigos, Spiritism); pp. 77-79, Trinidad (Shango, Rada, Shouters); pp. 83, Jamaica (Myallism, Obeah, Angelism, Convince cult, Ras Tafari); U.S. (black religion, Black Muslims, etc.); briefly on several other Latin American countries.

79 Desmangles, Leslie Gérald. Review of *Black religions in the New World,* by G. E. Simpson (entry 141). *Sociological Analysis* 40, no. 3 (1979): 269-72.

80 Drake, St. Clair. Foreword to *Garveyism as a religious movement,* by R. K. Burkett. Metuchen, N.J.: Scarecrow Press; American Theological Library Association, 1978, pp. xi-xxvi.

81 Drake, St. Clair. *The redemption of Africa and black religion.* Black Papers Series. Chicago: Third World Press, 1970, 80 pp.
     Pp. 71-75, 78, Ethiopianism and religious-political movements in Africa, North America, and Jamaica; pp. 31ff., Richard Allen; 38ff., Nat Turner; 54ff., E. W. Blyden. This represents the first chapter of his then-expected book, *The Black Diaspora.*

82 Dyke, Annette Joy Van. "Feminist curing ceremonies: The goddess in contemporary spiritual traditions." Ph.D. thesis, University of Minnesota, 1987, 219 pp.
     Pueblo Indian, Afro-American, Celtic.

83 Fichte, Hubert (text), and Mau, Leonore (photos). *Petersilie: Santo Domingo, Venezuela, Miami, Grenada.* Die Afroamerikanischen Religionen, 4. Frankfurt: S. Fischer Verlag, 1980, 403 pp., many color plates, with notes.
     Combines travelogue with journalistic style, and includes limited references to San Pedro cult (Dominican Republic), Maria Lionza cult (Venezuela). Yoruba-based Cuban religions in Miami, and Shango in Grenada.

84 Franco, José Luciano. "La presencia negra en el Nuevo Mundo: Glosario afroamericano." *Casa de las Américas* (Havana), nos. 36-37 [6] (May-August 1966): 7-22.
   By a Cuban historian.

85 Glazier, S[tephen] D[avey]. Review of *Black religions in the New World*, G. E. Simpson (entry 141). *Review of Religious Research* 22, no. 1 (1980): 96-97.

86 Goeje, C. H. de. "Negers in Amerika." *West-Indische Gids* (Amsterdam) 28 (1947): 217-21.

87 Gomes, Lindolfo. "Afro-Negrismo." *Revista de Philologia e de Historia* (Rio de Janeiro) 2 (1934): 378-92.

88 Gonzalez-Wippler, Migene. *Santería: African magic in Latin America*. New York: Julian Press, 1973, 181 pp., illus., glossary, bib.
   Claims to be the first book in English on the subject, and appears to focus on Cuba, but is a generalized account with emphasis on magical aspects, and sections on Brazilian forms (pp. 134-36) and on Puerto Rican magic (pp. 136-43); pp. 149-71 contain detailed formulae for various spells.

89 Gräbener, Jürgen, ed. *Klassengesellschaft und Rassismus: Zur Marginalisierung der Afroamerikaner in Lateinamerika*. Interdisziplinäre Studien, 4. Dusseldorf: Bertelsmann Universitäts-Verlag, 1971, 342 pp.
   See digest by K. J. Jäcklein in English in *Mundus* 10, no. 2 (1974), 109-12.

90 Herskovits, Melville J[ean]. "African gods and Catholic saints in New World belief." *American Anthropologist* 39, no. 4 (1937): 635-43. Reprinted in *The New World Negro*. Bloomington: Indiana University Press, 1966, pp. 321-29. Reprinted in *Reader in Comparative Religion*, edited by W. A. Lessa and E. Z. Vogt. New York: Harper & Row, 1958, pp. 492-98. 2d ed. 1965, pp. 541-47. Portuguese translation. "Deuses africanos e santos catholicos nas crenças do Negro do Novo Mundo." In *O Negro no Brasil*, compiled by E. Carneiro and A. do Couto Ferraz. Rio de Janeiro, Civilazação Brasileira, 1940, pp. 19-29.

91 Herskovits, Melville J[ean]. "The a-historical approach to Afroamerican Studies: A critique (1960)." *American Anthropologist* 62, no. 4 (1960): 559-68. Reprinted in *The New World Negro*. Bloomington: Indiana University Press, 1966, pp. 122-34.

92 Herskovits, Melville J[ean]. "The ancestry of the American Negro." *American Scholar* 8, no. 1 (1938-39): 84-94. Reprinted in *The New World Negro*. Bloomington: Indiana University Press, 1966, pp. 114-22.

93 Herskovits, Melville J[ean]. "The contribution of Afroamerican studies to Africanist research (1948)." *American Anthropologist* 50, no. 1, pt. 1 (January-March 1948): 1-10. Reprinted in *The New World Negro*. Bloomington: Indiana University Press, 1966, pp. 12-23.

94 Herskovits, Melville J[ean]. "The Negro in the New World: The statement of a problem." *American Anthropologist* 32, no. 1 (1930): 145-55. Reprinted in *The New World Negro*. Bloomington: Indiana University Press, 1966, pp. 1-12.

95 Herskovits, Melville J[ean]. *The New World Negro*. Selected papers in Afro-American Studies, edited by F. S. Herskovits. Bloomington: Indiana University Press, 1966, 370 pp.
   Posthumous collection of essays – see separate entries.

96 Herskovits, Melville J[ean]. "The present status and needs of Afroamerican research (1951)." *Journal of Negro History* 36, no. 2 (1951): 123-47. Reprinted in *The New World Negro*. Bloomington: Indiana University Press, 1966, pp. 23-41.

97 Herskovits, Melville J[ean]. "Problem, method, and theory in Afro-American studies." *Afroamerica* (Mexico City) 1 (1945): 5-24. Reprinted in *The New World Negro*. Bloomington: Indiana University Press, 1966, pp. 43-61.

98 Herskovits, Melville J[ean]. "The significance of West Africa for Negro Research (1936)." *Journal of Negro History* 21, no. 1 (1936): 15-30. Reprinted in *The New World Negro*. Bloomington: Indiana University Press, 1966, pp. 89-101.

99 Herskovits, Melville J[ean]. "What has Africa given America?" *New Republic*, no. 1983 [84] (1935), 92-94. Reprinted in *The New World Negro*. Bloomington: Indiana University Press, 1966, pp. 168-74.
   Pp. 173-74, possession in worship–whether it came from the whites to the blacks, or vice versa, and the differences between the two forms.

100 Horowitz, Michael M. "A comparative study of several Negro cults in the New World." M.A. thesis, Columbia University, 1956.

Includes Afro-American cults in Brazil and the Caribbean, observing that the degree of African retention was higher in Roman Catholic areas than in Protestant.

101 Hunt, Carl Monroe. *Oyotunji village: The Yoruba movement in America*. Washington: University Press of America, 1979, 130 pp.

The Order of Damballa Hwedo; Santo in Cuba; Shango in Harlem; a Yoruba village in South Carolina founded to express African religion and philosophy by a Yoruba, Adefunmi (Walter Serge King). See review by T. O. Beidelman in *Anthropos* (entry 68).

102 Italiaander, Rolf. *Schwarze Magie – Magie der Schwärzen: mehr als schwarze Magie. Begegungen mit religiösen Phänomenen in Cuba, Brasilien und Westafrika*. Freiburg: Aurum, 1983, 176 pp.

103 Kilson, Martin, and Rotberg, Robert I., eds. *The African diaspora: Interpretative essays*. Cambridge: Harvard University Press, 1976, 510 pp., maps.

The relevant essays have been placed in the appropriate sections of vols. 5 and 6 of this series.

104 Maggie, Yvonne. "Afro-Brazilian cults." In *The Encyclopedia of Religion*, edited by M. Eliade. Vol. 1. New York: Macmillan, 1987, pp. 102-5.

105 Marks, Morton. "Uncovering ritual structures in Afro-American music." In *Religious movements in contemporary America*, edited by I. I. Zaretsky and M. P. Leone. Princeton: Princeton University Press, 1974, pp. 60-134 (pp. 117-134, musical texts).

Pp. 67-75, Afro-Brazilian carnivals; pp. 75-82, slave religion in Cuba (Santeria, Lucumi, etc.); pp. 82-87, these Cuban forms in New York; pp. 87-98, Afro-American gospel music, and "shouting"; pp. 98-109, themes collected; pp. 109-16, conclusions.

106 Marks, Morton. "'You can't sing unless you're saved': Reliving the call in Gospel music." In *African religious groups and beliefs . . . in honor of William R. Bascom*, edited by S. Ottenberg. Meerut, India: Archana Publications for the Folklore Institute (Berkeley, Calif.), [1982], pp. 305-31.

Christian content shaped by West African trance-based religion, as represented by three songs (with texts) describing conversion through a possession-trance.

107 Massajoli, Pierleone. "L'Afro-Americanistica in Italia." *Etnologia/Antropologia Culturale* (Naples), no. 9 (1981), 1-10, bib.
     Pp. 2-3, on Afro-Brazilian cult studies, and otherwise on the whole area.

108 Massajoli, Pierleone. "Studi italiani di Afro-Americanista." In *La antropologia americanista en la actualidad: Homenaje a Raphael Girard*. Vol. 2. Editores Mexicanos Unidos, [1980], pp. 119-29, bib.
     Pp. 120-21, on Afro-Brazilian cult studies; otherwise on the whole area.

109 Mau, Leonore (photos), and Fichte, Hubert (text). *Petersilie: Santo Domingo, Venezuela, Miami, Grenada*. Die Afroamerikanische Religionen, 3. Frankfurt: S. Fischer Verlag, 1980, 199 pp. (140 pages being color and black-and-white photos).
     Pp. 167-93, a detailed essay on the relation of local Afro-American religions to the socialist revolution in Grenada in 1979; good photos especially of Shango, Spiritual Baptists (Grenada), Maria Lionza (Venezuela), and Santeria (Cuban exiles in Miami), as well as various forms of African religions.

110 Melton, J. Gordon. (1) "African Orthodox Church." (2) "African witchcraft." In *The Encyclopedia of American Religions*. Wilmington, N.C.: McGarth Publishing Co., 1978, vol. 1, p. 75, vol. 2, pp. 168-70, respectively.
     McGuire's African Orthodox Church; Yoruba religion as practised in Oyotunji Village in South Carolina; Afro-American Vodou as in Madam Arboo, Harlem, New York.

111 Mintz, Sydney Wilfred, and Price, Richard. *An anthropological approach to the Afro-American past: A Caribbean perspective*. Occasional Papers in Social Change, 2. Philadelphia: Institute for the Study of Human Issues, [ca. 1976], 64 pp., bib. (pp. 51-64).

112 Nida, Eugene A. "African influence in the religious life of Latin America." *Practical Anthropology* 13, no. 4 (1966): 133-38.
     Shango, Vodou, Candomble ("Carnivalism").

113 Nodal, Roberto A. "El sincretismo afrocatólico en Cuba y Brasil." *Anuario Científico* (San Pedro de Macoris, Dominican Republic, Universidade Central del Este) 3, no. 3 (1978): 207-22. Reprinted in *Estudos Ibero-Americanos* (Pôrto Alegre) 5, no. 2 (1979): 207-18.
     Includes discussion of Santeria and Candomble.

114 Palau-Marti, Montserrat. "Africa en America a traves de sus dioses."
     Actas y Memorias XXXVI Congrese Internacional de Americanistas,
     España, 1964. Seville, pp. 627-32. French translation. "L'Afrique en
     Amérique grâce à ses dieux." *Revue de l'Histoire des Religions* (Paris)
     168, no. 2 (1965): 165-73, bib.
         Africa still lives in America through its gods – especially in Brazil,
     Cuba, and Haiti.

115 Palau-Marti, Montserrat. "Noirs d'Amérique et dieux d'Afrique." *Revue*
     de l'Histoire des Religions (Paris) 156 (1959): 189-201.
         Historical background – origins in Africa, and population figures
     in Americas at various times; survival of African religions, with
     examples from Haiti and Brazil.

116 Palau-Marti, Montserrat. "Oba so, ko so (le roi s'est pendu, le roi ne
     s'est pas pendu)." *Bulletin du Bureau d'Ethnologie* (Port-au-Prince), 3d
     ser., nos. 23-25 (1960): 56-64.
         Yoruba Shango deity in Africa and in the New World.

117 Pavan, Adalberto. "Processo alla chiesa della 'conquista.'" *Nigrizia* 104,
     no. 9 (1986): 50-52.

118 Paxon, Barbara. "Mammy water: New World origins." *Baessler-Archiv*
     31, no. 2 (1983): 407-46.
         The water spirit, of African origin, but with European, Indian
     and Islamic elements in the iconography.

119 Pereda Valdés, Ildefonso. *Línea de color (Ensayos afro-americanos).*
     Santiago de Chile: Ediciones Ercilla, 1938, 248 pp. + 5 pp. (bib.).
         Collected essays: part 2 (Brazil) includes "Las danzas frenéticas
     de los negros Brazil"; part 4 includes "Rituales de los Afroamericanos"
     (in Bahia, Pernambuco, Cuba and Haiti); and "Los Negros en el Brasil"
     (festivals, songs, etc.).

120 Pollak-Eltz, Angelina. *Afroamerikaanse godsdiensten en culten.*
     Roermond, Holland: Romen & Zonen, 1970, 221 pp., plates. Spanish
     translation. *Cultos afroamericanos.* Caracas: Universidad Católico
     Andrés Bello, 1972, 270 pp. New ed. Colección Manoa, 8. 1977, 344
     pp., bib.
         Surveys cults in Brazil and the Antilles; Trinidad, Grenada,
     Jamaica, Haiti, Cuba; and Venezuela, Surinam.

121 Pollak-Eltz, Angelina. "Attualitá dell'Afroamericanstica." *Terra Ameriga* (Genoa), 18-19 (1970): 5-7.

122 Pollak-Eltz, Angelina. "Las culturas negras en las Americas." *Ego* (Bogotá) 15, no. 4 (1967): 430-52.

123 Pollak-Eltz, Angelina. "Instituciones de ayuda mutua en Africa occidental y entre afroamericanos." *Boletín Bibliográfico de Antropología Americana* 38, no. 47 (1976): 185-206.
    Structures and functions of black mutual-aid societies, including cofradias.

124 Pollak-Eltz, Angelina. "Kulturwandel bei Negern der Neuen Welt." *Umschau in Wissenschaft und Technik* (Frankfurt am Main) 67, no. 19 (1967): 623-26.
    A general survey.

125 Pollak-Eltz, Angelina. "Negerprobleme in Nord- und Suedamerika." *Aconcagua* (Madrid) 5, no. 2 (1969): 176-83.

126 Pollak-Eltz, Angelina. *Panorama de estudios afroamericanos.* Serie de Religiones Comparadas, 20. Caracas: Instituto de Investigaciones Historicas, Universidad Catolica Andrés Bello, 1972, 64 pp.
    A survey of methods of study, problems, and literature; pp. 24-46, cults in Brazil, Venezuela, Caribbean.

127 Pollak-Eltz, Angelina. "Religiones africanas en las Américas." *Boletin de la Asociación Cultural Humboldt* (Caracas) 4 (1968): 57-66.
    General survey of Afro-American rites and their African origin.

128 Pollak-Eltz, Angelina. "Seelenvorstellung und Totenriten der Afroamerikaner." *Mitteilungen der Anthropologische Gesellschaft in Wien* 111 (1981): 47-74.

129 Pollak-Eltz, Angelina. "Voodoo heute. Lateinamerika: Afrikanische Religionskulte breiten sich aus." *Umschau in Wissenschaft und Technik* (Frankfurt am Main) 75, no. 18 (1975): 574-75, illus.
    A brief popular survey of Afro-American religions.

130 Pollak-Eltz, Angelina. "Woher stammen die Neger Suedamerikas?" *Umschau in Wissenschaft und Technik* (Frankfurt am Main) 67, no. 8 (1967): 244-49, illus.

A survey of the diverse African origins of the Negro population in the Americas, and of the various Afro-American cults in Latin America and the Caribbean.

131 Pollak-Eltz, Angelina. "Yoruba religion and its decline in the Americas." In *Proceedings, 38th International Congress of Americanists 1968.* Vol. 3, *Afro-Amerikanistik.* Munich: Klaus Renner, 1971, pp. 423-427.

A description of Yoruba religion, followed by brief accounts of Afro-American cults and their degrees of acculturation in Brazil and the West Indies.

132 Price, Richard, ed. *Maroon societies: Rebel slave communities in the Americas.* Garden City, N.Y.: Doubleday, Anchor Books, 1973, 429 pp.

An extensive survey–Spanish, English, Dutch, French, and U.S. areas; see index, "Religion."

133 Raboteau, Albert J[ordy]. "Afro-American religions." In *The Encyclopedia of Religion,* edited by M. Eliade. Vol. 1. New York: Macmillan, 1987, pp. 96-100.

134 Raboteau, Albert Jordy. "'The invisible institution': The origins and conditions of black religion before emancipation." Ph.D. dissertation (religion), Yale University, 1974, 320 pp.

Pt. 1, the African heritage and its influence in Latin America, the Caribbean, and the U.S., with discussion of the discrepancy between degrees of African retention in North and in Latin America.

135 Ranger, Terence Osborn. "Recent developments in the study of African religious and cultural history and their relevance for the historiography of the diaspora." *Ufahamu* (Los Angeles, African Activist Association, UCLA) 4, no. 2 (Fall 1973): 17-34.

136 Richards, Dona. "Let the circle be unbroken: The implications of Afro-American spirituality." *Présence Africaine,* nos. 117-18 (1981), 247-92.

Includes African retentions in Candomble (Brazil), Vodou (Haiti), and Obeah (Caribbean).

137 Roback, Judith. [Comment on English translation of Bastide's *Les Amériques noires.*] *American Anthropologist* 77, no. 3 (1975): 602.

The errors, inconsistencies, etc., in the original are more numerous in the translation (e.g., "les caraïbes" means "West Indians," not "Caribs," and "les caraïbes nègres" means "black West Indians," not the people known as "Black Caribs" in English); there is very little on Rastafarians.

138 Scott, William R[andolph]. *Going to the Promised Land: Afro-American immigrants in Ethiopia, 1930-1935*. Atlanta: Institute of the Black World, 1975, 16 pp.
    Pre-Rastafarian immigrants and visitors, with similar motivation. "Rabbi" Arnold Ford, a Harlem black Jewish leader, and other black settlers.

139 Senghor, L. S. "Latinité et négritude." *Political Affairs* (New York), no. 52 [22, no. 4] (1964): 5-13.

140 Simpson, George Eaton. "Afro-Caribbean religions." In *The Encyclopedia of Religion*, edited by M. Eliade. Vol. 3. New York: Macmillan, 1987, pp. 90-98.

141 Simpson, George Eaton. *Black religions in the New World*. New York: Columbia University Press, 1978, 415 pp., maps, bib.
    The revised and extended version of much of his earlier publications, representing a lifetime of work. See especially chap. 3 (pp. 51-110), "Neo-African religions and ancestral cults of the Caribbean and South America"; chap. 4 (pp. 111-46), "Revivalist and other cults of the Caribbean"; chap. 6 (pp. 171-212), "Neo-African and African-derived religions of South America"; also see index for individual movements and leaders. Note that Amerindian movements are not included.

142 Steger, Hanns-Albert. "Revolutionäre Hintergründe des kreolischen Synkretismus." In *Internationales Jahrbuch für Religions-Soziologie* 6, edited by J. Matthes. Cologne and Opalden: West-deutscher Verlag, 1970, pp. 99-139 (English summary, pp. 139-41). Spanish translation. *El trasfondo revolucionario del sincretismo criollo. Aspectos sociales de la transformación clandestina de la religión en Afroamerica colonial y postcolonial*. Translated by N. Muñoz and H.-A. Steger. CIDOC: Sondeos 86. Cuernavaca, Mexico: Editions du CIDOC, 1972, 87 pp.
    The relation between Afro-American religions ("Creole syncretism") and Catholicism is explored as analogous to that between Gnosticism and Greek philosophy. Creole syncretism, however, lacks messianic and speculative features; is oriented nostalgically to the African past; and, being fatalistic concerning the present, does not lead to revolutionary action.

143 Szwed, John F., and Abrahams, Roger D., eds. *Afro-American folk culture: An annotated bibliography of materials from North, Central, and South America and the West Indies*. Publications of American Folklore Society, Bibliography and Special Series, 31 and 32. Philadelphia: Institute for the Study of Human Issues, 1978.
See especially the essay by S. L. Jones.

144 Thompson, Robert Farris. *Flash of the spirit: African and Afro-American art and philosophy*. New York: Random House, 1983; Vintage Books, 1984, 317 pp., illus.
Pp. 111-15, mystic drawings in various countries among black populations.

145 Thornton, John K. "On the trail of Voodoo: African Christianity in the Americas." *Americas* 44, no.1 (1988).

146 Truluck, Jack L. "Voodoo: In an African village near Beaufort the king has seven wives and residents sacrifice animals to gods." *State Newspaper* (Columbia, S.C.), 23 September 1979, pp. 12-13, illus.
A very journalistic account of a Negro community since 1969 practicing an ersatz form of Yoruba religion in South Carolina at "Oyotunji African Village" under Walter Serge King, now known as King Efuntola, formerly as Chief Baba.

147 Verger, Pierre. "African cultural survivals in the New World: The examples of Brazil and Cuba." *Tarikh* (London, etc.) 5, no. 4 (1978): 79-91, illus.
Pp. 82-86 on the syncretist cults.

148 Verger, Pierre. "Afro-Catholic syncretism in South America." *Nigeria Magazine*, no. 78 (September 1963), 211-16.
The *Yemanja* festival of the Virgin of Regla in Havana, Cuba, and in Bahia, Brazil, with general discussion.

149 Walker, Sheila S[uzanne]. "African gods in the Americas: The black religious continuum." *Black Scholar* (Sausalito, Calif.) 11, no. 8 (1980): 25-36, illus., bib.
On possession of the faithful by their deities as the basic religious act; this provides a common unifying feature across black churches in the U.S. and African cults in Latin America and the Caribbean.

150 Walker, Sheila S[uzanne]. *Ceremonial spirit possession in Africa and Afro-America: Forms, meanings, and functional significance for individuals and social groups*. Leiden: E. J. Brill, 1972, 179 pp.
An important study by a black anthropologist.

151 Waterman, Richard Alan. "African influence on the music of the Americas." In *Acculturation in the Americas. Proceedings of the 29th International Congress of Americanists, New York, 1949*, edited by S. Tax. Vol. 3. Chicago: University of Chicago Press, 1952, pp. 207-18. Reprint. New York: Cooper Square Publications, 1967.
P. 217, African religious music persisting intact in the Afro-American cults, and in more reinterpreted fashion in less syncretistic religions, especially those affected by Protestantism.

152 Whitten, Norman E., Jr., and Szwed, John [F.]. "Anthropologists look at Afro-Americans. Introduction." *Trans-Action* (St. Louis, Mo.) 5, no. 8 (1968): 49-56, illus.
A critique of anthropological approaches since M. J. Herskovits. Portions reprinted in entry 153.

153 Whitten, Norman E., Jr., and Szwed, John [F.]. Introduction to *Afro-American anthropology: Contemporary perspectives*. New York: Free Press; London: Collier-Macmillan, 1970, 468 pp.
Pp. 23-39, portions reprinted from their article in *Trans-Action* (entry 152).

154 Williams, Ethel L., and Brown, Clifton F. *The Howard University bibliography of African and Afro-American religious studies, with locations in American libraries*. Wilmington, Del.: Scholarly Resources, 1977, xxi + 525 pp.

155 Wittkower, E. D. "Trance and possession states." *International Journal of Social Psychiatry* 16, no. 2 (1970): 153-60.
Possession states described in Vodou, Bahian Candomble and Monrovian prophet-healers, and interpreted as having "distress relieving, integrative, adaptive functions" and therefore as prophylactic in mental illness.

156 Zaretsky, Irving I., and Shambaugh, Cynthia L. *Spirit possession and spirit mediumship in Africa and Afro-America: An annotated bibliography*. Reference Library of Social Science, 56. New York: Garland Publishing Co., 1978, 470 pp.

Central America

Theory and General

There is so little material that "Theory" and "General" have been grouped together. The black or Negro population is small and the Indian population, although a majority group in Guatemala and some 20% in Mexico, is also small elsewhere.

This group, however, has in the past produced a large range of political and military revolts in which a messianic or inspired prophetic figure was an important source of validation or initiative, and where there was some nativistic or syncretistic religious form and content. These were distinguishable as protest movements from the general diffused process of syncretism under a Catholic veneer that has produced the widespread "Christo-paganism" (as some anthropologists and others have called it) characteristic of both Indian and ladino (or mestizo) populations. For a table of these revolts see M. S. Edmonson (entry 159) and also the equivalent movements among the Indian peoples of Northern Mexico who are included in the North American volume, the second in this series.

For the most part many aspects of Christo-paganism have not been included – the modern shamans with a following, the folk-curers or healers, and the popular saints' fiestas. The main exception is the inclusion of a selection of the more interesting or significant movements in Mexico.

The Black Caribs of the Caribbean coast in Honduras and Belize have a separate section within the category of Particular Movements at the end of volume 6, *The Caribbean*.

The two items by W. J. Moreno (entries 160 and 161) are a useful general introduction, and the item by S. Tax (entry 164), although set in Guatemala, is included here for its general theoretical value. The item by J.

29

Theory and General

Nash (entry 163) spans Mexico and Guatemala and therefore appears in this general section. A few items allocated to different countries also refer to neighboring areas but have been placed in the country of primary concern.

157 Beals, Ralph L[eon]. "Acculturation." In *Handbook of Middle American Indians*, edited by M. Nash. Vol. 6, *Social Anthropology*. Austin: University of Texas Press, 1967, pp. 449-68.
Pp. 461, 466, religious revitalization movements in outline.

158 Carrasco, David. "Towards the splendid city: The study of Mesoamerican religions." *Religious Studies Review* 14, no. 4 (October 1988): 289-302, bib.

159 Edmonson, Munro S. "Nativism, syncretism, and anthropological science." In *Nativism and syncretism*, by M. S. Edmonson, et al. Middle American Research Publications, 19. New Orleans: Tulane University, 1960, 203 pp., bib.
Pp. 183-97 have a table of resistance movements from the sixteenth to twentieth centuries, many with a religious dimension; also theoretical discussion.

160 Jiménez-Moreno, Wigberto. "Las religiones mesoamericanas y el cristianismo." *Verhandlungen des XXXVIII Internationalen Amerikanistenkongresses, Stuttgart-München, 1968*. Vol. 3. Stuttgart and Munich: Klaus Renner, 1971, pp. 241-45.
A general survey of "christo-paganism."

161 Jiménez-Moreno, Wigberto. "Sincretismo, identidad y patrimonio en Mesoamérica." In *Cultural tradition in Caribbean identity*, edited by J. K. Wilkerson. Gainesville: Center for Latin American Studies, University of Florida, 1980, pp. 353-69; English summary (pp. 370-71); French summary (pp. 372-73).

162 Nachtigall, Horst. "Entwicklungsprobleme der Cofradias in Guatemala und Mexico." *Verbum SVD* 1 (1986): 53-66.

163 Nash, June. "The passion play in Mayan Indian communities." *Comparative Studies in Society and History* 10, no. 3 (1968): 318-27, bib.
Studies in Amatenango del Valle (Mexico), and Cantel and Santiago Atitlán (both in Guatemala); the competition between, and different interpretations of the play in Easter Week, in the four religious systems: folk Catholicism, formal Catholicism, Protestantism

Theory and General

(as a reaction against all Catholicism), and esoteric cults associated with shamans and healers.

164 Tax, Sol. "World view and social relations in Guatemala." *American Anthropologist* 43, no. 1 (1941): 27-42.
Indian peoples of Guatemala as possessing a typical "primitive" world-view and a "civilized" form of social and economic relations (i.e., a distinction can occur between world-view and social relations; in such a case contact with Western "civilized" social systems is less traumatic, less acculturation occurs, and no new cults arise).

Belize (except Black Caribs)

Of the two articles in this brief section the first is historical, on the War of the Castes and the Talking Cross cult, with an account of sources for the Belizean part of a movement set primarily in Mexico, and should be read in conjunction with the main materials about this movement as found in the Mexican section below.

The other article concerns the recent development of an independent Pentecostal movement among descendants of refugees from the same mid-nineteenth century War of the Castes.

Groups with a suggested total of 2,000 people have been spoken of as "Afro-American Spiritists" involved in Obeah, as in the Caribbean context, but no literature has been discovered for our purposes.

165 Birdwell-Pheasant, Donna. "The power of Pentecostalism in a Belizean village." In *Perspectives on Pentecostalism: Case studies from the Caribbean and Latin America*, edited by S. D. Glazier. Washington, D.C.: University Press of America, 1980, pp. 95-109.

166 Buhler, Richard. "Belize ecclesiastical archives and the War of the Castes." *Actes du 43e Congrès International des Américanistes ... Paris, 1976*. Paris: Société des Américanistes, Musée de l'Homme, 1978, pp. 45-51.
The War of the Castes and Talking Cross, as presented in the Jesuit archives, and the difference from the British government record.

Costa Rica

Over 80% of the population is white, and there are only a few thousand Indians, among whom "spiritists" have been reported, and a somewhat larger

Costa Rica

number of black peoples who are mainly in churches of mission or of black
North American origin.

The two items included give a general picture of black religion,
including the brotherhoods and other forms akin to those in the Caribbean,
such as Pocomania and Obeah.

167 Biesanz, Richard; Biesanz, Karen Zubris; and Biesanz, Mavis Hiltunen.
     The Costa Ricans. Englewood Cliffs, N.J.: Prentice-Hall, 1982, 246 pp.,
     illus.

     Chap. 8 (pp. 137-57), religion: mostly on Catholicism – pp. 150-54,
     the cult of the saints, *curanderismo* and the occult; pp. 154-56,
     Protestantism, a useful current survey.

168 Melendez Chaverri, Carlos. *El Negro en Costa Rica*. San José: Editorial
     Costa Rica, 1972. 2d ed. 1974. Reprint. 1982, 262 pp.

     Pp. 100-108, on Negro religion – its syncretism, its brotherhoods,
     Pocomania, Obeah, Catholic forms, "popular theology," and
     "superstitions."

Guatemala

Indians make up about half the population, but the black peoples form only
about 1% to 2%. The characteristic *cofradías*, or brotherhoods, occur among
the latter; see S. L. Orellana (entry 173) and the United States Government
Army Handbook (entry 176). A similar feature is reported among the Maya
Indians; see P. Massajoli and A. Ghidinelli (entry 171).

For general theoretical background see S. Tax (entry 164) in the
introductory section on Central America above. The U.S. Army Handbook
provides the best overview.

For the assertion that Mayan Christo-paganism does form a new
functioning religious system see M. Siegel (entry 175). O. LaFarge (entry
170) studies Mayan religion in a remote village, with Cult of the Cross and
other syncretist features. Otherwise the Cult of the Cross is best studied
where it occurs in the materials on Mexico. Further relevant Indian items
seem to be in short supply.

169 Dahlin, Bruce Harrison. "An anthropologist looks at the pyramids: A
     late classical revitalization movement at Tikal, Guatemala." Ph.D.
     dissertation (anthropology), Temple University, 1976, 396 pp.

     Rapid culture change administered by a single prophet or
     charismatic leader to people relatively deprived as against the lowland
     Maya in the seventh century A.D. – a "nativistic revitalization"

movement, included as a possible example of precontact movement, although religious dimensions are not prominent.

170 LaFarge, Oliver. *Santa Eulalia: The religion of Cuchumatán Indian town*. Publications in Anthropology, Ethnological Series. Chicago: University of Chicago Press, 1947, 211 pp., bib.

The Mayan survivals and acculturation aspects in a remote village (e.g., "formal Christianity," "Christian-derived deities," a "Cult of the Cross," "formal non-Christian ceremonies," magic, shamanism, divination).

171 Massajoli, Pierleone, and Ghidinelli, Azzo. "Le confraternite religiose presso i Pokoman orientali del Guatemala." *L'Universo* 58, no. 1 (1978): 141-79, illus.

These religious fraternities represent a syncretism between the ancient agro-religion of the Maya and the solar cult of their priesthood, and Hispano-Catholicism of the "campesinos."

172 Mendelson, E. M. "The king, the traitor, and the cross: An interpretation of a highland Maya religious conflict." *Diogenes* 21 (Spring 1958): 1-10.

Mayan "Judas Iscariot worship."

173 Orellana, Sandra L. "La introducción del sistema de cofradía en la región de lago Atitlán en los altos de Guatemala." *América Indígena* 35, no. 4 (1975): 845-56; English summary.

Origin and development of the Indian brotherhood system, which had its own identity, gave stability, and contributed to religious syncretism.

174 Sapper, Karl. "Die Gebräuche und religiösen Anschauungen der Kekchi-Indianer." *International Archiv für Ethnographie* 8 (1895): 195-215.

Pp. 205f., Juan de la Cruz and the Guatemalan Kekchi troubles of 1885, with an inspired woman oracle.

175 Siegel, Morris. "Religion in Western Guatemala: A product of acculturation." *American Anthropologist*, n.s. 43 (1941), pp. 62-76.

The village of San Miguel Acatán, 11,000 Indians plus 155 whites or others. Its religion is *new*, as a product of Mayan and Roman Catholic elements, and not merely Mayan with a Catholic overlay; a new functional entity with its system of feasts. Occasionally visited by a Catholic priest, but really independent.

Guatemala

176 United States Government, Department of the Army. *Handbook for Guatemala*, edited by J. Dombrowski, et al. Foreign Area Studies Division, the American University. DA PAM 550-78. Washington, D.C.: Government Printing Office, 1970, xiv + 361 pp.

Pp. 83-85, cofradias; pp. 88-89, Black Caribs; pp. 113-15, 120-31, Indian (Mayan) culture, religion, and syncretism with Catholicism.

177 Wagley, Charles. "The social and religious life of a Guatemalan village." *Memoirs of the American Anthropological Association*, no. 71 (1949) [*American Anthropologist* 51, no. 4, ii (1949)]: 150 pp., illus.

Pp. 50-78, the "Christo-paganism" or syncretist religion, with Mayan and Catholic aspects in Chimaltenango village.

178 Ximenez, Francisco. *Biblioteca Guatemala, historia de la Provincia.* . . . 3 vols. Guatemala: Tipografia Nacional, 1929-31.

Vol. 3, Book 6, chaps. 58-64: pp. 226-64, Tzotzil revolt; pp. 265-67, 1711 revolt; pp. 267ff., Maria Candelaria; p. 297, Tila Indian "Christ."

Mexico (except Northern Mexico)

As explained in vol. 2 of this series, on North America, northern Mexico is included in that volume for cultural reasons, so that this section concerns central and southern Mexico. About a quarter of the population may be regarded as Indian, and there is a long history of the kinds of religiously-inspired revolts described in the introduction to Latin America.

On these revolts the following may be mentioned: H. H. Bancroft (entry 181) on the Tzeltal revolt; A. M. Barabas (entry 182); V. Riefler de Bricker on the Caste War (entry 252), and on rewriting the history of five Mayan revolts (entry 254); D. G. Brinton (entry 187), a historical drama idealizing Candelaria, the prophetess-founder of the Tzeltal revolt – see also H. S. Klein (entries 224 and 225) on the same subject; M. T. Huerta and P. Palacios (entry 219) surveys thirteen movements from 1523 to 1761, and the documentation they provide on two of them is included here; D. E. Thompson (entry 262) gives an overview.

On Aztec and Mayan syncretism see W. Madsen (entry 231). For the Mayan Talking Cross/War of the Castes/Cuzcat revolt see J. A. Burdon (entry 190), archival materials; T. W. F. Gann's items (entries 203-205); D. Heyden (entry 218) for a popular introduction; N. Reed (entry 250) for a vivid history sympathetic to Indians; A. Villa Rojas, in Spanish and English versions (entries 269 and 270); C. Wilson (entry 273), a historical novel; C. Zimmerman (entries 275 and especially 276, a valuable theoretical and

Central America

Mexico

historical article on the interpretation of interaction between cultures and cosmologies). On other Indian peoples (e.g., the Tarasco), see P. Carrasco (entry 192).

On folk-curing see R. G. Wasson, et al. (entry 272). For items on Spiritism: S. Ortiz Echanez (entry 240) on the history; K. Finkler (entry 200), rural areas; M. Kearney (entry 222), Baja California; B. J. Macklin (entry 230) includes forms of Spiritism among Hispanics and others in the United States and the influence of Kardecism (on which see later in Brazil, especially on Umbanda).

For ex-Catholic movements see K. Finkler (entry 198), where the founder was half-Indian.

The black population is under 1%. For Negro movements with cofradias and syncretist features see C. A. Palmer (entry 241).

For indigenous Pentecostalism among both ladinos and Indians see M. J. Gaxiola (entry 207), a long-time bishop in the earliest Pentecostal Church, and F. D. Goodman (entry 211) on the same Iglesia Apostolica de la Fe en Cristo Jesus. For an indigenous non-Pentecostal but evangelical and strongly biblical Church among ladinos see R. S. Greenway (entry 216) on the "Luz del Mundo" movement.

179 Ancona, Eligio. *Historia de Yucatán, desde la época más remota hasta nuestros días.* 4 vols. Mérida, Yucatan: M. Heredia Arguelles, 1879. Reprint. 1889.

Vol. 4 on the War of the Castes in Yucatan 1847-55: along with his friend Baqueiro (1878), a standard source with much reprinting of documentary materials, and, directly or indirectly, the authority for most later accounts in English; by a Yucatecan with the contemporary local view of the Maya.

180 Archer, Christon J. *El ejército en el México borbonico, 1760-1810.* Mexico City, 1983.

Pp. 132-35, Indian prophet Mariano, in detail.

181 Bancroft, Hubert Howe. *The history of Central America.* Vol. 2, *1530-1800.* Works, vol. 7. San Francisco: A. L. Bancroft & Co., 1883, 766 pp.

Chap. 37, Guatemala and Chiapas: pp. 696-705, on Tzeltal revolt of 1712, based on contemporary manuscript account of Fr. Marselino García, "Informe sobre la sublevacion de los Zendales. . . ."

182 Barabas, Alicia M[abel]. "Profetismo, milenarismo y mesianismo en las insurecciones mayas de Yucatan." *Cuadernos de los Centros Regionales,* no. 4. Mexico: Instituto Nacional de Antropologia e Historia, 1974.

Mexico

Mimeo. Also in *Actas del XLI Congreso Internacional de Americanistas, Mexico, 1974*. Mexico City: 1974, pp. 609-22.
Colonial revolts from 1546; pp. 615-22, the War of the Castes.

183 Bartolome, Miguel [Alberto]. "La iglesia maya de Quintana Roo." *Cuadernos de los Centros Regionales*, no. 4. Mexico: Instituto Nacional de Antropologia e Historia, 1974. Also in *Estudios Indígenas* (Coyoacón, Mexico) 4, no. 2 (1974): 177-94.
Shows how the Iglesia Maya provides the basis for an integrated recording of society, with its own administrative, religious, military, political and judicial structures.

184 Bartolome, Miguel Alberto, and Barabas, Alicia Mabel. *La resistencia: Relaciones interétnicas en el oriente de la península de Yucatán.* Coleccion Cientificá, Etnologia, 53. Mexico, D. F.: Centro Regional del Sureste, Instituto Nacional de Antropología e Historia, 1977, 136 pp., illus.
Pp. 19, 29-33, 36, 56-57, 60-61, 68-77, 114, deal with the Talking Cross and Mayan "church," passim.

185 Bennett, Anne K. "La Cruz Parlante." *Estudios de Cultura Maya* (Mexico, Centro de Estudios Mayas, UNAM) 8 (1970): 227-37.
Talking Cross cult.

186 Bollra, Adolfo Ecarrea de. "Maria, la hija del sublevado (leyenda historia)." *Registro Yucateco* 1 (1845): 394-422.
A romantic literary account of the Maya revolt of 1761 written when the 1847 Maya rising was close at hand, but without any anticipation.

187 Brinton, Daniel G[arrison]. *Maria Candelaria: An historic drama from American Aboriginal life*. Philadelphia: David McKay, 1897, xxix + 98 pp., illus.
Historical introduction and religious background, pp. v-xxix (pp. xxvii-xxix on sources); text in the form of a three-act verse play, on the Tzeltal "new religion" of 1712, and its founder, Maria Candelaria; from a viewpoint idealizing the prophetess in terms of one overarching world religion.

188 Brinton, Daniel G[arrison]. "Nagualism: A study in Native American folklore and history." *Proceedings, American Philosophical Society*, no. 144 [33] (January 1894): 11-73. Reprinted separately. Philadelphia: D. McKay, 1894, 65 pp.

Pp. 14-17 (first printing), use of peyote; pp. 34-41, 58-60, limitations and parodies of Christian practices; Indian revolts, sixteenth-eighteenth centuries; text of illustrative prayer.

189 Brooks, Francis Joseph. "Parish and Cofradia in eighteenth century Mexico." Ph.D. dissertation, Princeton University, 1976, 320 pp.

Indian cofradias as buffers between Indian and Spanish cultures, being both a "white" and "non-white" institution, with the parish priest performing very different roles within it as compared with his church and parish, and depending on it financially; hence the clergy opposed government attempts to control cofradias and their funds.

190 Burdon, John Alder. *Archives of British Honduras*. Vol. 3, *1841-1884*. London: Sifton Praed & Co., 1935.

Sundry references to Santa Cruz ("Talking Cross") Indians – pp. 24, 35, 237-40, 242, 253, 259, 296-97; includes a visit of a British delegation, which was ill-treated.

191 Burns, Allan F. "The Caste War in the 1970s: Present day accounts from village Quintana Roo." In *Anthropology and history in Yucatan*, edited by G. D. Jones. Austin: University of Texas Press, 1977, pp. 259-73.

192 Carrasco, Pedro. "Tarascan folk religion, Christian or Pagan?" In *The social anthropology of Latin America: Essays in honour of Ralph Beals*, edited by W. R. Goldschmidt and H. Hoijer. Latin American Studies, 14. Los Angeles: University of California Latin American Center, 1970, pp. 3-14.

Discusses his own and R. A. M. van Zantwijk's different interpretations of the same data, so that Carrasco sees an essentially Christian religion and Van Zantwijk a still essentially primal one. See further literature in the bibliography.

193 Castellanos, Rosario. *Officio de Tinieplas*. Mexico, D.F.: J. Martiz, 1962, 368 pp.

A novel that sets many events of the War of Santa Rosa (the Cuzcat revolt) in a later period.

194 Collins, Anne C. "The *Maestros Cantores* in Yucátan." In *Anthropology and history in Yucatán*, edited by G. D. Jones. Austin: University of Texas Press, 1977, pp. 233-47.

Pp. 233-34, Talking Cross cult.

Mexico

195 Cortez Ruiz, Efraim C. *San Simón de la laguna: La organización familiar y lo mágico-religioso en el culto al oratoria.* Colleción SEP-INI. Mexico: Secretaría de Educación Publica, Instituto Nacional Indigenista, 1972, 165 pp., bib., illus., maps.

A religious complex among the Mazahua, with crosses of malevolent significance (requiring propitiatory offerings), chapels that unite groups of families, rituals reminiscent of baptism, Christian godparents, and community saints.

196 Dumond, Don E. "Independent Maya of the late nineteenth century: Chiefdoms and power politics." In *Anthropology and history in Yucatan*, edited by J. D. Jones. Austin: University of Texas Press, 1977, pp. 103-38.

Pp. 106, 108-9, 119-23, 125-26, the Talking Cross.

197 Dumond, Don E. "The Talking Crosses of Yucatan: A new look at their history." *Ethnohistory* 32, no. 4 (1985): 291-308.

There was no unitary cult, but four independent centers between 1853 and the 1890s, corresponding to political divisions.

198 Finkler, Kaja. "Dissident sectarian movements, the Catholic Church, and social classes in Mexico." *Comparative Studies in Society and History* 25, no. 2 (1983): 277-305.

Research into a "mother" temple in Mexico City, and three rural temples, of a movement founded in the nineteenth century by a half-Indian, "Father Elias."

199 Finkler, Kaja. "Non-medical treatments and their outcomes." *Culture, Medicine, and Psychiatry* (Dordrecht, the Netherlands) 4, no. 3 (September 1980): 271-310, bib.

A study of healing at a spiritualist temple in rural Mexico, with more failures than successes, and a restricted category of diseases proving responsive.

200 Finkler, Kaya [sic]. "Spiritualism in rural Mexico." In *Religión y sociedad*. Mexico: Departmento de Etnología y Antropología Social, Instituto Nacional de Antropología e Historia, 1972, 72 pp. in various pagings. In summary form in *Actes du 42e Congrès International des Américanistes, Paris, 1976.* Paris: Musée de l'Homme, 1979, pp. 99-105.

201 Frankowska, Maria. "Z problematyki synkretyzmu religijnego Indian Meksyku" [Some problems of religious syncretism among Mexican Indians]. *Etnografia Polska* (Warsaw) 5 (1979): 99-113.

In Polish.

202 Frankowska, Maria. [The sanctuaries and pilgrimages – Their meaning for the evangelization of Mexican Indians and . . . religious syncretism.] *Etnografia Polska* (Warsaw) 30, no. 2 (1986):95-127.
In Polish.

203 Gann, Thomas [William Francis]. *Glories of the Maya.* London: Duckworth, 1938, 279 pp., illus.
Pp. 19-20, the "Talking Cross" cult or "Santa Cruz," with quotation of letter to the Superintendent of Belize, from the Chief of the Santa Cruz Indians – from letter-book at Government House. See also entry 205.

204 Gann, Thomas [William Francis]. *In an unknown land.* London and New York: Duckworth & Co., 1924, 363 pp., illus.
Pp. 32-34, Holy Cross cult as observed in 1859.

205 Gann, Thomas [William Francis]. *The Maya Indians of Southern Yucatan and Northern British Honduras.* Bureau of American Ethnology Bulletin 64. Washington, D.C.: Government Printing Office, 1918, 146 pp.
Pp. 40-42, "Religion" – including, pp. 41-42, the "Talking Cross" of Santa Cruz, with extract from Henry Fowler's narrative, Belize, 1879.

206 Gaxiola, Maclovio L. *Historia de la Iglesia Apostólica de la Fe en Cristo Jesús de Mexico.* Mexico, D.F.: Libréria Latinoamericana, 1964.
The earliest Pentecostal independent Church (1914), among ladinos and Indians; by a long-time bishop.

207 Gaxiola, Manuel J. "Letter." *Mission Studies* (Leiden), no. 1 (1984), 68-70.
An updating report on his own activities as a bishop in the Iglesia Apostólica de la Fe en Cristo Jesús.

208 Gaxiola, Manuel J. *La serpiente y la paloma.* South Pasadena, Calif.: Carey Library, 1970, 177 pp.
On the Iglesia Apostólica de la Fe en Cristo Jesús.

209 Gonzalez Navarro, Moisés. "La guerra de castas en Yucatán y la venta de Mayas a Cuba." *Historia Mexicana* (Mexico, D.F.), no. 69 [18, no. 1] (July-September 1968): 11-34, bib., notes.

Mexico

Mainly on the government's outlook; otherwise similar to entry 250.

210 Gonzalez Navarro, Moisés. *Raza y tierra: La Guerra de Castas y el henequén*. Centro de Estudios Historicos, n.s. 10. Guanajuato: El Colegio de México, 1970, 392 pp., bib.
Pp. 21-31, "Evangelizacion y obvenciones"; pp. 31-42, "Las rebeliones indigenas."

211 Goodman, Felicitas D. "Apostolics of Yucatán: A case study of a religious movement." In *Religion, altered states of consciousness, and social change*, edited by E. Bourguignon. Columbus: Ohio State University Press, 1973, pp. 178-218.
A Maya congregation of the Iglesia Apostólica de la Fe en Cristo Jesús de Mexico; the earliest Pentecostal independent church, here among Mayan peasants.

212 Goodman, Felicitas D. "Disturbances in the Apostolic Church: A trance-based upheaval in Yucatan." In *Trance, healing, and hallucination*, edited by F. D. Goodman, et al. New York: John Wiley & Sons, 1974, pp. 227-364.

213 Gossen, Gary H. "Translating Cuscat's war: Understanding Maya oral history." *Journal of Latin American Lore* 3, no. 2 (1977): 249-78.

214 Gow, David D[rummond]. "Simbolo y protesta: Movimientos redentores en Chiapas y en los Andes peruanos." *América Indígena* 39, no. 1 (1979): 47-80.
Mexican and Peruvian Indian movements compared.

215 Greenleaf, Richard E. "The Inquisition in Colonial Mexico: Heretical thoughts on the spiritual conquest." In *Religion in Latin American life and literature*, edited by L. C. Brown. Waco, Tex.: Markham Press Fund, 1980, pp. 70-82.
Pp. 71-75, on Amerindian resistance through nativistic and syncretistic religious developments.

216 Greenway, R. S. "The 'Luz del Mundo' movement in Mexico." *Missiology* 1, no. 2 (April 1973): 113-24.
A one-ness Pentecostal but strongly biblical and evangelical indigenous church among ladinos, founded by prophet Joaquin, named Aaron (hence "Aaronistas") after a vision, about 1940.

217 Hellbom, Anna-Britta. "Reflejos de 'sincretismo' en el valle de México." In *Actes du 42e Congrès International des Américanistes, Paris, 1976.* Vol. 6. Paris: Musée de l'Homme, 1979, pp. 73-84.

218 Heyden, Doris. "Birth of a deity: The Talking Cross of Tulum." *Tlalocan* (Mexico, La Casa de Tlaloc, with Instituto Nacional de Antropología) 5, no. 3 (1967): 235-42.

219 Huerta, Maria Teresa, and Palacios, Patricia, eds. *Rebeliones indígenas de la época colonial.* Mexico: SEP-INAH, 1976.
    A seminar at Instituto Nacional de Antropología e Historia. Documents and bibliography for all thirteen revolts from 1523 (Panuco) to 1761 (Yucatan) in an area of modern Mexico.

220 Jiménez-Moreno, Wigberto. "Popular religious expression in Latin America." In *The religious dimension in the new Latin America*, edited by J. J. Considine. Notre Dame, Ind.: Fides Publishers, 1966, pp. 43-57.
    Mexico as representative; veneration of the Cross, the cult of the Virgin of Guadaloupe; other similar sanctuaries as pilgrimage centers – all as Indian independent developments.

221 Jones, G[rant] D. "Levels of settlement alliance." In *Anthropology and history in Yucatan*, edited by G. D. Jones. Austin: University of Texas Press, 1977, pp. 139-83.
    Pp. 172-73, Talking Cross cult of 1850.

222 Kearney, Michael. "Oral performance by Mexican spiritualists in possession trance." *Journal of Latin American Lore* 3, no. 2 (1977): 309-238.
    Spiritualism as ecstatic cult movements. As found around city of Ensenada, Baja California, brought by migrants from elsewhere in Mexico.

223 Kelly, Isabel. "Mexican Spiritualism." *Kroeber Anthropological Society Papers* 25 (1961): 191-206.

224 Klein, Herbert S[anford]. "Peasant communities in revolt: The Tzeltal republic of 1712." *Pacific Historical Review* (Los Angeles) 35, no. 3 (1966): 247-63.
    Tzeltal Indians in Chiapas and their capacity for organization, in the revolt that Maria Candelaria encouraged. See entry 225 for Spanish translation.

Central America

Mexico

225 Klein, Herbert S[anford]. "Rebeliones de las communidades campesinas: La República Tzeltal de 1712." In *Ensayos de antropología en la Zona Central de Chiapas*, compiled by N. A. McQuown and J. Pitt-Rivers. Mexico, D.F.: Instituto Nacional Indigenista, 1970, pp. 148-70.
The origins and course of the revolt inspired by Maria Candelaria and a syncretist religion.

226 Lafaye, Jacques. "L'utopie mexicaine / Mexico according to Quetzalcoatl: An essay of intra-history." *Diogène* (Paris), no. 78 (Summer 1972), pp. 20-39; also in *Diogenes* (Florence), no. 78 (Summer 1972), 18-37.
The interplay between indigenous Indian and Christian politico-religious myths, including messianism, in Mexico.

227 Lagarriga Attias, Isabel. "Un ejemplo de religiosidad de los marginales de México: El espiritualismo trinitario Mariano." In *Religión y sociedad*. Mexico: Departmento de Etnología y Antropología Social, Instituto Nacional de Antropología e Historia, 1977, 72 pp. in various pagings. Summary in *Actes du 42e Congrès International des Américanistes, Paris, 1976.* Paris: Musée de l'Homme, 1979, pp. 111-17.

228 Lagarriga Attias, Isabel. *Medicina tradicional y espiritismo: Los espiritualistas trinitarios marianos de Jalapa, Veracruz.* Sep. Setentas, 191. Mexico: Secretaría de Educación Pública, Dirección General de Divulgación, 1975, 158 pp., bib., illus., maps.
Spiritualists' rites, diagnosis, and healing methods.

229 Laurencio, Juan. [Letter to Padro Rodrigo de Cabredo in 1609.] Reprinted by Pérez de Ribas in *Córonica* . . . , vol. 1, pp. 284-92 (see entry 244), and from his source, in Francisco Javier Alegre. *Historia de la Provincia de la Compañía de Jesús en la Nueva España.* Rome, 4 vols. 1956-60; vol. 2, pp. 175-83.
A Jesuit eye-witness account of a Maroon community in 1609 in the mountains near Veracruz, which retained its freedom and a form of Catholicism.

230 Macklin, [Barbara] June. "Belief, ritual, and healing: New England Spiritualism and Mexican-American spiritism compared." In *Religious movements in contemporary America*, edited by I. I. Zaretsky and M. P. Leone. Princeton: Princeton University Press, 1974, pp. 383-417.
Pp. 385-88, history of Spiritualism; pp. 388-93, Rivail and Kardecism; pp. 394-402, a Mexican-American cult in a small Indian

town, with El Niño Fidencio as the active spirit; pp. 402-11, New England Spiritualism; pp. 411-16, analysis.

231 Madsen, William. *Handbook of Middle American Indians*, edited by M. Nash.. Vol. 6, *Social anthropology*. Austin: University of Texas Press, 1967, pp. 369-91, illus.

Especially among the Aztecs and Maya, with pp. 387-89 on cult of the Talking Cross.

232 Maler, Teobert. "Mémoire sur l'état de Chiapa (Mexique)." *Revue d'Ethnographie* (Paris) 3 (1885): 295-342.

Pp. 308-11, on Tzotzil revolt of 1869 and "Santa Rosa" leader.

233 Miller, William. "A journey from British Honduras to Santa Cruz, Yucatan." *Proceedings of the Royal Geographical Society* (London), n.s. 11, no. 1 (January 1889): 23-28, map.

Pp. 26-27, on a "talking cross" among Maya Indians of Santa Cruz, near Tulum.

234 Molina, Cristóbal. *War of the Castes: Indian uprisings in Chiapas, 1867-70*. Middle American Series, Tulane University, Pamphlet 8, Publication 5. New Orleans: Tulane University, 1934, pp. 359-401, map.

Pp. 365-85, 389-401, the more religious aspects.

235 Mondloch, J. "Sincretismo religioso maya-cristão en la tradición oral de una communidad quiché." *Mesoamérica* 3 (1982): 107-23.

Maya-Christian religious syncretism in the oral tradition of a Quiche community. No particular movement described.

236 Mondragon, Sergio. "Los espiritualistas." *Revista de América* (Paris), 2 September 1961.

237 Mondragon, Sergio. "Patraña, poesia o fraude a los humildes? La alucinante aventura de los espiritualistas." *Revista de América* (Paris), 27 May 1961.

238 Nebel, Richard. "Christological aspects of the ancient Mexican-Christian popular piety in modern Mexico." *Verbum S.V.D.* 27, no. 1 (1986): 43-52.

Cultural-historical background and popular "Christo-paganism" as basis for a local Christology; current "Jesusology" emphasizes the suffering Christ but not His resurrection.

Mexico

239 Nutini, Hugo G. "Syncretism and acculturation: The historical development of the cult of the patron saint in Tlaxcala, Mexico." *Ethnology* 15, no. 3 (July 1976): 301-21.
     The cult of the Virgin of Ocotlán as exhibiting a "guided syncretism," especially in its symbolic aspects, during the first century and a half after the conquest.

240 Ortiz Echanez, Silvia. "Origen, desarrollo y características del espiritismo en México." *América Indígena* 39, no. 1 (January-March 1979): 147-70.
     Mexican Spiritualism began in 1866 when Roque Rojas founded the Iglesia Mexicana Patriacal del Elías with himself as the new messiah; later split in several groups, but some 500 temples exist, mostly in Mexico City, and their poor followers combine Judaism, folk Catholicism, and nationalism.

241 Palmer, Colin A. *Slaves of the white god: Blacks in Mexico, 1570-1650.* Cambridge: Harvard University Press, 1976, 234 pp., map.
     Pp. 54-55, black cofradias; pp. 162-66, religious syncretism in a folk Catholicism among blacks.

242 Paniagua, Flavio [Antonio]. *Florinda.* Chiapas, Mexico: 1889.
     A romance about the Cuzcat revolt of 1867-70–by a native of San Cristobal where the revolt centered.

243 Perez Castro, Ana Bella. "Mitos y creencias en los movimientos mesiánicos y luchas campesinas en Chiapas." *Anales de Antropologia* (Mexico) 17, no. 2 (1980): 185-95; English summary (p. 194).
     Pp. 187-88, the Cancuc movement (1712); pp. 188-90, the Chanula Tzajalhemel movement (1867); discussion of associated myths.

244 Pérez de Ribas. *Corónica y historia religiosa de la provincia de la Compañía de Jesús de México en Nueva España.* 2 vols. Mexico City, 1896.
     Vol. 1, pp. 285, 288-90, the Catholic features in the free Maroon settlement on 1609 near Veracruz; see further under J. Laurencio (entry 229).

245 Pineda, Vicente. *Historia de las sublevaciones indígenas habidas en el estado de Chiápas.* San Cristóbal de las Casas, Mexico: Tipografia del Gobierno, 1888.

Based on an unpublished contemporary official report of the War of the Castes by President Cocio, and on local oral traditions, including accounts of the Tzeltal revolt, 1712.

246 Porro, Antonio. "Millenarismus der Maya während der Kolonialzeit." *Ethnologia Americana* (Dusseldorf) 15, no. 6 (1979): 895ff.
Surveys movements in what is now Guatemala in 1524.

247 Porro, Antonio. "Un nuevo caso de milenarisimo maya en Chiapas y Tabasco, Mexico, 1727." *Estudios de Historia Novohispana* (Mexico City, Universidad Nacional Autónoma de Mexico, Instituto de Historia, Seminario de Cultura Nahuatl) 6 (1978): 109-17, map.
The unsuccessful 1712 revolt in Chiapas and Tabasco, as forerunner of the 1727 rising and of many later uprisings of a messianic nature.

248 Pozas, Ricardo Arciniega. *Juan the Chanula: An ethnological re-creation of the life of a Mexican Indian.* Berkeley and Los Angeles: University of California Press, 1962, 115 pp., illus.
A novel, set in the time of the rebellion, 1867-70, in southern Mexico under Cuzcat. Religious references are more on general Christo-paganism.

249 Price, William J. "The Costumbre – a Maya-Christian syncretism." In *The Religious Dimension in the new Latin America*, edited by J. J. Considine. Notre Dame, Ind.: Fides Publishers, 1966, pp. 88-101.
Maya Costumbre "the sum of Maya religious culture"; see especially pp. 88-101 on the new system with its Cult of the Cross.

250 Reed, Nelson. *The Caste War of Yucatán.* Stanford: Stanford University Press, 1964, 308 pp., illus.
Maya revolts of 1847 to 1855 led to the syncretistic cult of the Talking Cross: a vivid history based on extensive local and archival research. On the cult see especially pp. 132-45, the appearance of the cult (1850-52); pp. 159-84, activities (1855-61); pp. 206-24, development and later history; pp. 275-80, contemporary surviving beliefs; pp. 223-24, Maria Uicab's rival Talking Cross at Tulum in 1870s-80s.

251 Riefler de Bricker, Victoria. "Algunas consecuencias religiosas y sociales del nativismo maya del siglo XIX." *América Indígena* (Mexico, D.F.) 33, no. 2 (April-June 1973): 327-48, bib.
Analysis of a fiesta still held by Indians of Chamula (Chiapas State) commemorating events in the Cuzcat revolt of 1868-70, and

other troubles: pp. 330-37, Cuzcat and the War, based on V. Pineda (entry 245), C. Molina (entry 234), N. Reed (entry 250) and contemporary newspapers; pp. 337-46, interpretation as historical representation.

252 Riefler de Bricker, Victoria. "The Caste War of Yucatán: The history of a myth and the myth of history." In *Anthropology and history in Yucatan*, edited by G. D. Jones. Austin: University of Texas Press, 1977, pp. 251-58.

253 Riefler de Bricker, Victoria. *The Indian Christ, the Indian king: The historical substrate of Maya myth and ritual.* Austin: University of Texas Press, 1981, xiv + 368 pp., bib., maps.
   The "First 'Rebellions' (1511-1697)"; Colonial rebellions – four early eighteenth century highland Chiapas religious movements (including Cancuc) associated with saint worship, the 1761 Jacinto Canek revolt, and a purported Guatemalan revolt in 1820 (of Totonicapán); two postcolonial revolts – the Caste War 1847-1901, and the War of Santa Rosa in Chanula (1867-70). Uses Lévi-Strauss's structuralism for interpretation of Maya cyclic and Spanish pacification views.

254 Riefler de Bricker, Victoria. "Les insurrections des Mayas: La pensée sauvage." *Actes du 42e Congrès International des Américanistes, Paris, 1976.* Paris: Société des Américanistes; Musée de l'Homme, 1978, pp. 33-43.
   On rewriting the history of the five Maya revolts from 1712 to 1867 to include the Indian viewpoint; pp. 34-36, Tzeltal revolt; pp. 36-38, Totonicapán (Guatemala), 1820; pp. 38-41, War of the Castes, 1847-53.

255 Riefler de Bricker, Victoria. "Movimientos religiosos indígenas en los altos de Chiapas." *América Indígena* 39, no. 1 (1979): 17-46.
   New saints' cults introduced since the early eighteenth century; their relation to the Tzeltal revolt of 1712 and the 1869 Chamulan rising.

256 Roys, Ralph L[oveland]. *The Book of Chilam Balam of Chumayel.* Washington, D.C.: Carnegie Institution, 1933, 229 pp., illus. Reprint. Norman: University of Oklahoma Press, 1967.
   Chilam Balam, the last and greatest of the Mayan prophets, late fifteenth-early sixteenth centuries, prophesied the coming of strangers from the east to establish a new religion: see pp. 182-87 on Maya

prophecies, and pp. 164-69, translation of the prophecies of a new religion, with explanatory notes; the prophecies probably referred to the return of Quetzalcoatl, the culture-hero, but were later applied to the Spaniards and Christianity, and formed a validation for new religious movements.

257 Rubio Mane, Jorge Ignacio. "La guerra de castas según un escritor angloamericano." *Revista de la Universidad de Yucatán* (Mérida) 61 [11] (January-February 1969): 9-20.
    A review article on N. Reed (entry 250) as oversympathetic to the rebels.

258 Sapper, Karl. "Independent Indian states of Yucatan." *Bulletin, Bureau of American Ethnology* 28 (1904): 625-34. Translated and reprinted from *Globus* 67, no. 13.
    A favorable report on the Mayan "states" resulting from the War of the Castes, as found in a journey in 1894; little on religion, but see p.628 on church services led by a Mayan layman.

259 Scholes, France V., and Roys, Ralph [Loveland]. "Fray Diego de Landa and the problem of idolatry in Yucatan." In *Cooperation in Research*. Carnegie Institution Publication no. 501. Washington, D.C.: Carnegie Institution, 1938, pp. 585-620.
    Pp. 604-8, early examples of primal cults surviving in the Christian period by the admixture of some Christian elements.

260 Taylor, William. "La Indiada: Peasant uprisings in central Mexico and Oaxaca, 1700-1810." *Actes du 42e Congrès International des Américanistes ... Paris, 1976.* Paris: Société des Américanistes; Musée de l'Homme, 1978, pp. 189-91, 196.
    P. 191, "New Saviour" millennial neoprimal movement in 1769 in Hidalgo state; p. 196, notes for this.

261 Thays, Carmen Delgado de. "Religión y magia en Tupe (Yauyos)." CIDOC: Sondeos, 28. Cuernavaca, Mexico: Centro Intercultural de Documentación, 1968, various pagination [ca. 260 pp.]. Mimeo.
    Full ethnographic description of the syncretistic religious, etc., activities of a town at the center of Canqui culture.

262 Thompson, Donald E[ugene]. *Maya paganism and Christianity: A history of the fusion of two religions.* Middle American Research Institute Publications, 19. New Orleans: Tulane University, 1954, pp. 1-

Mexico

35. Reprinted in *Nativism and syncretism*, by M. S. Edmonson, et al. New Orleans: Tulane University, 1960, pp. 1-36.

Pp. 11-22, the imposition of Christianity and its results; pp. 16-16, nativism; pp. 17-18, Talking Cross; pp. 18-20, Cuzcat and Tzotzil revolt; pp. 20-21, Tzeltal revolt, 1712: all good outlines quoting earlier sources. Pp. 23-30, present-day Maya religion, syncretistic, with a personified cross; pp. 31-32, conclusion.

263 Trens [Marentes], Manuel B[artolmé]. *Historia de Chiapas, desde los tiempos mas remotos hasta la caida del Segundo Imperio*. 2d ed. Mexico City, 1957.

Pp. 189-90, the Zinacantan Tzotzil religious revival, 1708-10; pp. 190-95, the Maria Candelaria movement.

264 Van Young, Eric. "Millennium on the northern marches: The mad messiah of Durango and popular rebellion." *Comparative Studies in Society and History* 28, no. 3 (1986): 385-413.

On Indian rebels preceding the Hidalgo revolt for independence in 1810, especially José Bernado Herrada, active 1800-1801. Also useful for further references on Indian popular revolts.

265 Vanderwood, Paul J. "Crisis cult at Tomóchic, 1891-1892" [summary of informal presentation]. In *International Colloquium: The Indians of Mexico in pre-Colombian and modern times. Leiden . . . 1981*, edited by M. E. R. G. N. Jansen and Th. J. J. Leyenaar. Leiden: Rutgers B.V., 1982, pp. 259-62 + illus., pp. 263-68.

State military conflict with a section of the Teresa Urrea movement.

266 Velasco Toro, José. "Indigenismo y rebelión Totonaca de Papantla, 1885-1896." *América Indígena* 39, no. 1 (1979): 81-105.

In State of Veracruz, armed risings against forced decommunalization of land, in 1885, 1892 and 1896. The leader of the first, Antonio Diaz Mantfort, known as the "holy doctor," advocated return to Catholic religion, expulsion of foreigners, reduced taxes, and land rights; pp. 100-102, text of his proclamation.

267 Ventur, Pierre. Review article on *The Indian Christ, the Indian king*, by V. Riefler de Bricker (entry 253). *Latin American Indian Literature* 6, no. 2 (1982): 133-40.

268 Villa Rojas, Alfonso. "El culto de la Cruz que habla entre los Mayas del Territorio de Quintana Roo." *Diario del Sureste* (Mérida), 20 November 1937, pp. 5ff., illus.
By a historian at the Carnegie Institution, Washington, D.C.

269 Villa Rojas, Alfonso. *Los elegidos de Dios: Etnografía de los Mayas de Quintana Roo.* Appendix by Howard E. Cline, "Sobre la Guerra de Castas." Serie de Antropología Social, 56. Mexico, D.F.: Instituto Nacional Indigenista, 1978, 574 pp., illus., map.
Pp. 97-103, cult of the Talking Cross; chap. 10 (pp. 277-311), "El complejo religioso pagano-christiano"; pp. 459-69, "Appendix B. Sermon de la Cruz que Habla. Traducido de un manuscrito redactado por los Mayas de Chan Santa Cruz."

270 Villa R[ojas], Alfonso. *The Maya of East Central Quintana Roo.* Publication 559. Washington, D.C.: Carnegie Institution, 1945, 182 pp.
Pp. 20-25, cult of the Cross; pp. 30-31, survival of the cult; pp. 97-110, the pagan-Christian religious complex, with references to the place of the Cross; p. 161-64, sermons of the Talking Cross (translated from the Maya) containing the "commandments" of Juan de la Cruz; pp. 167-72, bibliographic remarks on the War of the Castes. For Spanish version, see entry 269.

271 Vogt, Evon Z. "Gods and politics in Zinacantan and Chamula." *Ethnology* 12, no. 2 (1973): 99-113, illus.
Pp. 103-4, revolts associated with new religious developments.

272 Wasson, R. Gordon; Cowan, George [M.]; Cowan, Florence [H.]; and Rhodes, Willard. *María Sabina and her Mazatec mushroom velada.* New York: Harcourt Brace Jovanovich, 1974, 282 pp., music (79 pp. of musical transcriptions, 4 cassettes of field recordings), illus., maps.
A Christian-Indian syncretist shamanist healing rite in Oaxaca, performed by a shaman, or *curandera*, during a *velada*, or night vigil. See pp. xiii and xv for brief comments on Christian aspects.

273 Wilson, Carter. *A green tree and a dry tree.* New York: Macmillan, 1972, 300 pp., maps, notes.
Rebellion of 1867-70 in Southern Mexico under mystical leader, Cuzcat – a syncretist Maya-Christian revitalization movement: a historical reconstruction as a novel based on careful research. For the religious aspects see especially Part 3, "God's play, 1867-1870" (pp. 159-285).

Mexico

274 Ximénez, Francisco. *Historia de la Provincia de San Vicente de Chiápa y Guatemala de la Orden de Predicadores*. Vols. 1-3. Biblioteca Guatemala. Guatemala: Tipografía Nacional, 1929-31.

About 1721, Ximénez, the discoverer of Popol Vuh, wrote on the Tzeltal revolt of 1712–in vol. 3, pp. 257-358: see Book 6, chaps. 58-64; also on the Tzotzil religious revival of 1708-10, pp. 226-64; on a similar cult in 1711, pp. 265-67; on the Maria Candelaria movement, pp. 267ff.; p. 297, a Tila Indian claiming to be Christ.

275 Zimmerman, Charlotte. "The cult of the Holy Cross: An analysis of cosmology and Catholicism in Quintana Roo." *History of Religions* 3, no. 1 (Summer 1963): 50-71.

Among Maya Indians of the Yucatan from 1850–a military and religious cult arising after defeat, not Christian but rather cosmological and pre-Christian in origin (thus differing from R. Redfield's views), although Christian symbolism is used.

276 Zimmerman, Charlotte. "The hermeneutics of the Maya cult of the Holy Cross." *Numen* 12, no. 2 (April 1965): 139-59.

A valuable theoretical and historical article: pp. 139-43, theory of hermeneutics; pp. 143-147 et passim, history of the cult from 1950 to its contemporary decline; pp. 147-50, interpretation as an authentic religious response by an archaic or "cosmological" culture to Christianity and Western technological superiority.

Nicaragua

The small Indian population of some 4% is concentrated among the Miskito people of the east coast, also referred to as Moskitos or Mosquitos. Here the first Protestant mission was commenced by the Moravians in 1849 and has led to the largest Protestant church in Nicaragua. Some 95% of its members, however, are black. This section of the population forms about 8% of the whole and comes largely from Jamaica; some Jamaican movements therefore are found here.

The literature seems concentrated on reports of what is called the "awakening" or "revival" among the Miskito Indians in 1881-96, after the translation of the New Testament in 1880: see T. A. Good (entry 278) and J. E. Hutton (entry 280), and also *Missionary Review of the World* (entry 277).

One item, M. W. Helms (entry 279), discusses the Miskito Indians in relation to the Moravians and also mentions a semi-independent Miskito church, the Iglesia de Dios, which is related to the Church of God, Cleveland, Tennessee.

277 "Central America: Mosquitoland is a part of Nicaragua." *Missionary Review of the World*, o.s. 11, no. 3 [n.s. 1, no. 3] (March 1888): 230.
   The revival of 1881 among Moravian mission Indians after the translation of the New Testament in 1880.

278 Good, Thelma A. "Now–what? 125 years of Moravian missions in Bluefields." Bluefields: N.p., 1974, 25 pp. Mimeo.
   Pp. 10-12, the 1881 awakening in Bluefields on the Mosquito Coast, resembling the Jamaica revival of 1860, but among Moravian mission Indians.

279 Helms, Mary W. *Asang: Adaptations to culture contact in a Miskito community.* Gainesville: University of Florida Press, 1971, 168 pp., illus., maps, bib.
   A village in northern Nicaragua in 1964-65; discusses adaptation to Christian missions by Moravians, and the semi-independent Iglesia de Dios (from Church of God, Cleveland).

280 Hutton, Joseph Edmund. *A history of Moravian missions*. London: Moravian Publications Office, [ca. 1922], 550 pp.
   Pp. 334-39, the revival of 1881-96 among Miskito Indians.

281 Wilson, John. *Obra morava en Nicaragua: Trasfondo y breve historia.* San José, Costa Rica: Seminario Biblico Latinoamericano, 1975.
   P. 205, the 1880s "awakening" among Moravian Miskitos.

Panama

The black population is some 14%, about a third of which is Jamaican in origin and therefore there are some movements from the same source. The only item here on a black movement is R. S. Bryce-Laporte (entry 284), which includes the "Jump-Up" or "Benjinite" church.

Of the Indian population of some 7%, over half belong to the Guaymi people. An important movement began among the Western Guaymi or Ngawbe about 1962, the Mama Chi (Little Mother) movement under Delia Atencio, but this was in decline by 1973: see the New Tribes Mission agent H. Sheffield (entry 287), the anthropologist P. D. Young (entry 288) and the Survival International Review (entry 286).

282 Alphonse, Ephraim J. S. "Some reminiscences of Guaymi cults." Transcription of interview by Rev. Dr. D. Dunn Wilson, June 1987, 3 pp.

Panama

Mama Chi cult, founded 1960, described by Panamanian pioneer Methodist evangelist among the Guaymi Indians. Includes dream descriptions.

283 Bort, John Roger. "Guaymí innovators: A case study of entrepreneurs in a small scale society." Ph.D. dissertation (anthropology), University of Oregon, 1976, 214 pp.
    Primarily on economic entrepreneurs and change as background to the Mama Chi movement.

284 Bryce-Laporte, R. S. "Crisis, contraculture, and religion among West Indians in the Panama Canal Zone." In *Afro-American anthropology: Contemporary perspectives*, edited by N. E. Whitten, Jr., and J. F. Szwed. New York: Free Press, 1970, pp. 103-18.
    Includes "Jump-Up" or "Benjinite" Church – with African, Roman Catholic and evangelical Protestant elements.

285 Drolet, Patricia Lund. "The Congo ritual of Northeastern Panama: An Afro-American expressive structure of cultural adaptation." Ph.D. dissertation (cultural anthropology), University of Illinois at Urbana-Champaign, 1980, 296 pp.
    A large-scale annual six-week ritual among Spanish-speaking blacks in eight small towns in the area of Costa Arriba – providing a world-view, social solidarity and cultural adaptation; the religious dimension (e.g., baptism) shows syncretism with Catholicism, but is not dealt with at length.

286 "The Guaymi Comarca." *Survival International Review*, no. 39 [7, no. 1] (Spring 1982): 44-45.
    English translation of article in *Dialogo Social*, April 1981, on the Guaymi demands for recognition of their region, "the Comarca"; p. 45, brief account of failure of an earlier movement, with wider demands, inspired by the Mama Chi new religion.

287 Sheffield, Henry. "Mama Chi – Little Mother." *Brown Gold* (Woodworth, Wis., New Tribes Mission) 30, no. 9 (1973): 4-5.
    A missionary account of origins and present decline of the movement begun by Delia Atencio in 1962 – based on her cousin's version.

288 Young, Philip D[onald]. *Ngawbe: Tradition and change among the Western Guaymi of Panama*. Illinois Studies in Anthropology, 7. Urbana: University of Illinois Press, 1971, 257 pp., illus., maps.

Pp. 212-25, et passim, new Mama Chi cult, 1961, among the Ngawbe or western Guaymi; San Felix district, Chiriqui Province.

South America

Theory

Much of the material placed under Latin America: Theory also applies to South America. M. M. Marzal (entry 293) is a simple introduction. A. Dorsinfang-Smets (entry 289) is the Spanish version of her 1954 French original and has an English summary; she surveys the varieties and degrees of acculturation among Indians, Negroes and whites in all South American countries.

A. Posern-Zielinski (entry 295) provides a theoretical discussion of syncretist socioreligious movements and their ideologies, classification, and millennial, nativistic and prophetism features. This item examines why there are so few religious interaction movements among South American Indians in the present century (see especially pp. 158-59) and looks at such factors as geographical accessibility or inaccessibility, types of colonization and of slavery, Indian cultural types (e.g., the special nature of Guarani millenarianism), the power of the Inca restoration myth or hope, and the economic base of hunting or farming. Other factors are the susceptibility to contagious diseases and the consequent extermination of populations, loss of territory, of social identity and hence of the will to survive, and the exodus to the "civilized" world in search of better conditions. Although many of these factors appear among the causes of new religious movements in tribal peoples in other parts of the world, there seems to have been a peculiar conjunction of traumatic factors in this continent which has operated in the opposite direction.

M. I. P. de Queiroz (entry 296) discusss R. Bastide's contribution; although his work was focused on Brazil, it has theoretical value for the whole continent. The same applies to M. Eliade (entry 290), which is a more

Theory

theoretical discussion of the Guarani (Paraguay, Brazil and adjacent areas) search for a lost paradise, and to R. C. de Oliveira (entry 294), who discusses acculturation theories in relation to a study of the Tukuna people in Brazil. The item by B. Ertle (entry 291) has a general reference to tribal peoples and the causes of these movements among them, but has South American, and especially Brazilian, examples – the Guarani, the Santidade movements, messianism among the Canela, as well as rural mestizos' messianic movements; these latter, however, as we explain in the introduction to the Latin America and Caribbean volumes, do not come within the agenda of this series.

As always, there is much theoretical material contained in items classified in other ways.

289 Dorsinfang-Smets, A. "Contacts de cultures et problèmes d'acculturation en Amérique du Sud." *Revue de L'Institut de Sociologie Solvay* (Brussels) 27, no. 3 (1954): 647-66. Spanish version in *América Indígena* (Mexico, D.F.) 15, no. 4 (1955): 217-91; English summary.

Survey of varieties and degrees of acculturation among Indians, Negroes, and whites in all South American countries.

290 Eliade, Mircea. "Paradise and Utopia: Mythical geography and eschatology." In *Utopias and Utopian thought*, edited by F. E. Manuel. Boston: Beacon Press, 1967, pp. 260-80. Reprinted from "Paradis et utopie: Géographie mythique et eschatologie." In *Vom Sinn der Utopie, Eranos Jahrbuch 1963*. Zurich: Rhein-Verlag, 1964. Reprinted in *The Quest*. Chicago: University of Chicago Press, 1969, pp. 101-11.

Pp. 270-78, a more theoretical discussion of the Guarani search for the Lost Paradise.

291 Ertle, Brigitte. "Uber Ursachen messianischer Bewegugnen unter Naturvölken." *Zeitschrift für Ethnologie* (Brunswick) 97, no. 1 (1972): 61-73.

A good survey of causal theories and criteria for these; South American illustrative examples: Guarani "terre-sans-mal" movements as indigenous millennialism accentuated by white contact; Santidade movements and the Canela messianism as syncretistic, after disintegrating contact; Brazilian rural messianisms using a "bastard Catholicism" for social renewal.

292 Kostash, Janis Mary. "Indians on the edge of the Spanish empire: The Yaquis and Mapuche in relation to nativistic and revitalization theory." M.A. thesis, Tulane University, 1968, 99 pp.

Theory

293 Marzal, Manuel M. "Religions populaires d'Amérique du Sud." *Recherches de Sciences Religieuses* (Paris) 63 (1975): 215-42.

Catholic, Andean and African traditions–their beliefs, rites and organization, syncretist features, and contributions to modernity.

294 Oliveira, Roberto Cardoso de. *O índio e o mundo dos brancos: A situaçio dos Tukúna do alto Solimies.* Corpo e almo do Brasil, 12. São Paulo: Difusão Europeia do Livro, 1964, 143 pp., illus., bib.

Important discussion of acculturation in Brazil, reviewing and criticizing existing theories and adding his own–"inter-ethnic friction." Essential for specialists in culture change.

295 Posern-Zielinski, A[leksander]. "From comparative studies of the socio-religious movements of the Indians in Spanish South America." *Ethnologia Polona* 1 (1975): 151-70.

Four categories of movements: sectarian, escapist-millenarian, revolutionary-millenarian, secular protest movements with millenarian elements. The factors of ideology or myth, charismatic leaders, and relative deprivation are interwoven.

296 Queiroz, M[aria] I[saura] Pereira de. "Principe de participation et principe de coupure: La contribution de Roger Bastide à leur définition sociologique." *Archives de Sciences Sociales des Religions* 47, no. 1 (1979): 147-57; English summary (p. 147).

Based on her study of Afro-Brazilian religions.

General

There are few general surveys, mostly in French, and these often include the messianic movements among mestizos or whites that do not fall within our definition; the latter, however, have a certain value for comparative purposes. V. Lanternari, *The religions of the oppressed* (London: MacGibbon & Kee, 1963), may serve as a start. A. Métraux (entries 303, with French translation, and 305, with Spanish translation) has a heavy emphasis on messianism but includes examples from the tribal peoples with whom we are concerned. M. I. P. de Queiroz (entry 307) is a good descriptive and interpretative survey.

General literature on the Guarani is included here in view of their ranging over much of central South America, through Bolivia, northern Argentina, Paraguay, and Brazil. They form a marginal case, important because of their precontact millenarianism but much less clear as to their interaction with Christianity. See P. Clastres (entry 298); E. Schaden (entry 309); M. I. P. de Queiroz (entry 306); and also B. R. Wilson (entry 312).

General

297 Clastres, Hélène. *La terre sans mal: Le prophétisme tupi-guarani*. Recherches Anthropologiques. Paris: Éditions du Seuil, 1975, 157 pp.

On the question of the Tupi-Guarani migratory quests for paradise as a precontact indigenous feature or a postcontact millennial reaction to oppression; adopts the former position and presents the quest as an impressive manifestation of religion. Based on a Sorbonne dissertation (3e cycle), 1972.

298 Clastres, Pierre. "Prophètes dans la jungle." In *Exchanges et communications ... offerts à Claude Lévi-Strauss*, compiled by J. Pouillon and P. Miranda. The Hague: Mouton, 1970, vol. 1, pp. 535-42.

On the Tupi-Guarani, especially the Mbya section, and their messianism.

299 Clastres, Pierre. "Religions et sociétés indiennes de l'Amérique du Sud." *Annuaire École Pratique des Hautes Études* (Paris) 85 (1977-1978): 53-54.

Tupi-Guarani prophetic movements; a report on the school's 1977-78 seminar.

300 Hurzeler, Richard Paul. "Messianic movements among American aborigines." M.A. dissertation, 1965, Columbia University, 108 pp.

Describes these activities among Indians of North and South America.

301 Imazio, Alicia. "Una hipotesis de trabajo referida al San La Muerte." *Folklore Americano* (Lima) 19-20 (1971-72): 110-16.

A secret syncretistic spiritist cult in Paraguay, Argentina, and Brazil. Based on field work.

302 Métraux, Alfred. "Jésuites et Indiens en Amérique du Sud." *Revue de Paris* (Paris), June 1952, pp. 201-13.

With special reference to Paraguay and Bolivia.

303 Métraux, Alfred. "Messiahs of South America." *Inter-American Quarterly* (formerly *Quarterly Journal of Interamerican Relations*) 3, no. 2 (1941): 53-60. French translation. "Les messies de l'Amérique du Sud." *Archives de Sociologie des Religions* 4 (1957): 108-12.

304 Métraux, Alfred. [Messianism.] In *Handbook of South American Indians*, edited by J. H. Steward. Vol. 3, *The tropical forest tribes*. Bureau of American Ethnology Bulletin 143. Washington, D.C.: Smithsonian Institution, 1948.

Pp. 77, 93-94, Guarani messianism; pp. 98, 131, Tupinambo revivalism; pp. 436-37, Guarayu messianism; p. 468, Chiriguano messiah, p. 512, Atahualpa as messiah.

305 Métraux, Alfred. *Religions et magies indiennes d'Amérique du Sud* (édition posthume . . . par Simone Dreyfus). Bibliothèque des Sciences Humaines. Paris: Gallimard, 1967, 290 pp., illus., map, bib. Spanish translation. *Religión y magias indígenas de América del Sur*. Madrid: Aguilar, 1973.

Chap. 1, Indian messiahs, pp. 10-41: Tupi-Guarani, pp. 15-22; Paraguay Guarani (and Obera), pp. 23-27; Messiahs and Jesuits, pp. 27-32; Chiriguano, pp. 32-35; Tukuna 1941 movement, pp. 35-38, and other Amazonian messiahs; Andes Region–Santos Atahualpa, pp. 39-40; Gauchos movement led by Solares, 1872, pp. 40-41; plates 1-7 on Hallelujah religion in Akawaio Indians; plates 8-11 on Kayova-Guarani Indians and their travel to Paradise (i.e., the coast).

306 Queiroz, Maria Isaura Pereira de. "O mito da Terra sem Males. Uma utopia guaraní?" *Revista de Cultura Vozes* (Petrópolis) 67, no. 1 (1973): 41-50, bib.

307 Queiroz, Maria Isaura Pereira de. "Mouvements messianiques dans quelques tribus sud-américaines." *L'Homme et la Société* 8 (April-May-June 1968): 229-36, bib.

Describes the Guarani "terre-sans-mal" movements independent of contact, and those related to white contacts such as Santidade de Jaguaripe, Obera's movement, that of Yaguacaporo, the Chiriguano "hommes-dieux" movements, that of "Christ-Alexander," etc.; discusses the similarities and differences of the two types. A useful descriptive and interpretative survey.

308 Queiroz, Maria Isaura Pereira de. *Réforme et révolution dans les sociétés traditionelles: Histoire et ethnologie des mouvements messianiques*. Paris: Éditions Anthropos, 1968, 394 pp., illus., bib. Spanish translation. *Historia y etnología de los movimientos mesianicos: Reforma y revolución en los sociedades tradicionales*. Mexico, D.F.: Siglo Veintiuno, 1969. German translation. *Reform und Revolution in traditionalen Gesellschaften*. Geissen: A. Achenback, 1974.

Surveys movements in various continents, but on pp. 136-38 notes the absence of messianism from Brazilian blacks; pp. 195-206, South American aboriginal movements including Guarani; pp. 206-15, acculturated Indian movements (the messianic Santidade de Jaguaripe ca. 1650, the synthetist movement of Chief Yaguacaporo, 1635-37,

General

Obera's millennialism of 1579, the Loreto area messianism, and the messianic "new Christs" of the Rio Negro area of Amazonas from 1850); pp. 289-375, general account of social dynamics. An important collation of information.

309 Schaden, Egon. "Le messianisme en Amérique du Sud." In *Histoire des religions*, edited by H.-C. Puech. Encyclopédie de la Pléiade, vol. 3. Paris: Gallimard, 1976, pp. 1051-1109, bib.
Pp. 1051-70, Tupi-Guarani; pp. 1070-78, Andine region movements; pp. 1104-7, causes of messianism; pp. 1108-9, bibliography. A major article.

310 Schaden, Egon. "A religião o guaraní e o cristianismo: contribuição ao estudo de um processo histórico de communicação intercultura." *Revista de Antropología* (São Paulo) 25 (1982): 1-24.

311 Schaden, Egon. "Uberlieferung und Wandel in der Religion der Guarano." *Actes du IVe Congrès International des Sciences Anthropologiques et Ethnologiques, Vienna, 1952.* Vol. 2. Vienna, 1955, pp. 379-84.
In Paraguay and Brazil.

312 Wilson, Bryan R[onald]. *Magic and the millennium: A sociological study of religious movements of protest among tribal and third-world peoples.* London: Heinemann Educational Books; New York: Harper & Row, 1973, 547 pp. Reprint. Frogmore, St. Albans: Granada Publishing, Paladin Books, 1975.
Pp. 206-14, Tupi-Guarani movements.

313 Winz, Antônio Pimental. "Notas histórico söbre Nossa Senhora de Copacabana." *Anais do Museo Histórico Nacional* (Rio de Janeiro) 15 (1965): 87-220, illus., bib.
Origins of this cult in present-day Bolivia; its spread to the Peninsula and thence to Brazil and Rio, and its subsequent history in Rio.

Argentina

The black population is very small and items here are confined to G. R. Andrews (entry 314) on the cofradias as still dominated by the priests, and B. Kordon (entry 327) and N. Ortiz Oderigo (entry 337) as representative of black studies, which tend to focus more on cultural than on religious aspects.

The Indian population is also small, under 200,000, and concentrated partly in the far south but primarily in the far north. Most literature is on the important Toba people and with reference to the influence of the Mennonite settlement and later of Pentecostalism upon them. The Iglesia Evangélica Unida, embracing the majority of the Toba as well as some other peoples, is a resultant independent church. On this we note I. Antognazzi et al. (entry 315); three items from Mennonite sources – J. A. Loewen et al. (entry 329), E. S. Miller (entry 334) and Mennonite Board of Missions reports (entries 330 and 331); W. D. and M. F. Reyburn (entry 340); and B. R. Wilson (entry 343).

Other items on earlier messianic movements among Indians are E. J. Cordeu et al. (entry 323) and A. Siffredi (entry 341); see also G. Wolf (entry 344) on Guarani monotheism. Messianism among mestizos is not included, except for the *gauchos* (Indian-European) where the Solares movement in the 1870s was antiwhite, syncretist and utopian – see A. Métraux (entry 303, pp. 59-60) located in South America: General.

As an introduction to Spiritism, in which some blacks and Indians will also probably be involved, see A. M. Centeno (entry 321) for a general account of this form and its presence in Argentina, together with B. Kloppenberg (entry 326), a review of Centeno.

314 Andrews, George Reid. *The Afro-Argentines of Buenos Aires, 1800-1900*. Madison: University of Wisconsin Press, 1980, 286 pp.
   Pp. 138-42, 154-55, cofradias, as still dominated by the priests.

315 Antognazzi, Irma; Garbulsky, E.; Franco, R. di; Laurino, E.; and Regueiro, B. Nuñez. "El proceso de aculturación de las communidades tobas de la Provincia del Chaco: Informe preliminar." *Rehue* (Chile, Unversidad de Concepción) 1 (1968): 69-87, illus., maps, bib.
   The acculturation situation in the Tobas of the Argentine Chaco as in 1964-65; the Toba-led Protestant church as the one unitive institution.

316 Barroso, Haydée [M.] Jofré. *Los hijos del miedo: Reportaje a las supersticiones y creencias del porteño*. Buenos Aires: Emecé Editores, 1975, 256 pp.
   Popular religious forms – spiritist, occult, astrological, etc.

317 Bartolomé, L. J. "Milenarismo y 'Culto a la Mercadería' en grupos indígenas del Chaco argentino." *Revista Latinoamericana de Sociologia* (Buenos Aires) 2a entrega 1970 en prensa.
   Cited by E. J. Cordeu and A. Siffredi (entry 323), but possibly inaccurate. Reported to refer to a millenarian rebellion early in the

South America

Argentina

twentieth century among the Mocovi in Santa Fé Province, owing to cultural disintegration following a changeover from a forestry to an agricultural economy.

318 Cáceres Freyre, Julián. "El encuentro o Tincunaco: Las fiestas religiosas traditionales de San Nicolás de Bari y el Niño Alcade en la cuidad de la Rioja." *Cuadernos del Instituto Nacional de Antropología* (Buenos Aires) 6 (1966-67): 253-388, illus., music, bib.
    Detailed study of a Spanish-Indian festival among the Quichua of Argentina.

319 Carozzi, Maria Julia. "De los santos porteños." *Sociedad y Religion* 3 (1986): 34-47.
    A study of "Santos" in Buenos Aires.

320 Casamiquela, Rodolfo M. *Estudio del nillatún y la religión araucana.* Bahia Blanca, Argentina: Instituto de Humanidades, Universidad Nacional del Sur, 1964, 271 pp., illus., map, bib.
    Pp. 250-52, the *nillatún* rite described, analysed, interpreted – a rite of communication with the gods or spirits through priests and shamans for various purposes; history, acculturative changes, influence of Christianity.

321 Centeno, Angel M. *El espiritismo.* Colección Lector. Buenos Aires: Artes Graficas Moderna, 1955, 190 pp.
    Part 1, "What is spiritism?"; Part 2, "Truth and error of spiritism"; Part 3, "Spiritism in Argentina." See also B. Kloppenberg's comments (entry 326).

322 Cordeu, Egardo Jorge. "El ciclo de Metzgoshé. Nota sobre una respuesta mesiánica de los Toba Argentinos." *Revista del Museo Americanista* (Lomas de Zamora) 1 (1969): 29-43.

323 Cordeu, Egardo Jorge, and Siffredi, Alejandra. *De la algarroba al algodón: Movimiento mesíanico de los Guaycurú.* Buenos Aires: Juárez Editor, 1971, 173 pp., map, bib.
    Includes anthropological account of emergence of millennial and syncretist movements in the Chaco region, among the Guaycuru; pp. 57-107, Napalpi movement among the Toba, from 1924 (using E. S. Miller, entry 335); pp. 109-13, the El Zapaltar movement under Natochi, 1931-1934 (based on L. J. Bartolomé, entry 317); pp. 114-17, the Pampa del Indio movement under Tapanaik, as a "cargo-cult," 1933-34; pp. 119-52, syncretist salvation movements from the 1940s,

under white Pentecostal influences; pp. 153-66, Guaycuru millennialism.

324 Frigerio, Alejandro. "With the banner of Oxalá: Social construction and maintenance of reality in Afro-brasilian religions in Argentina." Ph.D. dissertation (cultural anthropology), University of California at Los Angeles, 1989, 392 pp.

Umbanda and Batuque as practiced simultaneously in more than three hundred temples in Buenos Aires; socialization into the religious worldview; social stigmatization, and sources of conflict both within and between temples.

325 Frigerio, Alejandro, and Carozzi, Maria. "Mamãe Oxum y la Madre Maria Santos, curanderos y religiones afro-brasileiros." *Afro-Asia* 15 (1989).

326 Kloppenberg, Boaventura. "O espiritismo na Argentina." *Revista Eclesiástica Brasileira* (Petrópolis) 15, no. 3 (1955): 663-66.

Review of *El espiritismo*, by Angel M. Centeno (entry 321).

327 Kordon, Bernardo. *Candombe: Contribución al estudio de la raza negra en el Rio de la Plata.* Buenos Aires: Editorial Continente, 1938, 61 pp.

Sections on Candombe dances and Negro religion (e.g., pp. 21-25, 59-60).

328 Lagar, John R. "Toba Indians of Argentina." *Missionary Digest* (Dayton, Ohio) (1946).

First report of the Toba mass movement by the faith-healing missionary who was influential in its beginnings. Cited by E. S. Miller (entry 334), p. 159.

329 Loewen, Jacob A., et al. "Shamanism, illness, and power in Toba church life." *Practical Anthropology* 12, no. 6 (1965): 250-80.

The Iglesia Evangélica Unida of over 40 churches: pp. 246-68, history, and church services; pp. 268-75, sickness, leadership, dancing; pp. 275-79, pre-Christian forms continuing; pp. 279-80, contrasting relations to Pentecostal and Mennonite missionaries.

330 Mennonite Board of Missions. *Annual report, 1983.* Elkhart, Ind.: The Board, 1984.

Pp. 116-19, the semi-independent Iglesia Evangélica Unida in the Chaco and Formosa provinces – its relation to development and the Indian freedom movement, and to Mennonite missionaries.

Argentina

331 Mennonite Board of Missions. *Go where I send you: Annual report,*
1980. Elkhart, Ind.: The Board, 1981, pp. OM-5-80 to OM-7-80 [i.e.,
pp. 5-7].

On the Iglesia Evangélica Unida, mainly Toba, Mocoví, and
Pilagá, with some Mataco (different language group), in about 75
congregations; their securing government registration, their friendly
demands for participation by Mennonite missionaries, and ecstatic
revival in 1980 among young members with personal problems.

332 Métraux, A[lfred]. "La obra de las misiones inglesas en el Chaco."
Journal de la Société des Américanistes (Paris), n.s. 25 (1933): 205-9.

Pp. 205-6, Messianic movements among the Toba-Pilagá.

333 Millán de Palavecino, Mariá Delia. "Religiosidad indigena y visión
protestante en los Indios del Chaco: Documentos etnográficos."
Megafon. Revista Interdisciplinaria de Estudios Latinoamericanos
(Buenos Aires) 4, no. 8 (1978): 85-98, bib.

The encounter of Argentine Chaco Indians with Western society
in Protestant missions; the ensuing transculturation.

334 Miller, Elmer S. "The Argentine Toba evangelical religion service."
Ethnology 10, no. 2 (1971): 149-59, bib.

History of the syncretistic mass movement from the 1940s and
how congregations were formed; Mateo Quintana, "visionary prophet";
description of rites and beliefs; decline since mid-1960s in favor of
political action.

335 Miller, Elmer S. "Pentecostalism among the Argentine Toba: Analysis
of a religiously orientated social movement." Ph.D. dissertation
(anthropology), University of Pittsburgh, 1967, 283 pp.

(1) Syncretism of traditional and Pentecostal elements in the
intense religious movement among the Toba of North
Argentina – when earlier contacts with Catholics, Emmanuel (British)
and Mennonite (North American) missions had not produced such a
reaction. (2) Religious belief systems have a primary role in such
movements and cannot be treated as mere expressions of other social
and economic factors.

336 Miller, Elmer S. "Shamans, power symbols, and change in Argentine
Toba culture." *American Ethnologist* 2, no. 3 (1975): 477-96, bib.

Healing beliefs, and practices; Pentecostal missions' success
among the Toba as connected with similarities between their view of

supernatural power and Pentecostal views as manifest in healing and in glossolalia.

337 Ortiz Oderigo, Nestor [R.]. *Aspectos de la cultura africana en el Río de la Plata*. Colección Ensayos, 9. Buenos Aires: Ne Plus Ultra, 1974, 200 pp.
A comprehensive study: chap. 1 (pp. 15-52), on religion and magic, details black rites and festivals; pp. 51-52 are on transculturation. Note also pp. 59-60 on Yemanja.

338 Ratier, Hugo E. "Candombes porteños." *Vicus cuadernos, arqueología, antropología, cultura, etnologia*. Vol. 1. Amsterdam: J. Benjamins B.V., 1977, pp. 87-149.
Candombe, an extinct Afro-Argentine festivity; its history and relation to Brotherhoods, Societies and Nations; pp. 130-31, its religious reference.

339 Reyburn, William D. *The Toba Indians of the Argentine Chaco: An interpretative report*. Elkhart, Ind.: Mennonite Board of Missions and Charities, 1954. Reprint. 1959, 84 pp.
Pp. 43-50, 59-68, 75-78, et passim: the independent Toba Pentecostal Christianity, its relation to Mennonite missions and to Pentecostalists.

340 Reyburn, William D., and Reyburn, Marie F. "Toba caciqueship and the Gospel." *International Review of Missions* 45, (2d Quarter 1956): 194-203.
Toba numbered about 10-15,000 in some 35 settlement areas, and accepted Christianity after contact with Pentecostals from 1935; healing emphasis and syncretism, but no nativism.

341 Siffredi, Alejandra. "Movimenti socio-religiosi fra gli Indios del Chaco argentino." *La Critica Sociologica* (Rome), no. 36 (1975-76), pp. 167-204, bib.
On four movements in the twentieth century.

342 Vuoto, P. "Los movimientos de Pedro Martinez y Luciano: Dos cultos de transición entre los Toba Taksek." *Scripta Ethnologia* (Buenos Aires) 10 (1984).

343 Wilson, Bryan R[onald]. *Magic and the millennium: A sociological study of religious movements of protest among tribal and third-world peoples*. London: Heinemann Educational Books; New York: Harper & Row,

Argentina

1973, 547 pp. Reprint. Frogmore, St. Albans: Granada Publishing, Paladin Books, 1975.
Pp. 121-23, Pentecostalism reinterpreted.

344 Wolf, Gemmea. "Report from Argentina." *International Review of Mission*, no. 247 [62] (July 1973): 381-20.
A Guarani Indian group in Misiones Province (far northeast) near Puerto Piray, with a monotheistic worship that seems akin to or influenced by Christianity.

345 Wright, P[ablo] G[erardo]. "Presencia protestante entre aborígenes del Chaco argentino." *Scripta Ethnologica* (Buenos Aires) 7 (1983), Supplement 2, pp. 73-84.

346 Wright, Pablo Gerardo. "Tradición y aculturación en una organización socio-religiosa toba contemporánea." *Cristianismo y Sociedad* (Buenos Aires), no. 95 [26, no. 1] (1988): 71-87.
On the Iglesia Evangélica Unida independent Toba church.

Bolivia

For a general account see the United States Army Handbook (entry 353). There is no black community and some two-thirds of the population are Indians.

More attention has been paid in the literature to the earlier Indian movements, often associated with revolt against the Spaniards, as in J. A. Dabbs (entry 348) on the Santiago movement of the 1570s among the Chiriguano. A. Métraux (entry 349) describes the virtually independent Indian churches among the Aymara. There are many unreported independent churches, often Pentecostal, among the Aymara and others, especially in the area around the capital.

See J. Riester (entry 351) on messianism but with little syncretism among the Guarani since white contact; but compare J. Riester (entry 352) for syncretism among the Guarani-speaking Guarayos. On the Guarani see also within Brazil and Paraguay.

347 Cardüs, J. *Las missiones franciscanas entre los infieles de Bolivia.* Barcelona: Librería de la Immaculada Concepción, 1896.
Pp. 90-94, on Bolivian revolt of 1779, by Chamava se Luís.

348 Dabbs, J[ack] A[utrey]. "A messiah among the Chiriguanos." *Southwestern Journal of Anthropology* 9 (1953): 45-58.

A tribe between Paraguay and Parana, in modern Bolivia, in the 1570s; Santiago, a reformer, as agent of Jesus.

349 Métraux, A[lfred]. "Paganism and Christianity among the Bolivian Indians." *Inter-American Quarterly* 2, no. 2 (1940): 53-60.

Inca-Catholic syncretism among Aymara Indians, with virtually independent "churches" (see especially pp. 58-60).

350 Mujía, Ricardo. *Exposición de los titulos que consagran el derecho territorial de Bolivia sobre la zona comprendida entre los ríos Pilcomayo y Paraguay. Ediçion oficiel. Anexos.* La Paz: Editora "El Tiempo," 1914. Reprint. São Paulo: Livraria Martins, 1945.

Vol. 2, pp. 102-8, on the Governor's orders for the enquiry into messianic movement, 1573; pp. 108-29, the report; see extracts in J. A. Dabbs (entry 348), pp. 46-50, 57 et passim.

351 Riester, Jürgen. *Die Pauserna-Guarasug wä Monographie eines Tupí-Guaraní-Volkes in Ostbolivien.* Collectanea Instituti Anthropos, 3. St. Augustin-bei-Bonn: Anthropos Institut, 1972, xviii + 562 pp.

A very religious Guarani culture, with great religious mystical faith, which exhibits the "terre-sans-mal" messianism, but which has rejected Christianity and not developed any syncretic forms. Pp. 240ff., on religion, et passim (see especially pp. 246ff. on the heart of their religion); pp. 19-34, history of the tribes and of their culture-contact with whites; pp. 329-34, attempts at Christianizing, and the claims of Gurasu religion; pp. 354-58, social and religious change.

352 Riester, Jürgen. "Uberlieferung und Wandel in der Religion der Chiquitanos." *Verhandlungen des XXXVIII Internationalen Amerikanistenkongresses, Stuttgart-München, 1968.* Vol. 3. Stuttgart and Munich: Klaus Renner, 1971, pp. 65-75, illus.

The Catholic syncretism, with baptism, processions, festivals, saint-cults, and preachings, among Guarani-speaking Guarayos.

353 United States Government, Department of the Army. *Area Handbook for Bolivia*, edited by T. E. Weil, et al. Foreign Area Studies, The American University. DA PAM 500-66. Washington, D.C.: Government Printing Office, 1974, xiv + 417 pp., maps.

Pp. 129-36 on religion.

Brazil

Brazil presents a vast, complex, and distinctive religious world. It is difficult to distinguish the religious developments that belong to our specific agenda amid the complex of many interrelated forms, which run from survivals of African religions through the numerous varieties of Spiritism to the sophisticated versions of Umbanda. In principle we are concerned with movements arising against the background of the indigenous Amerindian tribal peoples and of the imported peoples of African origin. The former are now few in number, probably nearer 100,000 than 200,000; the black population is estimated at from 12% to 15% of a total population reaching some 130 million in the 1980s and possibly reaching 200 million by the end of the century. In addition there is a mulatto (i.e., white-Negro) sector variously estimated to comprise from 12% to 22% of the population. The high degree of racial mixing in Brazil means that such boundaries are imprecise and the mestizo population (in various racial combinations) is extensive. There are also some one million Japanese immigrants, who have introduced a number of the new religions of Japan, but these are not within our subject.

The great variety of religious movements and of their interrelationships, and their different forms and names in different parts of this vast country, result in a problem of terminology. On the Afro-Brazilian section of the problem see the dictionary of O. G. Cacciatore (entry 467, pp. 21-23 and following definitions); F. G. Sturm (entry 998); and F. O'Gorman (entry 839, p. 103-6), introducing the literature and various terms. A further problem occurs through variations in the forms of personal names; in addition, word spelling varies due to the phonetization of spellings during the 1930s and 1940s, which simplified many words (for example "philosophia" became "filosofia").

For *general introductions or surveys* see: R. Bastide (entries 404, 430, and 431), for overview; Bill/Guillermo Cook (entry 538) and his summary (entry 539) of *Os deuses do povo*, by C. R. Brandão (entry 457); R. H. Chilcote (entry 530) lists and classifies all "protest movements" in Brazil and in Angola; E. Fülling (entry 619); W. C. van Hattem (entry 650) on new movements being accepted from Japan but not from Europe or North America; M. Mörner (entry 814), a survey with theoretical value; M. I. P. de Queiroz (entry 877, in French) and especially entry 882; T. L. Smith (entry 983, in English); A. Q. Tiller (entry 1002, in English) on healing and healers. For *messianism* in relation to all races, see E. Léonard (entry 747) and R. Ribeiro (entry 921, in English).

Movements among the Amerindians reach back to the sixteenth century; there have been many small local movements with indigenous "Christs," especially in Amazonia, and a messianic aspect has been common. The pre-

and postcontact millennialism of the Guarani is dealt with more extensively in the literature on Paraguay and on Bolivia, but for a Brazilian context see W. H. Lindig (entry 756), A. Métraux (entry 807) and more generally entry 806, and K. U. Nimuendajú (entry 829). Otherwise see W. H. Crocker (entries 553 and 554), also M. C. da Cunha (entry 555) on a Canela movement of the 1960s; E. E. Galvão (entry 626) on Amazonia; M. Gerbert (entry 630, pp. 1-35), also on mestizo movements; F. A. Knobloch (entry 722, in English), an independent church among the Baniwa; J. C. Melatti (entry 792) on the Kraho; M. V. de Queiróz (entry 885), seven movements among the Tukuna, interpreted as resistance to "civilization"; K. U. Nimuendajú (entries 831 and 832, in English) on the Tukuna; M. I. P. de Queiroz (entries 880, 881, and especially 882); E. Schaden's French encyclopaedia article (entry 967), especially on the Tukuna and Ramkokamekra, and his other items. Although messianic movements among the mestizo and white populations, especially in the north-east, do not fall within our category, they do appear more marginally in some of the above literature.

Movements primarily or by origin in the Negro population, usually called Afro-Brazilian, occur mainly on the eastern littoral. These "cults," as they are designated, began organizing about the 1830s and spread especially among the freed Negroes in the cities in the late nineteenth century. Now it has been estimated that one in three Brazilians, including many others besides those who may be regarded as black, participates in some form of Afro-Brazilian cult.

Much of the extensive literature deals with the more *cultural aspects* such as folklore, customs, songs, dances, music and festivals. Here we concentrate on the more distinctly religious materials. For background see R. Bastide, *Le prochain et le lointain*, in the Latin America: Theory Section (entry 2). As *general introductions or surveys* see O. da Costa Eduardo (entries 570, briefly, and 569) for northern Brazil; selections from G. Freyre (entries 599 and 601, both in English translation); A. Ramos (entries 890 and 900, both in English); J. Ribeiro (entry 915); R. Nina Rodrigues (enty 834) – although writing from 1896 he was not recognized until the intellectuals began to "discover" the Afro-Brazilian cults in the 1920s; S. Rodman (entry 938, in English).

For *more specific studies* see especially R. Bastide, particularly his major French work (entry 431, with English translation); and his survey (entry 435). Other items: Conferencia Nacional dos Bispos (entry 536) for changing Catholic Church attitudes; R. Flasche (entry 591 for healing and healers; M. Gerbert (entry 630, pp. 35-46); S. Leacock (entries 741, 742, and 743 on Batuque in Belém); K. Oberg (entry 838, in English); J. Ribeiro (entry 915), comprehensive yet succinct; J. E. dos Santos (entry 954); G. E. Simpson, selections in English (entry 982); P. V. A. Williams (entry 1055); N. R. Sales (entry 946) is by a cult leader with a social science degree.

Brazil

On *Candomble* movements (a fairly wide term) see J. Amado (entry 366); R. Bastide (entry 406, pp. 7-52); E. Carneiro's various items, especially especially entries 488 and 507; E. F. Frazier (entry 594, in English); M. J. Herskovits (entries 658 and 661, both in English); N. O. Oderigo (entry 845); F. O'Gorman (entry 839, in English); D. Pierson (entry 861, in English).

On *Macumba* forms see R. Bastide (entries 422 and 431, pp. 294-303 of the English translation), on urban Macumba; K. E. Koch (entry 723), a case history of Christian conversion from Macumba.

On *Umbanda* itself there is an extensive literature, which is drawn upon for the special section on Umbanda as a Particular Movement at the end of this volume. Many items included in this section on Brazil also contain valuable material on Umbanda along with other movements (see index of movements).

On *Spiritism* in general, and therefore on the above three forms, see P. Avann (entry 392) for a missionary view; E. Benz (entry 441, with English summary); C. P. F. de Camargo (entry 473); A. G. Fernandes (entry 578); M. Gerbert (entry 630, pp. 47-59); R. Ireland (entry 677); the pioneer Catholic researcher B. Kloppenburg (entry 714, in English) for a pastoral approach; P. McGregor, himself a medium (entry 769); and E. Willems (entry 1052, in English).

For discussion of the fictional but authentic accounts in the famous *novels of Jorge Amado*, see A. A. Bourdon (entry 450) for table of Afro-Brazilian references, R. G. Hamilton (entry 646), and M. L. Nunes (entry 837), both in English.

On the *lack of messianic movements*, with explanations, see R. Bastide (entry 425); M. I. P. de Queiroz (entries 874, 881, and 882, p. 76).

On the *survival of African religions*, either explicitly (especially Yoruba) or under a veneer of Catholicism, see W. Abimbola (entry 355, in English), J. R. Barros (entry 396), R. Bastide (entry 419), J. U. Gordon (entry 634, in English), E. L. Lasebikan (entry 738, in English).

On the *cofradías*, or brotherhoods, see M. S. Cardozo (entry 481, in English) for early examples, R. Ribeiro (entry 932, in English, pp. 470-71, 474), J. Scarano (entry 958, in English), J. C. de O. Tórres (entry 1008, pp. 71-77).

On *revolts* and their religious dimensions, see J. C. Ferreira (entry 585), and on the communities of escaped slaves (quilombos) see R. Bastide (entry 431, pp. 88-95 of the English translation).

On *Islamic-related* movements, see R. Bastide (entry 420), E. I. Brazil (entry 462) W. Valente (entry 1018, pp. 46-52), C. A. Winters (entry 1060, in English).

On *folk Catholicism* in relation to Afro-Brazilian forms and influences, see C. Ott (entry 846), and A. Ramos (entry 901). On *Pentecostalism*, which may be regarded as a Christian alternative to Spiritism, see M. Gerbert (entry 630, pp. 67-82), and D. T. Monteiro (entry 810) on healing in São Paulo.

354 Abbeville, Claude d'. *Histoire de la mission des Pères Capucins en l'Isle de Maraguan et terres circonvicines.* Paris: 1614. Portuguese translation. *Historia da missão dos padres capuchinhos na Ilha do Maranhão.* . . . São Paulo: Livraria Martins Editôra, 1945. 2d ed. 1951.

Pp. 252-53, a millennial movement in a whole tribe, promised to be led to the "terre-sans-mal" in the centre of the earth; work stopped, there was continual dancing, many perished en route, the rest abandoned the leader who was allegedly a reincarnation of the culture-hero; extract reprinted in A. Métraux, *Religions et magies indiennes d'Amérique du Sud* (Paris: Gallimard, 1967), pp. 20-21. By a French missionary.

355 Abimbola, Wande. "Yoruba religion in Brazil: Problems and prospects." In *Actes du 42e Congrès International des Américanistes Paris, 1976.* Vol. 6. Paris: Société des Américanistes, Musée de l'Homme, 1979, pp. 619-39.

356 Abreu, Julio [Filho]. "A influência negra na religião brasileira." *Problemas* (São Paulo) 1, no. 5 (1938): 28-35.

357 Acuña, Christoval de. *Nuevo descubrimiento del gran Rio de las Amazonas . . . en el ano de 1639.* . . . Madrid: Royal Press, 1641. French translation. 1682. English translation. 1698. New Spanish ed. Coleción de Libros que Tratan de America (raros o curiosos). Madrid, 1891. English translation. *A new discovery of the Great River of the Amazons.* . . , translated by C. R. Markham. Hakluyt Society Works, 1st series, no. 24. London: 1859. Reprint. New York: Burt Franklin, n.d.

Vol. 2: Spanish 1891 edition, pp. 9-91, English translation, pp. 84-85, Acuña's early seventeenth-century encounter with a "man-god" on the upper Amazon who returned nightly to his father the sun to receive instructions for government of the world. No evidence as to being pre- or postcontact or a "movement."

358 Albergaria, Ezio, Jr. "Orixás na cidade é um fato." *Revista de Cultura Vozes* (Petrópolis), February 1939.

359 Albuquerque, Américo de. "Como aprender a religião negra." *Seiva* (Salvador), no. 4, 1939.

Brazil

360 Almeida, Renato. *Candomblé em cordel*. Salvador: Departamento de Assuntos Culturais, Secretaria Municipal da Educação e Cultura, 1978, unpaged, illus.

A praise-poem on Bahia, with detailed account of many Candomble beliefs.

361 Alva, Antonio de. *Como desmanchar trabalhos de quimbanda*. Rio de Janeiro: Editôra Eco, 1966, 158 pp.

362 Alva, Antonio de. *O livro dos Exus (Kiumbas e Eguns)*. Rio de Janeiro: Editôra Eco, 1967, 158 pp.

363 Alvarenga, Oneyda, ed. *Tambor-de-mina e tambor-de-crioulo*. Registros Sonoros de Folclore Musical Brasileiro, 2. Discos FM 15 a 28-A. Notas e grafica dos textos feitas por Oneyda Alvarenga. São Paulo: Disoteca Publica Municipal, 1948.

Mina referred originally to slaves from the Guinea Coast in West Africa, and now to Batuque-type cults in Belém, highly syncretized and Yoruba-derived; also popularly known in Maranhão as *tambor*. These songs were collected by a folklore research team under Mario de Andrade. Brief critique in R. Bastide, *The African religions of Brazil* (Baltimore: John Hopkins University Press, 1978), pp. 443-44.

364 Alvarenga, Oneyda, ed. *Xangô*. Discos FM 1 a 14. Notas e grafica dos textos feitas por Oneyda Alvarenga, chefe da Discoteca Publica Municipal. São Paulo: Discoteca Publica Municipal, 1948.

365 Alvarenga, Oneyda, ed. *Babassuê*. Discos FM 39 a FM 51 [por] Oneyda Alvarenga, chefe da Discoteca Publica Municipal. São Paulo: Discoteca Publica Municipal, 1950.

Meaning "St. Barbara," and a former name for Batuque cults in Belém; includes examples of *pagelance* cults in Amazonia, with Indian and African elements co-existent rather than syncretized. These songs were collected from Batuque cults.

366 Amado, Jorge. *Bahia de todos os santos: Quia das ruas e dos mistérios de cidade do Salvador*. Obras de Jorge Amado, 10. São Paulo: Livraria Martins, 1945, 306 pp., illus. Rev. ed. Lisbon: Publições Europa-América, 1970, 379 pp., illus. French translation. *Bahia de tous les saints*.

1970 edition, pp. 105-32, festivals; p. 135-40, Macumba; pp. 143-50 Candombles (over 600); pp. 153-55, Xango; p. 166, Spiritist centers.

By a famous novelist who has written many accounts in the form of novels.

367 Amado, Jorge. *Capitães da Areia, romance.* Rio de Janeiro: J. Olympio, 1937, 342 pp. Many later editions.
A novel featuring Yemanja, Xango, and Candomble in Salvador, shown as defending the oppressed.

368 Amado, Jorge. *Carybé: Mural do banco da bahía orixá de candomblé.* Bahía: Banco da Bahía, 1971, illus.

369 Amado, Jorge. "Elegio de um chefe de Seita." In *O Negro no Brasil*, compiled by E. Carneiro and A. do Couto Ferraz. Rio de Janeiro: Civilização Brasileira, 1940, pp. 325-28.
On M. E. Bomfim's "Pae Martiniano," a famous leader of Afro-Brazilian religion at Bahia.

370 Amado, Jorge. *Jubiabá, romance.* Rio de Janeiro: Ed. José Olympio, 1935, etc., 371 pp. Lisbon: Edição "Livros do Brasil." 14th ed. São Paulo: Livraria Martins, 1961. Many later editions.
A novel on lower-class life in the Bahian population that has preserved African religious and other elements; especially on Candombles and the life of a famous *Babalorixa*; by one of Brazil's best-selling authors, himself a Candomble priest.

371 Amado, Jorge. *Mar morto romance: Capa de Santa Rosa.* Rio de Janeiro: Livraria José Olympio, 1936, 346 pp. Many later editions.
A novel featuring the Yamanja cult.

372 Amado, Jorge. *O país do carnaval (romance).* Rio de Janeiro: Schmidt, 1932, 217 pp. Reprint. São Paulo: Martins, 1935, 347 pp.
Amado's first novel, already including the subject of Candomble, but as an onlooker and not yet a participant.

373 Amado, Jorge. *Os pastores de Noite.* São Paulo: Livraria Martins Editôra, 1964.
A mature novel, featuring Ogun and Exu in the Candombles in authentic fashion.

374 Amado, Jorge. *Suór. Romance.* São Paulo: Martins, 1934, pp. 225-412. Several later editions.
His third novel, but not yet with an inside view of Candomble.

Brazil

375 Amado, Jorge. *A tenda dos milagres*. São Paulo: Livraria Martins Editôra, 1969.
A novel featuring Candombles.

376 Amaral, Amadeu, Jr. "'Reisado,' 'Bumba meu boi' e 'Postorís.'" *Revista do Arquivo Municipal* (São Paulo), no. 64 (February 1940), pp. 273-84.
Macumba songs collected in 1937.

377 Amaral, Raul Joviano. *Os pretos do Rosário de São Paulo, subsídios*. São Paulo: Ed. Alarico, 1954.

378 Amorim, Deolindo. *Africanismo e espiritismo*. Collección Siglo Espirita, 3. Rio de Janeiro: Grafica Mundo Espirita, 1949, 79 pp., illus. Reprint. Buenos Aires: Editorial Constancia, 1958, 61 pp.
African-influenced and Kardecism-influenced movements.

379 Andrade, Mario de. "A Calunga dos Maracatús." *Estudos Afro-Brasileiros* (Rio de Janeiro) 1 (1935): 39-47.
By a music critic and folklorist. On a ritual object of Congolese origin used in Candomble dances.

380 Andrade, Mario de. "Os congos." *Lanterna Verde* (Rio de Janeiro), no. 2 (February 1935), pp. 36-53.
Analysis and description of the *Congos* dances.

381 Andrade, Mario de. "A entrado dos palmitos." *Revista do Arquivo Municipal* (São Paulo) 3, no. 32 (1937): 51-64.
One of the ceremonies that interested the writer was "The Entrance of the Little Palms," which took place in May 1939 in São Paulo.

382 Andrade, Mario de. "Geografia religiosa do Brasil." *Publições Médicas* (São Paulo), August 1941, pp. 71-84.
Main locations of Macumba, Candomble, Caboclo, Xango, Pagelança, Babassue, and other forms.

383 Andrade, Mario de. *Música de feitiçaria no Brasil*. São Paulo: Livraria Martins Editôra, 1963, 295 pp.
Pp. 25-72, general account–includes Afro-Brazilian cult songs (e.g., pp. 105, 233-34, 264, of Batuque from Belém).

384 Andrade, Mario de. "O samba rural paulista." *Revista do Arquivo Municipal* (São Paulo) 4, no. 41 (1937): 37-136.

A description by an eminent music critic and folklorist of the genuine expression of African folklore in the Negro dances during the annual Pirapóra festival in the state of São Paulo. Includes musical notations.

385 Aranha, Bento de Figueiredo Tenreiro. *Archivo de Amazonas*. 2 vols. Manaus, 1907.
   Vol. 2: p. 86, "native Christ" in Amazonia.

386 Araripe, Tristão de Alencar, Jr. *O reino encantado*. Rio de Janeiro: Gazêta de Noticias, 1878.
   A novel based on the 1837 Sebastian-type movement – shows a Negro *feiticeiro* ruling over a *quilombo* in the name of the Sebastianist prophet; highly imaginative descriptions of rituals similar to Macumba and Candomble, and regarded as illusory.

387 Araújo, Alceu Maynard. "Alguns ritos mágicos." *Revista do Arquivo Municipal* (São Paulo, Divisão do Arquivo Histórico), 1958.

388 Araújo, Alceu Maynard. "A congada nasceu em Roncesvales." *Revista do Arquivo Municipal* (São Paulo, Divisão do Arquivo Histórico), no. 163 (1959).

389 Araújo, Alceu Maynard. *Cultura popular brasileira*. 2d ed. São Paulo: Edições Melhoramentos, 1973, 198 pp. + illus.
   Pp. 35-35, Negro festivals; pp. 79-81, Batuque dances; pp. 147-49, Candomble. Similar to his *Folclore national* (São Paulo: Edições Melhoramentos, 2d ed., 1967).

390 Araújo, Alceu Maynard. *Folclore nacional*. 2d ed. 3 vols. São Paulo: Edições Melhoramentos, 1967, 487 pp., 457 pp., 423 pp., illus.
   Vol. 1, pp. 189-206, Negro festivals; vol. 2, pp. 231-37, Batuque dances in detail; vol. 3, pp. 38-45, Candomble, with some song texts.

391 Arcelrud, Isaac. *Novos profetas do Médio Oriente*. Rio de Janeiro: Instituto Brasileiro de Estudos Afro-Asiáticos, 1962.

392 Avann, Penny. "The fascination of the spirits." *Share* (Tunbridge Wells, Kent, South American Missionary Society), Summer 1979, pp. 9-10, illus.
   A missionary view of Spiritism as "the number one cult in modern Brazil," its appeal and its defects.

Brazil

393 Baldus, Herberto. "Ligeiras notas sobre os Índios Guaranys do littoral Paulista." *Revista do Museu Paulista* 16 (1929): 83-95.
Discusses state of acculturation in 1928 of a Guarani group who reached the ocean near Santos.

394 Barbieri, Sante Uberto. *Land of Eldorado*. New York: Friendship Press, 1961.
Pp. 123-24, Spiritism as a "hindrance to the march of the gospel."

395 Barbosa, Waldemar de Almeida. "O gongado no oeste mineiro." *Revista Brasileira de Folclore* (Rio de Janeiro), no. 11 [5] (January-April 1965): 5-22; English and French summaries.
Description, texts of songs, and music of a Minais Gerais version of a widespread festival of Negro origin.

396 Barros, Jacy Rêgo. *Senzala e macumba*. Rio de Janeiro: "Jornal do Commercio"; Rodrigues e Cia, 1939, 131 pp.
Pp. 49-79, the persistence of African religious elements among the slaves in Brazil; shows how Spiritism assists both assimilation and social ascent for the Negro.

397 Barroso, Haydée M. Jofré. *De la magia y por la leyenda*. Selección Emecé de Obras Contemporáneas. Buenos Aires and Barcelona: Emecé Editores, 1966, 181 pp., bib.
Negro folklore in Brazil: Part 2 (pp. 87-111), accounts of African divinities and Negro cults, including Candomble (pp. 104-6).

398 Barzaghi, Alberto. "I culti afro-brasiliani: Un mondo spirituale che ci interroga." *Monde e Missioni* (Milan) 105, nos. 11-12 (1976): 369-84, illus.

399 Bastide, Roger. "L'acculturation folklorique (Le folklore brésilien)." *Revue de Psychologie des Peuples* 5, no. 4 (1950). Reprinted in *Le prochain et le lointain*. Paris: Cujas, 1970, pp. 157-89.

400 Bastide, Roger. "Algumas consideraçoes em torno de uma 'lavagem de contas.'" Estudos Afro-Brasileiros, 3a série. *Boletim da Faculdade de Filosofia, Ciências Letras da Universidade de São Paulo*, 154: Sociologia (I) no. 3, 1933; French summary. Reprinted in *Estudos afro-brasileiros*. São Paulo: Editôra Perspectiva, 1973, pp. 363-74.
On the ritual baths to empower Candomble necklaces: "the baptism of the necklace," as mystical bonds with the supernatural.

401 Bastide, Roger. *Les Amériques noires: Les civilisations africaines dans le Nouveau Monde*. Paris: Payot, 1967. 2d ed. 1973, 236 pp. Spanish translation. *Las Américas negras: Las civilizaciones africanas en el Nuevo Mundo*. Madrid: Alianza Editorial, 1969, 226 pp. English translation. *African civilizations in the New World*. London: C. Hurst, 1971, 232 pp.

Chap. 3, Bush Negroes; chap. 4, Candomble, Macumba, Black Caribs, Caboclo; chap. 5, Afro-Brazilian; chap. 6, Vodou; chap. 7, syncretism.

402 Bastide, Roger. "L'Axêxê." In *Les Afro-Américains. Bulletin de l'IFAN*, no. 27. Dakar: Institut Français de l'Afrique Noire, 1952, pp. 105-10.
Funeral ceremony of the Xorubano (Nago) cult.

403 Bastide, Roger. "Le batuque de Pôrto Alegre." In *Selected Papers: 29th International Congress of Americanists*, edited by S. Tax. Vol. 3. New York, 1949. Chicago: University of Chicago Press, 1952, pp. 207-18. Reprint. New York: Cooper Square Publications, 1967, pp. 195-206.
The Afro-Brazilian "sects" in the South where "batuque" is the religious dance and "candomble" the secular dance; cf. the reverse terminology in the north.

404 Bastide, Roger. *Brésil, terre des contrastes*. Paris: Hachette, 1957, 343 pp., illus. Portuguese translation. *Brasil: Terra de contrastes*. Corps e Alma do Brasil, 2. São Paulo: Difusão Européia do Livro, 1959. Reprint. 1964, 261 pp. 6th ed. São Paulo: Difel, 1975, 283 pp.
In Portuguese translation, 6th ed.: pp. 68-85, the African presence; pp. 73-85, on religion; pp. 92-106, on messianic movements in the northeast; pp. 19-97, a Shinto-Catholic syncretism among Japanese immigrants in São Paulo state.

405 Bastide, Roger. "A cadeira de ogã e o poste central." Estudos Afro-Brasileiros, 1a série. *Boletim de Faculdade de Filosofia, Ciências e Letras da Universidade de São Paulo*, 59: Sociologia no. 1, 1946, pp. 44-49, illus. Reprinted in *Estudos afro-brasileiros*. São Paulo: Editôra Perspectiva, 1973, pp. 325-333.
On the furnishing and layout of Candomble cult centers.

406 Bastide, Roger. *Le candomblé de Bahia (rite nagô)*. Le Monde d'Outre Mer, Passé et Présent. Première série: Études, 5. The Hague: Mouton, 1958, 260 pp., illus., bib. Portuguese translation. *Candomblé de Bahia (rite Nagô)*. Brasiliana, 313. São Paulo: Companhía Editôra Nacional, 1961, 370 pp. (bib., pp. 359-70).

Brazil

Pp. 7-52, Candomble.

407 Bastide, Roger. "Cavalhos dos santos (Esboco de uma sociologia do transe mistico)." Estudos Afro-Brasileiros, 3a série. *Boletim de Faculdade de Filosofia, Ciências e Letras da Universidade de São Paulo*, 154: Sociologia (I) no. 3, 1953, photos. Reprinted in *Estudos afrobrasileiros*. São Paulo: Editôra Perspectiva, 1973, pp. 293-323.

408 Bastide, Roger. "Contribuição ao estudo do sincretismo católicofetichista." Estudos Afro-Brasileiros, 1a série. *Boletim de Faculdade de Filosofia, Ciências e Letras da Universidade de São Paulo*, 59: Sociologia no. 1, 1946, pp. 11-43, tables. Reprinted in *Estudos afrobrasileiros*. São Paulo: Editôra Perspectiva, 1973, pp. 159-91.

409 Bastide, Roger. "A cozinha dos deuses." *Cultura e alimentação* 1 (March 1950): 30-31.

410 Bastide, Roger. "Églises baroques et candomblés en fête." *Archives Internationales de Sociologie de la Coopération et du Développement* (Paris), no. 40 (1976), 35-51.

411 Bastide, Roger. "Ensaio duma estética afro-brasileira." *Estado de São Paulo* (São Paulo), 27 November, 4, 10, 22 December 1948; 4 January 1949.

412 Bastide, Roger. "Ensaios de metodologia afro-brasileira, o metodo linguistico." *Revista do Arquivo Municipal* (São Paulo) 59 (1939): 17-32.

413 Bastide, Roger. "Les esclaves des dieux." *Archives de Sciences Sociales des Religions* 38 [19, no. 2] (1974): 29-32 (pp. 29-31, comment by H. Desroches); also longer version in *Le sacré sauvage et autres essais* (Paris: Payot, 1975), pp. 210-13.

414 Bastide, Roger. "Estruturas sociais e religiões afro-brasileiras." *Anhembi* (São Paulo), no. 77 (year), 7 (vol.) [26, no. 4] (1957): 228-43.

415 Bastide, Roger. "Estudos afro-brasileiros." *Revista do Arquivo Municipal* (São Paulo) 98 (September-October 1944): 81-103. French translation. "Études afro-brésiliennes (études bibliographiques, 1939-1944)." *Bulletin des Études Portugaises de l'Institut Français au Portugal* (Coimbra), n.s. 10 (1945): 213-32.
      Pp. 81-90, "Monografias de candomblés"; pp. 91-100, "O ceremonial da polidez"; pp. 101-3, "O Lundum do padre."

416 Bastide, Roger. *Estudos afro-brasileiros*. Coleção Estudos, 18. São Paulo: Editôra Perspectiva, 1973, 384 pp., illus.
   Reprint of his own essays; see separate entries.

417 Bastide, Roger. "État actuel des études afro-brésiliennes: Le problème du contact des races." *Revue Internationale de Sociologie* 47 (January-February 1939): 77-89.
   Includes a critique of the work of A. Ramos (pp. 80-85) and of G. Freyre (pp. 85-89).

418 Bastide, Roger. *Imagens do nordeste místico em branco e prêto*. Rio de Janeiro: "Seção de Livros" da Emprésa Gráfica "O Cruziero," 1945, 247 pp., illus. Section "O mundo dos candomblés" reprinted in *Estudos afro-brasileiros*. São Paulo: Editôra Perspectiva, 1973, pp. 249-91.
   Afro-Brazilian religion in northeast Brazil–its rites and practices, and the cult of the Virgin Mary; pp. 202-22, on Catimbo cults.

419 Bastide, Roger. "Immigration et métamorphose d'un dieu." *Cahiers Internationaux de Sociologie*, n.s. 20 [3] (January-June 1956): 45-60. Reprinted in *Le prochain et le lointain*. Paris: Cujas, 1970, pp. 211-26.
   The Yoruba divinity Eshu (i.e., Legba, of the Ewe) as transplanted into Candombles of Bahia, and into Macumba and Umbanda with its Spiritism; latter regarded as reaction against white Spiritualism. A detailed study.

420 Bastide, Roger. "L'Islam noir au Brésil." *Hespéris* (Rabat) 3e et 4e trimestre, 1952, pp. 373-82.
   On the extent and manner of African Islam's survival in Brazil, for comparison with Afro-Christian movements.

421 Bastide, Roger. *Léxico das religiões africanas no Brasil*. Escola de Comunicações e Artes, Universidade de São Paulo, 1970.

422 Bastide, Roger. "A macumba paulista." Estudos afro-brasileiros, 1a serie. *Boletim de Faculdade de Filosofia, Ciências e Letras da Universidade de São Paulo*, 59: Sociologia no. 1, 1946, pp. 51-112, tables, maps. Reprinted in *Estudos afro-brasileiros*. São Paulo: Editôra Perspectiva, 1973, pp. 193-247.
   A major study of Macumba and various forms of Spiritism and curandeirismo in São Paulo–with historical background; local distribution; relation to African divinities and ethnic groups, to plants, animal sacrifices, etc., and to criminality.

Brazil

423 Bastide, Roger. "Medicina e magia nos candomblés." *Boletim Bibliográfico* (São Paulo) 16 (1950): 7-34.
The folk medicine aspect of Candomble: Appendix 1 (pp. 29-33), a table with botanical and popular names of herbal medicines, and their uses in cults in different areas (Ceara, Bahia); appendix 2 (p. 34), table of the relations between divinities, herbs, and ailments.

424 Bastide, Roger. "Le messianisme chez les noirs du Brésil." *Le Monde Non-chrétien*, n.s. 15 (July-September 1950): 301-8.

425 Bastide, Roger. "Le messianisme raté." *Archives de Sociologie des Religions*, 3e année (January-June 1958), pp. 31-37. Reprinted in *Le prochain et le lointain*. Paris: Cujas, 1970, pp. 267-74.
On why blacks in Brazil have not produced messianic movements; three examples where blacks have led *caboclos* in movements, or had visionary experiences.

426 Bastide, Roger. "Nicht-katholische Religionen und die ökonomische und soziale Entwicklung in Brasilien." In *Religion, Kultur und sozialer Wandel / Religion, culture, and social change ... Internationales Jahrbuch für Religionssoziologie*, 6, edited by J. Matthes. Cologne and Opladen: Westdeutscher Verlag, 1970, pp. 83-97; English summary (p. 98).
On the very limited verification of Marxist and Weberian theories of the relations between economics and religion; the social relationships of Spiritualism, Candomble, and Pentecostalism and their conservative social effects. They are not concerned with social change or modernization.

427 Bastide, Roger. *A poesia afro-brasileira*. São Paulo: Livraria Martins, 1943, 151 pp. Reprinted in *Estudos afro-brasileiros*. São Paulo: Editôra Perspectiva, 1973, pp. 3-113.

428 Bastide, Roger. "Os pontos riscados." *Estado de S. Paulo*, 22 and 29 December 1941.
On chalk drawings in Macumba, similar to Veve in Haiti.

429 Bastide, Roger. "Religiões africanas, estruturas da civilização." *Afro-Asia* (Salvador), nos. 6-7 (June-December 1968).

430 Bastide, Roger. "Religion and the church in Brazil." In *Brazil: Portrait of half a continent*, edited by T. Smith and A. Marchant. New York: Dryden Press, 1951, pp. 334-55.

Pp. 344-46, Messianism and the Muckers; p. 352, positivism; pp. 352-54, Spiritualism as an urban phenomenon.

431 Bastide, Roger. *Les religions africaines au Brésil: Vers une sociologie des interpénétrations du civilisations*. [Also issued as *Les religions afro-brésiliennes: Contribution à une sociologie des interpénétrations de civilisations*.] Bibliothèque de Sociologie Contemporaine. Paris: Presses Universitaires de France, 1960, 578 pp., no bib., but footnote references. German translation. *Die afrikanischen Religionen in Brasilien*. Geissen: Andreas Achenback, 1974, 400 pp. English translation. *The African religions of Brazil*. Baltimore: Johns Hopkins University Press, 1978, xxvii + 494 pp. Portuguese translation. *As religões africanas no Brasil*. ... 2 vols. São Paulo: Livraria Pioneira Universidade de São Paulo, 1971. 2d ed. 1985, 567 pp.
A major sociological study relating social, structural, and religious changes to the acculturation situation.

432 Bastide, Roger. Review of "Aspectos fundamentais da cultura guarani," by Egon Schaden (entry 963). *L'Année Sociologique* (Paris) 3d ser. (1961), pp. 340-41.

433 Bastide, Roger. "O ritual angola do axexê [*sic*]." Estudos Afro-Brasileiros, 3a série. *Boletim de Faculdade de Filosofia, Ciências e Letras da Universidade de São Paulo*, 154: Sociologia (I) no. 3, 1953, 104 pp., illus. Reprinted in *Estudos Afro-Brasileiros*. São Paulo: Editôra Perspectiva, 1973, pp. 335-62.
On a Candomble funeral rite in Bahia.

434 Bastide, Roger. "Le spiritisme au Brésil." *Archives de Sociologie des Religions* 24 [12, no. 2] (1967): 3-16.
"Upper class" Spiritism as Kardecist, middle class, and organized as a "church"; "lower class" Spiritism as Umbandist, unorganized, African-influenced, with possession more violent.

435 Bastide, Roger. "Structures sociales et religions afro-brésiliennes." *Renaissance* (New York) 5, nos. 2-3 (1944-45): 13-129.
Afro-Brazilian cults in relation to slavery and the various African "nations"–Candomble, etc., the latter in two forms (proletarian and among the wealthier); pp. 20-24 on Macumba and Umbanda.

436 Bastide, Roger. "La théorie de la réincarnation chez les Afro-Américains." In *Réincarnation et vie mystique en Afrique Noire*, edited by D. Zahan. Paris: Presses Universitaires de France, 1965, pp. 9-29.

Brazil

437 Bastide, Roger. "Ultima scripta: Textes recueillis et commentés par Henri Desroche. III: L'article pour *Présence Africaine*. Négritude et intégration nationale. La classe moyenne de couleur dans les religions afro-brésiliennes." *Archives de Sociologie des Religions*, no. 38 [19, no. 2] (July-December 1974): 12-18.

The changing situation in São Paulo with whites joining Candombles and making them more European, and tourism turning them into folk spectacles, while blacks join Umbanda and emphasize African elements.

438 Bastide, Roger. "Ultima scripta: Textes recueillis et commentés par Henri Desroche. IV: La communication pour le Colloque de Dakar (octobre 1973): La rencontre des dieux africains et des esprits indiens." *Archives de Sociologie des Religions* no. 38 [19, no. 2], (July-December 1974): 19-28. Reprinted in *Le sacré sauvage et autres essais*. Paris: Payot, 1975, pp. 186-200.

A typology covering Candomble, Catimbo, Macumba, and Umbanda: the two sets of spiritual beings are separated in the first of these cults, but united in the last. (With introduction by H. Desroche.)

439 Bastide, Roger, and Verger, Pierre. "Contribuição ao estudo da adivinhação no Salvador, Bahia." *Revista do Museu Paulista* (São Paulo), n.s. 7 (1953): 357-80.

440 Becco, Horacio Jorge. *Lexicografía religiosa de los Afroamericanos*. Buenos Aires: Editôra "Coni," 1952, 38 pp.

With Introduction, pp. 5-10, and bibliographical references within the annotations to the religious vocabulary.

441 Benz, Ernst. "Gebet und Heilung im brasilienischer Spiritismus." In *Der Religionswandel unserer Zeit in Spiegel der Religionswissenschaft*, edited by G. Stephenson. Darmstadt: Wissenschaftliche Buchgesellschaft, 1976, pp. 35-53; English summary (p. 53).

On Spiritism in general and Umbanda.

442 Bernabo, Hector Júlio Páride. *Festo do Bonfim*. 27 desenhos de Carybé [pseud.] Texto-Odorico Tavares. Salvador: Progresso, 1955, 32 pp., illus.

443 Bettencourt, Gastão de. *Os três santos de Juinho no folclore brasílico*. Rio de Janeiro: AGIR, 1947, 163 pp.

444 Beylier, Charles. "Une première enquête de Roger Bastide: Images du nordeste mystique en noir et blanc." *Archives Internationales de Sociologie de la Coopération et du Développement* (Paris), no. 40 (1976), pp. 15-34, bib.

445 Bezerra, Felte. *Etnias segipanas: Contribuição ao seu estudo*. Aracaju, 1950, 275 pp.
    Pp. 187-91, description of Xango in Alagoas.

446 Bezerra, Felte. "Um xangô de Aracajú." *Sociologia* (São Paulo) 10 (1948): 266-71.

447 Bittencourt, Dario de. "A liberdade religiosa no Brasil: A macumba e o batuque em face de lei." In *O Negro no Brasil*, compiled by E. Carneiro and A. do Couto Ferraz. Rio de Janeiro: Civilização Brasileira, 1940, pp. 160-99.

448 Bittencourt, José Maria. *No reino dos Exús, estudo cuidadoso sobre todas as entidades que baixam no terreiro*. Rio de Janeiro: Eco, 1970, 158 pp.

449 Bomfim, Martiniano do. "Os ministros de xangô." In *O Negro no Brasil*, compiled by E. Carneiro and A. do Couto Ferraz. Rio de Janeiro: Civilização Brasileira, 1940, pp. 233-236. Reprinted in *Antologia do Negro brasileiro*, compiled by E. Carneiro. Rio de Janeiro: Edições de Ouro, 1967, pp. 379-81.

450 Bourdon, A. A. "Les religions afro-brésiliennes dans l'oeuvre de Jorge Amado." *Bulletin des Études Portugaises*, nos. 35-36 (1974-75), pp. 145-203.
    With tables of Afro-Brazilian references in the fiction of J. Amado.

451 Brackman, Richard Willy. "Afro-fetischistische Feste in Brasilien." *Staden-Jahrbuch* (São Paulo), nos. 11-12 (1963-64), pp. 45-60.

452 Braga, Julio Santana. "Ifa au Brésil." *Annales de l'Université d'Abidjan. Série D: Littérature, Sciences Humaines* (Abidjan) 11 (1978): 323-35.
    The Ifa divination cult: history, idea of divinity, relations with other cults, especially Oxum; the role of women.

453 Braga, Julio Santana. "Prática divinatória e exercício do poder (O jogo de búzios nos candomblés de Bahia)." In *Afro-Asia* (Salvador, Centro

Brazil

de Estudos Afro-Orientais da Universidade Federal da Bahia) 13
(April 1980): 67-74; English and French summaries.

454 Braga, Rubem. "Um jongo entre os Maratimbas." *Revista do Arquivo Municipal* (São Paulo) 66 (April-May 1940): 77-80.
Festivals – *Catambá* and *jongo* as observed among Afro-Brazilians.

455 Braga, Zora. "Cérémonies secrètes au Brésil." *Horizons* (Paris), no. 59 (April 1956), pp. 68-74, illus.

456 Bramly, Serge. *Macumba. Forces noires du Brésil. Les enseignements de Maria-José, mère des dieux. Receuillis par Serge Bramly.* Maîtres et Mystiques Vivantes. Paris: Seghers, 1975, 152 pp. English translation. *Macumba: The teachings of Maria-José, mother of the gods,* translated by M. Bogin. New York: St. Martins Press, 1977. Reprint. New York: Avon Books, 1979, 214 pp., illus. German translation. *Macumba: Die magische Religion brasiliens.* Freiburg: Bauer, 1978, 175 pp.

457 Brandão, Carlos Rodrigues. *Os deuses do povo* [The gods of the people]. Rio de Janeiro: Editôra Brasilense, 1980, 260 pp.
Based on a doctoral dissertation, studying grass-roots religiosity in the small town of Itaipira, in interior of São Paulo state. The major Afro-Brazilian cults and larger Pentecostal denominations as well as some kinds of Catholic folk religion are "intermediate religions" for the upwardly mobile in society, rather than true "popular" or "peoples' religions." See summary by Guillermo Cook (entry 539).

458 Brazil, Etienne Ignace. *O culto das imagens.* São Paulo: A. Campos, 1910.

459 Brazil, Etienne Ignace. "Le fétichisme des Nègres du Brésil." *Anthropos* 3 (1908): 881-904, illus. Portuguese translation. "O fetichismo dos Negros do Brazil." *Revista do Instituto Histórico e Geográphico Brasileiro* (Rio de Janeiro) 74, no. 2 (1911): 192-260, illus., bib.
A systematic and clear exposition of the Candomble religion of Bahia Negroes early in the twentieth century – especially on the place of Olorun and the Orixas. Pp. 901-4, the mutual influence of Christians and "fetishists."

460 Brazil, Etienne Ignace. "Os Malês." *Revista do Instituto Histórico e Geográphico Brasileiro* (Rio de Janeiro) 72, no. 2 (1909): 67-126.

Revised and enlarged edition of the article in *Anthropos* (entry 462).

461 Brazil, Etienne Ignace. "A revolta dos Malês." *Revista do Instituto Histórico e Geográphico Brasileiro* (Rio de Janeiro), no. 14 (1907), 129-49.
Well-documented account of the revolt by African Muslims in Bahia in 1835.

462 [Brazil], Etienne Ignace. "La secte musulmane des Malès du Brésil et leur révolte en 1935." *Anthropos* 4, no. 1 (1909): 99-105; 4, no. 2 (1909): 405-15.
Detailed account of African Muslims in Brazil, especially their religion, based on personal experience and documentary sources; the second part is on the revolt of 1835.

463 Breeveld, M. M. "Aspects du syncrétisme religieux brésilien dans le cadre de son acculturation." Master's dissertation, Louvain University (Belgium), 1969.

464 Breeveld, M. M. "Uma revisão do conceito de sincretismo religioso e perspectiva de pesquisas." *Revista Eclesiástica Brasileira* 35 (1975): 451-23.

465 Brown, Ruth. Review of *Spirits of the deep*, by S. and R. Leacock (entry 743). *American Anthropologist* 75 (1973): 1042-43.

466 Bruneau, T[homas] C[harles]. *Political transformation of the Brazilian Catholic Church*. Cambridge: Cambridge University Press, 1974, pp. 62-63.

467 Cacciatore, Olga Gudolle. *Dicionário de cultos afro-brasileiros com origem das palavras*. Introduction by José Carlos Rodrigues. Rio de Janeiro: Forense-Universitária and Instituto Estadual do Livro, 1977, 279 pp., bib.
Pp. 1-25, introductions; pp. 21-23, classification tables; pp. 217-79, bibliographies.

468 Cadógan, León. "Ayvu Rapyta: Textos miticos de los Mbyá-Guaraní del Guairá." *Boletim de Faculdade de Filosofia, Ciências e Letras da Universidade de São Paulo* (Antropologia, 5) no. 227 (1959).
Mbya-Guarani myths and cosmology lying behind "terre-sans-mal" migrations.

Brazil

469 Cadógan, León. "Como interpretan los Chiripá (Avá Guaraní) la danza ritual." *Revista de Antropologia* (São Paulo) 7 (1959): 65-99.

470 Calazans, José. *A Santidade de Jaguaripe*. Bahia: S.A. Artes Gréficas, 1952.
Syncretistic millennial Indian movement, led by a halfbreed, 1585.

471 Calmon, Pedro. *Malês: A insurreição des senzalas*. Rio de Janeiro: Ed. Pro Luce, 1933, 154 pp.
A novel on the Malê or Muslim Negro revolt of 1835 in Bahia

472 Camargo, Cândido Procópio [Ferreira] de. *O movimiento de Natal*. Louvain and The Hague: Institute of Social Studies; Federação International dos Institutos de Pesquisas Sociais e Socio-Religiosas, 1968, 273 pp.

473 Camargo, C[ândido] P[rocópio] Ferreira de, and Labbens, J[ean]. "Aspects socio-culturels du spiritisme au Brésil." *Social Compass* 7, nos. 5-6 (1960): 407-30; English summary (p. 407).
"Mediumistic religion" in three main forms – Umbanda/White Magic, Quimbanda/Black Magic and Kardecist Spiritualism appealing to ascending order of socioeconomic groups; the position of the Catholic Church.

474 Camargo, Cândido Procópio [Ferreira] de, ed. *Católicos – protestantes – espirítas*. Petrópolis: Vozes, 1973, 185 pp., illus., bib.
Analyses based on government statistics, and therefore less adequate, on millennialisms, Afro-Brazilian cults, and spiritist movements.

475 Campos, João da Silva. "Costumes e crenças dos Afro-Bahianos." *Sociologia* (São Paulo) 11 (1949): 433-49; English abstract.
On the free blacks living in Salvador in the author's lifetime; pp. 440-47, religious activities, including Candomble.

476 Campos, Sabino de. *Catimbó*. Rio de Janeiro: Livraria Editôra Zélio Valverde, 1946, 399 pp.
A novel featuring African religious ceremonies.

477 Camps, Arnulf. *De weg, de paden en de wegen*. Baarn: Bosch & Keuning n.v., 1977, 103 pp.

Chap. 6 (pp. 57-66) on "popular religiosity in Latin America"–Spiritism and Umbanda in Brazil. Pp. 100-101, references.

478 "Le candomblé des Nègres de Bahia." *La Musée Vivante* (Istanbul), no. 8 (1956).

479 "Candomble, die Religion der Verdammten." *Kontinente* 15, no. 2 (1980): 22-23.

480 Canova, Pietro. "Dossier/riti afrobrasiliani: Tutto il mondo in una notte." *Nigrizia* 100, no. 7 (1987): 25-39, illus., map.

481 Cardozo, Manoel S. "The lay brotherhoods of colonial Bahia." *Catholic Historical Review* 33, no. 1 (1947): 12-30.
     Pp. 22-30, on the Negro cofradias, with detailed study of the statutes of the Brotherhood of St. Anthony of Catagerona, founded 1699.

482 Carise, Iracy. *A arte negra na cultura brasileira: Máscaras africanas*. Rio de Janeiro: Artenova, 1975, 159 pp., illus., maps, bib.
     Study of influence of African cultures on Brazilian culture. Contains a section on religion.

483 Carneiro, Edison [de Souza]. "Aninha." *Estado da Bahia* (Bahia), 25 January 1938. Reprinted in *Ladinos e crioulos*. Rio de Janeiro: Editôra Civilização Brasileira, 1964, pp. 207-8.

484 Carneiro, Edison [de Souza]. "Associação Nacional de Cultos Populares." *Jornal do Comércio* (Rio de Janeiro), 8 May 1960. Reprinted in *Ladinos e crioulos*. Rio de Janeiro: Editôra Civilização Brasileira, 1964, pp. 190-92.

485 Carneiro, Edison de Souza. "Candomblé." *Leitura* (Rio de Janeiro), September 1957. Reprinted in *Ladinos e crioulos*. Rio de Janeiro: Editôra Civilização Brasileira, 1964, pp. 198-200.

486 Carneiro, Edison [de Souza]. "Candomblés da Bahia." *Revista do Arquivo Municipal* (São Paulo), no. 84 [7] (July-August 1942): 127-37. Reprinted in *Antologia do Negro brasileiro*. Rio de Janeiro: As Nossas Edições, 1967, pp. 329-39.

487 Carneiro, Edison de Souza. "Candomblés da Bahia." *Revista do Arquivo Municipal* (São Paulo) 108 [11] (1943).

Brazil

488 Carneiro, Edison [de Souza]. *Candomblés da Bahia*. Publicações do Museo do Estudo, 8. Bahia: Museo do Estudo, 1948, 140 pp., illus. 2d ed., enlarged. Rio de Janeiro: Editorial Andes, 1954, 230 pp., illus. 3d ed. Rio de Janeiro: Conquista, 1961, 189 pp., illus. 4th ed. Rio de Janeiro: Edições de Ouro, 1967, 191 pp., illus. 5th ed., 1977, 145 pp.
   Chap. 1, cults of African origin; chaps. 2-10, Candombles of Bahia (not the Caboclo forms); chap. 11 (pp. 163-68, 3d ed.), Umbanda; pp. 175-89, vocabulary of terms used in Candomble.

489 Carneiro, Edison [de Souza]. "O Caruru de Cosme e Damião." *Província de São Pedro* (Pôrto Alegre), no. 5 (June 1946), pp. 79-81.

490 Carneiro, Edison [de Souza]. "Condoção social e econômica das 'filhas de santo.'" *Problemas* (São Paulo) 1 (1938): 19-21.

491 Carneiro, Edison [de Souza]. *Les cultes d'origine africaine au Brésil.* Translated from the Portuguese by Gilbert Schwartzenberg. Rio de Janeiro: Ministerio da Educação e Cultura, Biblioteca Nacional, 1959, 22 pp., bib.
   1. Vodou; 2. Negroes in Brazil.

492 Carneiro, Edison de Souza. "O culto nagô na Africa e na Bahia." *Diario da Bahia*, 16 and 23 December 1951. Reprinted in *Ladinos e crioulos*. Rio de Janeiro: Editôra Civilização Brasileira, 1964, pp. 174-181.

493 Carneiro, Edison [de Souza]. "Os cultos de origem africana no Brasil." Reprinted from *Decimália*. Rio de Janeiro: Publ. Ministério da Educação e Cultura, 1959, 20 pp. French translation. *Les cultes d'origine africaine au Brésil*. Publ. Ministério da Educação e Cultura, 1959, 22 pp. Reprinted in *Ladinos e crioulos*. Rio de Janeiro: Editôra Civilização Brasileira, 1964, pp. 121-42.

494 Carneiro, Edison [de Souza]. "As divinidades de Angola." *Brasil Açucareiro* (Rio de Janeiro) 78, no. 2 (1971): 144-47, illus.

495 Carneiro, Edison [de Souza]. "Uma falseta de Artur Ramos." *Diário Carioca* (Rio de Janeiro), 29 March 1964. Reprinted in *Ladinos e crioulos*. Rio de Janeiro: Editôra Civilização Brasileira, 1964, pp. 223-27.

496 Carneiro, Edison [de Souza]. *Ladinos e crioulos: Estudos sôbre o Negro no Brasil*. Retratos no Brasil, 18. Rio de Janeiro: Editôra Civilização Brasileira, 1964, 240 pp., illus., bib. (pp. 231-40).

Short essays on Negro life: reprints of his articles over the previous 30 years; includes African cults in the northeast.

497 Carneiro, Edison [de Souza]. "Liberdade de culto." *Quilombo* (Rio de Janeiro) 2, no. 5 (1950): 7. Reprinted in *Ladinos e Crioulos*. Rio de Janeiro: Editôra Civilização Brasileira, 1964, pp. 185-87.

498 Carneiro, Edison [de Souza]. "Linhas geraes da casa de candomblé." *Revista do Arquivo Municipal* (São Paulo) ano 6, vol. 71, 1940, pp. 129-40, illus.

The word *Candomble* is applied in Bahia to the meeting place of the religious festivals of the Negroes, although formerly restricted to the ceremonial proper. Description of the architectural features of one of these structures, said to be typical of most; the plans are rough sketches.

499 Carneiro, Edison [de Souza]. "Maes de Santo." *Província de São Pedro* (Rio de Janeiro), no. 11 (March-June 1948), pp. 51-53.

500 Carneiro, Edison [de Souza]. *Negros Bantús: Notas de etnographia religiosa e de folclore*. Biblioteca de Divilgação Scientifica, 14. Rio de Janeiro: Civilização Brasileira, 1937, 190 pp. 2d ed. 1981, illus., maps.

The second of his two basic studies of Negro life in Bahia. Pp. 133-41, 185-95, and extract, "A Reinha do Mar," reprinted in *Antologia do Negro brasileiro* (Rio de Janeiro: Edições de Ouro, 1967), p. 362.

501 Carneiro, Edison [de Souza]. "Nina Rodrigues." *Kriterion* (Faculdade de Filosofia, UMG), January-June 1958. Abridged in *Jornal de Letras* (Rio de Janeiro), December 1962. Reprinted in *Ladinos e crioulos*. Rio de Janeiro: Editôra Civilização Brasileira, 1964, pp. 209-17.

502 Carneiro, Edison de Souza. "Um orixa caluniado." In *Antologia do Negro brasileiro*. Pôrto Alegre: Edições Globo, 1950, pp. 344-45. Reprint. Rio de Janeiro: Edições de Ouro, 1967, pp. 367-78.

503 Carneiro, Edison [de Souza]. "Les religions du noir brésilien." *La contribution de l'Afrique à la civilisation brésilienne*. Marseilles: SOPIC, 1966, pp. 21-29.

504 Carneiro, Edison [de Souza]. *Religões negras: Notas de etnografia religiosa*. Biblioteca de Divilgação Scientifica, 7. Rio de Janeiro: Civilização Brasileira, 1936, 188 pp., illus. 2d ed. 1981, 113 pp.

Brazil

The religion of lower-class Negroes in Bahia city, including Candomble, Macumba, Xango, Yemanja, and the Malês or Muslims; pp. 94-98, syncretism; pp. 109-14, musical instruments; pp. 117-26, Orisha songs.

505 Carneiro, Edison [de Souza]. "Uma revisão na ethnographia religiosa afro-brasileira." In *O Negro no Brasil*, compiled by E. Carneiro and A. do Couto Ferraz. Rio de Janeiro: Civilização Brasileira, 1940, pp. 61-68.
   Mythology of Candomble's roots in Africa and in the worship of a high creator God.

506 Carneiro, Edison [de Souza]. "Situação do Negro no Brasil." *Estudos Afro-Brasileiros* (Rio de Janeiro) 1 (1935): 237-41.

507 Carneiro, Edison [de Souza]. "The structure of African cults in Bahia." *Journal of American Folklore* 53, no. 210 (1940): 271-78.
   Yoruba and Ewe influences strongest in over 100 Candombles.

508 Carneiro, Edison [de Souza]. "A 'teologia' dos cultos afro-brasileiros.'" In *Macumba: Cultos afro-brasileiros.* . . . , edited by C. F. Gomes. São Paulo: Edições Paulinas, 1976, pp. 39-53.

509 Carneiro, Edison [de Souza]. "Xangô." In *Novos estudos afro-brasileiros*, edited by G. Freyre, et al. Vol. 2. Biblioteca de Divilgação Scientifica, 9. Rio de Janeiro: Civilização Brasileira, 1937, pp. 139-45.
   Shango in Bahia – an outline.

510 Carneiro, Edison de Souza. *Xangos de Maceió, parecer ao govêrno de Alagoas.* 1952. Reprinted in *Ladinos e crioulos*. Rio de Janeiro: Editôra Civilização Brasileira, 1964, pp. 188-89.

511 Carneiro, Edison [de Souza]. "Yêmanjá e a mae-d'água." Paper presented at Congresso do Negro Brasileiro. Rio de Janeiro, 1950. Reprinted in *Ladinos e crioulos*. Rio de Janeiro: Editôra Civilização Brasileira, 1964, pp. 164-67.

512 Carneiro, Edison de Souza, comp. *Antologia do Negro brasileiro*. Pôrto Alegre: Edições Globo, 1950, 432 pp. Reprint. Coleção Brasileira de Ouro. Rio de Janeiro: Edições de Ouro, 1967, 466 pp., illus., music.
   Pp. 329-83, reprinting of short selections from important writings on black religion in Brazil; see separate entries under M. do Bomfim

(449), E. Carneiro (486, 500, 502), M. J. Herskovits (659, 664) R. Landes (733, 734) D. J. Nery (827), A. Ramos (896), J. do Rio (937).

513 Carneiro, Edison [de Souza], and Ferraz, Aydano do Couto, comps. *O Negro no Brasil.* Biblioteca de Divilgação Scientifica, 20. Rio de Janeiro: Civilização Brasileira, 1940, 367 pp.
    Report of the 2d Congresso Afro-Brasileiro, Bahia, 1937. Pp. 19-29, M. J. Herskovits on African gods and Catholic saints (entry 652); pp. 61-68, E. Carneiro on the revision of Afro-Brazilian religious ethnography (entry 505); pp. 129-37, R. Guimarães on Bantu syncretistic elements (entry 640); pp. 169-99, D. de Bittencourt on Macumba and the law (entry 447); pp. 233-36, M. do Bomfim on Shango ministers (entry 449); pp. 325-28, J. Amado on a famous cult leader in Bahia (entry 369); pp.343-47, M. V. dos Santos on Bahia Negroes (entry 956); pp. 349-56, M. B. Paixão on the Congo nation (entry 847).

514 Carriker, Charles Timothy. "Evangelização de espíritas." Paper presented at consultation on Brazilian Spiritism in Belo Horizonte, October 1985. For publication with the Proceedings (ca. 1989).

515 Carvalho, Alfredo de. "A magia sexual no Brasil." *Revista do Instituto Archeológico, Histórico e Geográfico* (Pernambuco) 21 (1919): 406-22.
    On Catimbo cults and magical practices of African origin.

516 Carvalho, J. J. de. "Ritual and music of the *sango* cults of Recife, Brazil." Ph.D. thesis, The Queen's University of Belfast, 1984.

517 Carybé [Héctor Júlio Páride Bernabó]. "Candomblés of Bahia." *Americas* (Union Pan Americana) 2 (January 1959): 16-19.
    By an artist who is an *ogan*, or lay brother, of the Candomble shown in the illustrations.

518 Carybé [Hector Júlio Páride Bernabó]. *As sete portas da Bahia.* São Paulo: Martins Editôra, 1962. 4th ed., revised and amplified. Rio de Janeiro: Editôra Record, 1976, 346 pp., illus.
    New edition contains drawings of Bahia's Orixas, religious dances and street life, and enlarged glossary of Afro-Brazilian religious terminology, musical instruments, and cult objects.

519 Carybé [Hector Júlio Páride Bernabó]. *Temas de candomblé.* Salvador: Livraria Progresso, 1955, 32 pp. + 27 illus.

Brazil

520 Cascudo, Luis da Câmara. *Luanda! Luanda! Made in Africa: Pesquisas e notas*. Perspectivas do Homen, 3. Rio de Janeiro: Editôra Civilização Brasileira, 1965, 193 pp.

Despite title, historical essays in Portuguese on African influences in Brazil since the early colonial period; see especially pp. 10-16, "Sereias de Angola" (Luanda, Angola, and the Yemanja cult in Bahia, etc.); pp. 90-95, "Luanda!" (Luanda as representing the lost paradise of some Africans and Indians); pp. 105-12, "Ausencia do diabo Africano" (on the Devil in Africa and Brazil).

521 Cascudo, Luis da Câmara. *Meleagro: Depoimento e pesquisa sôbre a magia no Brasil*. Rio de Janeiro: AGIR, 1951, 196 pp., illus.

On the Catimbo cults.

522 Cascudo, Luis da Câmara. "Notas sôbre o catimbó." In *Novos estudos afro-brasileiros*, edited by G. Freyre, et al. Vol. 2. Biblioteca de Divilgação Scientifica, 9. Rio de Janeiro: Civilização Brasileira, 1937, pp. 75-129, bib.

With many texts of songs, a "pharmacopéa" of botanical items used, folk remedies for listed complaints, amulets, etc.; relation to Macumba.

523 Castro, Yeda Pessoa de. "Antropologia e linguistica nos estudos afro-brasileiros." *Afro-Asia* (Bahia) 12 (June 1976): 211-27.

Advocates interdisciplinary investigation of African customs and language in Brazil. Includes descriptions of some cults and comparison with Cuba and Haiti.

524 Cavalcanti, Pedro. "As seitas africanas do Recife." *Estudos Afro-Brasileiros* (Rio de Janeiro) 1 (1935): 243-57.

With glossary, rules, songs, liturgical calendars, and names, addresses, and leaders of thirteen registered cults.

525 Cavalcanti, Pedro. "Ulysses Pernambuco e as seitas africanas." *Estudos Pernambucanos* (Recife), 1937.

526 Cavalcanti, Pedro, and Lima, Denice C. "Investigações sobre as religiões no Recife." *Arquivos de Assistencia a Psicopatos de Pernambuco* (Recife), April 1932.

527 Cazeneuve, J. "Le candomblé de Bahia." *Revue d'Histoire et de Philosophie Religieuse* (Paris) 38 (1959).

528 César, J. V. "Aculturação religiosa dos Borodos de Méruri, Mato Grosso." *Arquivos de Anatomia e Antropologia* (Rio de Janeiro) 2, no. 2 (1977): 277-89, illus., bib.

529 César, J. V. "O Vale do Amanhecer." *Atu* 93-94 (1977): 367-91; 95-96 (1977): 451-506; 97-98 (1978): 58-107.
The movement also studied by I. Wulfhorst (entry 1066) near Brasilia.

530 Chilcote, Ronald H. "Protest and resistance in Brazil and Portuguese Africa: A synthesis and classification." In *Protest and Resistance in Angola and Brazil*, edited by R. H. Chilcote. Berkeley: University of California Press, 1972, pp. 243-301.
Primarily on political revolts but offers comprehensive classification of movements, including more religious ones.

531 Christopher, R. A. "The sacred waters of Oxalia: An eerie predawn visit to a Brazilian Voodoo ceremony." *Americas* (Washington, D.C., Pan American Union) 7, no. 1 (1955): 23-26, illus.

532 Claudio, Affonso. *As tribus negras importadas. Estudo ethnographico, sua distribuição regional no Brasil. Os grandes mercados de escravos*. Vol. 2. Actas, Congresso de Historia Nacional, Rio de Janeiro, 1914. Rio de Janeiro, 1915-17, pp. 595-657.
An ethnographic study of the African tribes from which slaves were captured for export to Brazil; contains much of interest to the study of folklore.

533 Clouzot, Henri-Georges. *Le cheval des dieux.* Paris: René Julliard, 1951, 239 pp.
On the Afro-Brazilian cults of Bahia. See R. Bastide, *Le candomblé de Bahia* (entry 406), for comment on Clouzot.

534 Conferencia Nacional dos Bispos do Brasil (CNBB). "Campagna nacional contra a heresia espiritista." *Revista Eclesiástica Brasileira* 13 (1953): 764-66.

535 Conferencia Nacional dos Bispos do Brasil (CNBB). "Condenação do espiritismo." *Revista Eclesiástica Brasileira* 13 (1953): 763.

536 Conferencia Nacional dos Bispos do Brasil (CNBB). *Macumba. Cultos afro-brasileiros: Candomblé, umbanda. Observações pastores*, edited by C. F. Gomez. Rio de Janeiro: Secretaria do Regional Leste-1 da

Brazil

CNBB, 1972, 68pp., bib. 2d rev. and enl. ed. São Paulo: Edições
Paulinas, 1976, 116 pp.
History, theology and liturgy of the cults; pastoral observations by
Valdeli Carvalho Costa, S.J., and Boaventura Kloppenburg, O.F.M.

537 Congresso Afro-Brasileiro. *Estudos afro-brasileiros*. Rio de Janeiro:
Editôra Ariel, 1935, 275 pp.
First volume of papers from the 1st Congresso Afro-Brasileiro at
Recife, 1934. Includes A. Ramos on the Brazilian forms of Yoruba
Shango legends (pp. 49-54) (entry 899); P. Cavalcanti on African cult
centers and their worship, etc., in Recife (pp. 243-57) (entry 524); E.
Braga on invocations to Shango in Recife.

538 Cook, Bill [A. William Cook, Jr.]. "An overview of religious pluralism
and syncretism in Brazil." *IAMS News Letter* (Leiden, Netherlands,
International Association for Mission Studies), no. 10 (March 1977),
pp. 37-41.
A survey of the origins, contributing religious and other
traditions, and social factors of syncretist Spiritism in its various forms;
by a member of the Institute of In-Depth Evangelization, São Paulo.

539 Cook, Guillermo [A. William Cook, Jr.]. Summary of *Os deuses do
povo* [The gods of the people], by Carlos Rodrigues Brandão (entry
457). *Missiology* 10, no. 2 (1982): 245-56.
A full summary. Shows that Spiritist (and Pentecostal) cults are
not truly grass-roots movements but "intermediate religions" serving
the upwardly mobile in society, and themselves in a hierarchy with
Kardecism at the top, Umbanda next, and increasing eclecticism down
the scale; there is an upward movement of both leaders and
movements. Pentecostalism is the main case study, but the theses also
apply to Spiritism in general.

540 Corrêa, A[rmando] Magalhães. *O Sertão Carioca*. Rio de Janeiro, 1936.
Pp. 217-22, Macumba.

541 Correa, Norton F. "As ilhas etnicas negras da zona rural do Rio
Grande do Sul." *Anual da ANPOCS* (Caxambu), no. 13, 1989.

542 Correa, Norton F. "Revisitando Herskovits e Bastide no batuque do
Rio Grande do Sul." Paper presented ath XVI Reunião Brasileira de
Antropologia Campinas, São Paulo, 27-30 March 1988.

543 Correa, Norton F. "Os vivos, os mortos e os deuses." Master's dissertation (anthropology), [1989?].
Popular version expected in 1990, as "Batuque do Rio Grande do Sul."

544 Corwin, Arthur F. "Afro-Brazilians: Myths and realities." In *Slavery and race relations in Latin America*, edited by R. B. Toplin. Westport, Conn.: Greenwood Press, 1974, pp. 385 et seq.
Pp. 414-17 (and notes p. 434), "Marginality and the Christian mission," includes Candomble, Macumba, and Umbanda.

545 Cossard-Binon, Gisèle. "Contribution à l'étude des candomblés au Brésil: Le candomblé Angola." Doctorat de troisième cycle, thesis (Directeur de Recherches: Roger Bastide), University of Paris, 1970.
An Angola cult house in Rio de Janeiro.

546 Cossard-Binon, Gisèle. "La fille de saint." *Journal de la Société des Américanistes* (Paris) 58 (1969): 57-78, illus.
Spirit mediumship in a Rio de Janeiro Candomble in 1946.

547 Cossard-Binon, Gisèle. "Origines lointaines du syncrétisme afro-catholique au Brésil et perspectives d'avenir." *Afro-Asia* (Bahia, Universidade Federal da Bahia, Centro de Estudos Afro-Orientais) 12 (June 1976): 161-66.
Emphasizes that large numbers of slaves had been baptized as Christians in Africa, prior to their deportation to Brazil.

548 Cossard-Binon, Gisèle. "Le rôle de la femme de couleur dans les religions afro-brésiliennes." In *La femme de couleur en Amérique Latine*, edited by R. Bastide. Paris: Éditions Anthropos, 1974, pp. 75-96; Introduction by the editor, pp. 9-47.

549 Costa, Esdras Borges. "Protestantism, modernization, and cultural change in Brazil." Ph.D. dissertation, University of California, Berkeley, 1979, 430 pp.
Protestant evangelical theology and "pure" liberal democracy assumed as necessarily connected – but the two concerns have sometimes worked against each other, and "liberalism" has been very conservative.

550 Costa, F[ernando]. *A prácticia do candomblé no Brasil.* Rio de Janeiro: Editoria Rines, 1974, 144 pp., illus.

Brazil

551 Costa, Neusa Meirelles. "O misticismo na experiência religiosa do candomblé." *Religiosidade popular e misticismo no Brasil. Ciências da Religião* (Edições Paulinas, São Paulo) 2, no. 2 (June 1984).

552 Costa, Valdeli Carvalho da. "Alguns marcos no evolução histórica e situação actual de Exu na umbanda do Rio de Janeiro." *Afro-Asia* (Salvador, Centro de Estudos Afro-Orientais, Universidade Federal da Bahia) 13 (April 1980): 87-105; English and French summaries.
    A study by a Jesuit professor.

553 Crocker, William H. "The Canela messianic movement: An introduction." In *Atas do Simpósio sôbre a Biota Amazônica, 1966*. Vol. 2, *Antropologia*. Rio de Janeiro: Conselho Nacional de Pesquisas, 1967, pp. 69-83.
    An attempt to leave traditional ways and become *civilizados*, among the Canela Indians in Maranhão, led by prophetess Keekhwëi in 1963; she contacted the culture hero through her unborn child, and expected an imminent inversion of the cultural situation. The symbolism of the rituals is analyzed in terms of traditional culture and current tensions.

554 Crocker, William H. "Extramarital sexual practices of the Ramkokamekra-Canela Indians: An analysis of socio-cultural factors." In *Native South Americans*, edited by P. J. Lyon. Boston: Little, Brown & Co., 1974, pp. 184-94.
    Pp. 192-94, the Ramkokamekra-Canela new religious movement.

555 Cunha, Manuela Carneiro da. "Logique du mythe et de l'action: Le mouvement messianique canela de 1963." *L'Homme* 13, no. 4 (1973): 5-37.
    The interactions between myth and ritual, and the importance of such movements in providing satisfying belief systems. Based on W. H. Crocker, "The Canela messianic movement: An introduction" (entry 553).

556 Cunha, Nobrega da. *Macumba*. Rio de Janeiro, 1960.

557 Curry, Donald Edward. "Lusiada: An anthropological study of the growth of Protestantism in Brazil." Ph.D. dissertation (anthropology), Columbia University, 1968, 293 pp.

558 Damascendo, Caetana. "Oxala e Jesus. Identidade étnica negra e o contexto cristão. Debate: Identidade étnica e religiosa." *Communicações do ISER* 5, no. 21 (1986): 4-11, 12-25.
   The efforts of black Protestant pastors and black Catholic religious in integrating elements of Afro-Brazilian cults into Christianity.

559 Denton, Roy. [Report on Spiritism in Belém, Brazil.] *Light and Life* (London, Unevangelized Fields Mission), April-June 1973, pp. 18-19.
   Spiritism equated with "voodooism," Umbanda, and Satan worship.

560 Desmangles, Leslie G[érald]. "African religions of Brazil." *Cross Currents* 30, no. 1 (1980): 81-83.
   A review of *The African religions of Brazil*, by R. Bastide (entry 431).

561 Diniz, Almacho. "O fetichismo des religios no Brasil." *A evolução* (Pernambuco), April 1909.

562 Dornas, João. *Capítulos da sociologia brasileira*. Rio de Janeiro: Edições da Organização Simões, 1955, 249 pp.

563 Dowell, M. "O candomblé da Bahia." *A Mascara* (Bahia) 11 (5 May 1942).

564 Doyon, Philippe. "Brazil's African cults." *Continent 2000* 22 (July 1971): 43-47, illus.

565 Duarte, Abelardo. "Sobrevivências do culto da Serpente (Dânh-Gbi) nas Alagoas et sobre o panteão afro-brasileiro." *Revista do Instituto Histórico de Alagoas* (Maceio, Alagoas) 26 (1948-50) [appeared 1952]: 60-79.

566 Duarte, Ophir Martins. "O desenvolvimento das religiões afro-brasileiras em Belém. *Boletino da Associação Atlética Banco do Brasil* (Belém) 1, no. 3 (1960-61).

567 Ebner, Carl Borromaeus. "Der Macumbakult–Africa in Brasilien." *Priester und Mission* (Aachen), 1972, pp. 167-69.

Brazil

568 Eco, Umberto. "Whose side are the orixa on?" In *Faith in Fakes*. Essays translated from the Italian by William Weaver. London: Secker and Warburg, 1987, pp. 103-12.

569 Eduardo, Octávio da Costa. *The Negro in Northern Brazil: A study in acculturation*. Monographs, American Ethnological Society, 15. Seattle: University of Washington Press, 1948, 131 pp., map, bib.
   Mainly in the city of S. Salvador (i.e., Bahia). Chap. 5 (pp. 46-107), on religion, includes cult centers, dances, gods, rituals, etc.; chap. 6 (pp. 107-23), the soul, guardian angels, rites of death. Originally a Northwestern University thesis, 1946. The best source in English.

570 Eduardo, Octávio da Costa. "Three-way religious acculturation in a north Brazilian city." *Afroamerica Revista del Instituto Internacional de Estudios Afroamericanos* (Mexico) 2 (1946): 81-90.
   African (Dahomey and Yoruba) syncretistic cults; Indian-Catholic syncretisms.

571 Eduardo, Octávio da Costa. "O Tocador de Atabaque nas casas de culto afro-maranhenses." *Les Afro-Américains*. Mémoires de l'Institut Français de l'Afrique Noire, no. 27. Dakar: IFAN, 1952, pp. 119-23.

572 Espin, Orlando. "Iroko e Afá-Kolé: Commentário exegético a um mito Yorubá-Lucumi. Cientribução ao diálogo com as religões afro-americanas." *Perspectiva Teologica* (Belo Horizonte), no. 44 [18] (1986), 29-61.
   Redressing the neglect of Afro-American religions by Latin American theology, by examining one myth on origins of good and evil for values held in common with Christianity.

573 Fancello, Mauro. "Gli orixàs del candomblé." *Missioni Consolata* (Torino) 74, no. 7 (1972).

574 Fernandes, [Albino] Gonçalves. *O folclore mágico do nordeste*. Biblioteca de Divulgação Scientifica, 18. Rio de Janeiro: Civilização Brasileira, 1938, 179 pp.
   Chaps. 1, 7, 10, on Catimbo cults; especially the survival inside the Catimbo cult (which unites Indian, Negro and spiritist elements) of the old curative magic.

575 Fernandes, Albino Gonçalves. "Investigaçoes sobre cultos negros fetichistas do Recife." *Arquivos de Assistencia a Psicopatos de Pernambuco* 5, nos. 1-2 (1935): 87-132.

576 Fernandes, [Albino] Gonçalves. "Novas investigações sobre as seitas afro-brasileiras." *Neurobiologia* (Recife) 3, no. 2 (1940), 15 pp., illus.
Cultic and magic phenomena around Rio de Janeiro, including Macumba leaders (of white origin), black and mullato "terreiros."

577 Fernandes, [Albino] Gonçalves. "O sincretismo gêge-nagô-católico como expressão dinâmica dum sentimento de inferioridade." *Les Afro-Américains. Mémoires de l'Institut Français d'Afrique Noire* 27 (1952): 125-26.

578 Fernandes, [Albino] Gonçalves. *O sincretismo religioso no Brasil.* Estudos Nacionais, 1. Curitiba: Editôra Guaíra, 1941, 153 pp.; also 1942, 55 pp.
Mainly on the northeast (Xango, etc.) but includes accounts of Portuguese immigrants joining Macumba in Rio de Janeiro, and of the Universal Humanitarian Association, a "nippo-brésilien" group among Japanese immigrants.

579 Fernandes, [Albino] Gonçalves. *Xangôs do nordeste.* Biblioteca de Divilgação Scientifica, 13. Rio de Janeiro: Civilização Brasileira, 1937, 158 pp., illus.
Afro-Brazilian cults in Recife – details of their beliefs and rituals, rivalries and acculturation.

580 Fernandes, Florestan. "Congadas e batuques em Sorocaba." *Sociologia* (São Paulo), no. 138 (1951).

581 Fernandes, Florestan. *A integração do Negro na sociedade de classes.* 2 vols. São Paulo: Dominus Editôra, 1965, 261, 394 pp. Abridged English translation. *The Negro in Brazilian society.* New York: Atheneum, 1971, 489 pp., bib.
The most extensive sociological and historical study of Negro race relations in Brazil, with wide range of topics; passing references to Macumba as corrupted by whites.

582 Ferraz, Aydano do Couto. "Vestígos de um culto dahomeano no Brasil." *Revista do Arquivo Municipal* (São Paulo), no. 76 [7] (1941): 217-74.
Survival of the serpent cult from Bahia to Recife.

583 Ferraz, Aydano do Couto. "Volta à Africa." *Revista do Arquivo Municipal* (São Paulo), no. 54 [5] (February 1939): 175-78, illus.

Brazil

584 Ferreira, Climério Joaquim. *Uma festa pública de candomblé os orixas.* Ensaios/Pesquisas, 1. São Salvador de Bahia: Centro de Estudos Afro-Orientais da Universidade Federal da Bahia, 2d printing 1984, 8 pp.; English and French summaries.

585 Ferreira, José Carlos. "As insurreições dos Africanos na Bahia." *Revista do Instituto Geográphico e Histórico da Bahia*, no. 29 (1903), 90ff.
The Negro revolts, which usually had a religious dimension.

586 Ferretti, Mundicarmo. "La integracíon de 'caboclo' en el tambor de mina y el impacto del candomblé sobre el 'Linea de la Selva' (Estudio sobre el sincretismo afro-indígeno en cultos brasileiros)." *Montalban* (Caracas), 1987, pp. 161-67.

587 Figueiredo, Napoleão, and Vergolino e Silva, Anaíza. "Alguns elementos novos para o estudo dos batuques de Belém." *Atlas do Simpósio sôbre a Biota Amazônica* (Belém) 1 (1967): 101-22.

588 Figueiredo, Napoleão, and Vergolino e Silva, Anaíza. *Festas de santo e encantodos.* Belém: Academia Paraense de Letras, 1972, 37 pp., illus., bib.
Moju religious life and customs.

589 Flasche, Rainer. *Geschichte und Typpologie afrikanischer Religiosität in Brasilien.* Marburger Studien zur Afrika und Asienkunde, Serie A, 1. Marburg: Universitätsbibliothek Marburg/Lahn, 1973, 302 pp., tables, illus., maps, bib.
A *Religionswissenschaft* approach: Part 1, theoretical introduction on "new religions"; Part 2, historical and sociocultural background of Brazil's new religions – church and mission history, Iberian Catholicism, the slavery situation; Part 3, the Iberian Catholic and African religious traditions, the problem of their interpretation and the history of these; Part 4, structural typology: A.) Traditional African forms (Priestly = Candomble; healing = Macumba). B.) Afro-Western forms (Umbanda, as a church-form). Extensive bibliography.

590 Flasche, Rainer. "'Heil für den Einzelnen in der Gegenwart' – am Beispiel afro-brasilianischer Neureligionen." *Zeitschrift für Missions- und Religionswissenschaft* 60, no. 1 (1976): 16-28.
Three ways of viewing salvation from disaster: Priest-type (Candomble); Healer-type (Macumba); and Church-type (Umbanda).

591 Flasche, Rainer. "Vorläufige Bibliographie zu den synkretistischen Religionserscheinungen und Heilserwartungsbewegungen in Brasilien." In *Nachchristliche Bewegungen in Neuguinea und Brasilien: Ein Studienhefte*, edited by E. Dammann. Stuttgart: Evangelische Missionsverlag, 1968, pp. 40-51.
From Afro-Brazilian cults to Umbanda and messianisms.

592 Fonseca, Elias. "O mundo amoroso do candomblé." *Ela Ela* (Rio de Janeiro), December 1975.

593 Fontenelle, A[lvizio]. *Pontos riscados e cantados na umbanda e candomblé.* Rio de Janeiro: GB, 1962, 153 pp.
An Umbanda publication.

594 Frazier, E. Franklin. "The Negro family in Bahia, Brazil." *American Sociological* Review 7, no. 4 (1942): 465-78.
P. 469, description of Candomble cult place and its officiants; pp. 471-78, the Candomble in lower-class family life.

595 Freitas, João de. *Oxum marê: Nossa Senhora de Conceição.* Rio de Janeiro and São Paulo: Livraria Freitas Bastos, 1965, 304 pp.

596 Freitas, João de. *Xangô Djacutá: Historiá, mitologia, ritual, liturgia, culinária, curandeirismo, magia, doutrina, espiritismo, etc.* 2d ed. Rio de Janeiro: Edições Cultura Afro-Aborígene, 1957. 3d ed. 1968, 222 pp., illus.
Jakuta ("thrower of stones," i.e., thunderstones), is another name for Xango.

597 Freitas, Newton. *Macumba.* Curitiba: Ed. Guaira, 1949.

598 Frey, Hermann. "Afrika in Brasilien." *Die Katholischen Missionen* 78, no. 2 (1959): 48-50, illus.

599 Freyre, Gilberto [de Mello]. *Casa-grande [sic] & senzala.* Rio de Janeiro: Maia & Schmist, 1933, 517 pp., bib. 2d ed. 1936, 360 pp. 4th definitive ed. 2 vols. Rio de Janeiro: J. Olympio, 1943, 748 pp. English translation of the latter. *The masters and the slaves.* New York: A. A. Knopf, 1946. Reprint. 1956, lxxi + 537 + xliv pp., (bib., pp. 501-37); New York: A. A. Knopf, Borzoi Books, 1964.
English translation: pp. 81ff., Tupi religions; pp. 314-19, African religious influences; and see index, "Spiritualism."

Brazil

600 Freyre, Gilberto [de Mello]. *Mucambos do nordeste.* Rio de Janeiro: Ministerio da Eduão e Sande, 1937, 34 pp.

601 Freyre, Gilberto [de Mello]. *Sobrados e mucambos: Decadência do patriarcado rural no Brasil.* São Paulo: Companhia Editôra Nacional, 1936, 405 pp., illus. Enl. ed. 3 vols. Rio de Janeiro: J. Olympio, 1951, 1188 pp., illus. English translation. *The mansions and the shanties.* New York: A. A. Knopf, 1963, xxxvii + 431 pp., illus.
    Pp. 215, 315-16, 419-20, African cults and their religious influences on Brazilian religion and culture.

602 Freyre, Gilberto [de Mello], et al., eds. *Novos estudos afro-brasileiros.* Biblioteca de Divilgação Scientifica, 9. Rio de Janeiro: Civilização Brasileira, 1937, 352 pp., illus.
    Second volume of papers from the 1st Congresso Afro-Brasileiro at Recife 1934. Includes Luiz da Câmara Cascudo on Catimbo (pp. 75-129) (entry 522); Edison Carneiro on Xango (pp. 139-45) (entry 509), and Jacques Raymundo on the *Amburucu* Yoruba cult of Bahia and Pernambuco, its relation to Yemanja and various Christian saints (pp. 252-56).

603 Frickel, Protásius. "Die Seelenlehre der Gêge und Nagô [Yoruba]." *Santo Antonio. Provinzzeitschrift der Fraziskaner in Nordbrasiliene* (Bahia) 18-19 (1940-41): 192-212.
    A Franciscan opens up the neglected area of the ancestors and the cultic place of these, among the Brazilians of Yoruba and other descent.

604 Frickel, Protásius. "Traças de doutrina gêge e nagô sobre a crença na alma." *Revista do Arquivo Municipal de São Paulo* (São Paulo) 12 (1964): 51-81.

605 Friderichs, Edwin [A.] "Lá dove scendono gli spiriti. L''Instituto Scientifico di Parapsicologia' a San Pedro." *Monde e Missioni* (Milan) 105, nos. 11-12 (1976): 385-87.
    By the Jesuit co-founder of the Latin American Centre for Parapsychology at São Paulo, which studies Spiritism and holds popular courses to "unmask" seances.

606 Friderichs, Edvino [A.] *Onde os espíritos baixam: Orientação para os católicos sobre espritismo, umbanda e charlatanismo.* Col. Ideal Médico, 3. Pôrto Alegre: Edições Paulinas, 1965, 283 pp., illus.

A Catholic priest combatting various forms of Spiritism, but with valuable information about them.

607 Friderichs, Edwin A. "'Wo die Geister niedersteigen.' Der Spiritismus in Brasilien als pastorales Problem." *Die Katholischen Missionen*, 1975, pp. 189-93.
By a Jesuit.

608 Frigerio, Alejandro. "The search for Africa: Proustian nostalgia in Afro-Brazilian studies." M.A. thesis, University of California, Los Angeles, 1983.

609 Fry, Peter [H.] "Mediunidade e sexualidade." *Religião e Sociedade* (Rio de Janeiro) 1, no. 1 (1977): 105-23.
An anthropological study of homosexuality in Afro-Brazilian cults.

610 Fry, Peter H., and Howe, G[ary] N[igel]. "Duas respòstas a aflição: Umbanda e pentecostalismo." *Debate e Crítica* (São Paulo), no. 6 (July 1975), 75-94.

611 Fülling, Erich. "Ausserkirchliche religiöse Strömungen in heutigen Brasilien." *Jahrbuch Evangelischer-Mission 1961* (Hamburg), [1962?], pp. 64-76.
Pp. 68-71, Umbanda and Macumba; pp. 72-75, Spiritism and positivism.

612 Fülling, Erich. *Christus in sechsten Kontinent.* Weltweite Reihe, 19. Stuttgart: Evangelische Missionsverlag, 1966, 96 pp., illus., map, bib.
Pp. 43-56, Umbanda and Macumba; pp. 57-61, anti-Christian "Christian Spiritism."

613 Fülling, Erich. "Evangelische Kirche in Lateinamerika: Ihre missionarische und soziale Aufgabe." In *Evangelische Mission Jahrbuch 1969.* Hamburg: Verlag der Deutschen Evangelische Missions-Hilfe, [1970?], pp. 28-44.
Pp. 33-39, the "new religions" – Macumba, Umbanda, Spiritism.

614 Fülling, Erich. "Neue Religionen in Brasilien." *Lutherische Monatshefte* 8 (1969): 616-20.

Brazil

615 Fülling, Erich. "Neureligionen und Sekten im heutigen Brasilien." *Die Evangelische Diaspora* (Göttingen?), nos. 1-2 (1964), 55ff. Reprinted in *Mission und Unterweisung*, Beilage 3, 1966.

616 Fülling, Erich. "Die religiöse Lage im heutigen Brasilien." *Jahresbericht der Hermannsburger Mission*, 1970, pp. 73-82.

617 Fülling, E[rich]. "Südamerikanisches Christentum in Vergangenheit und Gegenwart, vor allem in Brasilien." *Estudos Teologicos* (São Leopoldo), 1957, pp. 40-53.
Pp. 44-48, on "syncretist cults."

618 Fülling, Erich. "Synkretistische Kulte afrikanischen Ursprungs in brasilianischen Grosstäden." *Evangelische Missionszeitschrift* 14, no. 5 (1957): 137-40.

619 Fülling, Erich. "Synkretische Neureligionen in Brasilien." In *Nachchristliche Bewegungen in Neuguinea und Brasilien: Ein Studienhefte*, edited by E. Dammann. Weltmission Heute 37-38. Stuttgart: Evangelische Missionsverlag, 1968, pp. 20-39.
Spiritism, Macumba, and Umbanda.

620 Fundação Cultural do Estado de Bahia. *Iconografia dos deuses africanos no candomblé de Bahia*. São Paulo: The Fundação, 1980, 268 pp.

621 Gabriel, Chester E. "Communications of the Spirits: Umbanda, regional cults in Manaus and the dynamics of mediumistic trance." Ph.D. dissertation (cultural anthropology), McGill University, 1981.
Spirit cults experiencing accelerated change under the influence of Umbanda, with its mediumistic trance, which is also assimilating to Spirit cults in their regions.

622 Gaçon, Annie. "Les vieux cultes africains du Brésil." *Europe, France Outre-Mer* (Paris) 32:26-29.

623 Galeano, Eduardo H. "Le diable dans les bidonvilles." *IDOC* (Rome), no. 39 (1 February), pp. 8-23.
Slum religion as a protest against the lot of the inhabitants.

624 Gallardo, Jorge E[milio]. "Cultos africanos no Passado Platino." *Communições do ISER* 21 (1986): 77-79.

625 Gallardo, Jorge Emilio. "Las religiones afrobrasileñas como objeto de investigación." *Cuadernos Nao* (Buenos Aires) 1, no. 3.

626 Galvão, Eduardo Eneas. "Aculturação indígena no Rio Negro." *Boletim do Museu Paranaense Emílio Goeldi* (Belém), n.s., Anthropologia, no. 7 (September 1959), pp. 1-60 + 18 plates; English summary, bib.

Pp. 53-54, "native Christs" in the nineteenth century and again under the influence of Protestant missions among the Baniwa as recently as 1950. With English translation of part of p. 54, and notes by Fr. A. Edwards, S.J.

627 Galvão, Eduardo Eneas. "The religion of an Amazon community: A study in culture change." Ph.D. dissertation (anthropology), Columbia University, 1952, 193 pp.

The folk religion of the *caboclo* (mixed Indian-Portuguese people) in a village on the mainstream of the lower Amazon River: (a) a cult of the saints within the Catholic context, and organized through the semi-independent lay brotherhoods, (b) Indian supernatural spirits, usually malevolent and in control of the natural environment, dealt with through *pagés* or shamans for curing or sorcery.

628 Galvão, Eduardo Eneas. *Santos e visagens: Um estudo da vida religiosa de Itá, Amazonas.* Biblioteca Pedagógica Brasileira, 5. São Paulo: Companhia Editôra Nacional, 1955, 202 pp.

Studies of three stages of syncretism in Amazonia – Indian tribal, small rural and small urban communities, emphasizing the analysis of the Indian and Catholic elements.

629 Garcia, Rodolfo. "Vocabulario nagô." *Estudos Afro-Brasileiros* (Rio de Janeiro) 1 (1935): 21-27.

630 Gerbert, Martin. *Religionen in Brasilien: Eine Analyse der nicht-katholischen Religionsformen und ihrer Entwicklung im sozialen Wandel der brasilianischen Gesellschaft.* Bibliotheca Ibero-Americana 13. Berlin: Colloquium Verlag, 1970, 127 pp., bib.

Pp. 23-30, pre- and postcontact Indian "messianism"; pp. 30-34, mestizo millennial movements such as Contestado; pp. 35-46, African-influenced cults, including Macumba; pp. 47-59, Spiritism, including Umbanda; pp. 67-82, Pentecostalism.

631 Girotto, P. D. "Il pericolo dello spiritismo nel Brasile cattolico." *Le Missioni Cattoliche* (Milan) 89 (1960): 351-54, 390-94.

Brazil

632 Gomes, Alfredo Dias. *O pagador de promessas*. Col. Teatro Moderno. Rio de Janeiro: AGIR, 1961. 2d ed., 1962, 168 pp.

Or, "The given word"–a hugely successful play suggesting that Candomble vows have more religious impact on the masses than those made under Catholic auspices.

633 Gonçalves, Martin. "A indumentária sagrada no candomblé da Bahia." *Revista da Música Popular* (Rio de Janeiro) 2 (1954).

634 Gordon, Jacob U. "Yoruba cosmology and culture in Brazil: A study of African survivals in the New World." *Journal of Black Studies* 10, no. 2 (1979): 231-44.

As seen in Candomble and other Afro-Brazilian religions, which are becoming more socially acceptable.

635 Griffiths, Mary. "The development of religious pluralism in Brazil." M. Litt. thesis, University of Glasgow, Latin American Institute, 1976, 262 pp.

636 Groppelli, Vito. "Un populo profondemente religioso." *Monde e Missione* 103, no. 10 (1974): 300-306, illus.

Pp. 302-3, "Spiritismo e protestantismo"; based on Porecatú, Paranà, S. Brazil.

637 Guariglia, Guglielmo. *Prophetismus und Heilserwartungs-Bewegungen als völkerkundliches und religionsgeschichtliches Problem*. Vienna: F. Berger, 1959, xvi + 332 pp., maps, bib.

Pp. 179-83, Tupi Guaraní; p. 184, Santidade de Jaguaripe (Bahia syncretist); pp. 187-88, Umbanda.

638 Guerra, Gregório de Mattos. *Obras completas*. 7 vols. São Paulo: Edições Cultura, 1943. Edited by J. Amado. Salvador, Bahia: Editoria Janaina, 1969, xxvii + 1782 pp.

639 Guerra, Gregório de Mat[t]os. *Obras completas*. 2 vols. São Paulo: Edições Cultura, 1945.

Poems by a seventeenth-century writer in Bahia, describing Negro religion (e.g., vol. 1, pp. 296-97, a Negro fiesta or carnival). Vol. 2, p. 304, similar to later Macumba; pp. 79-88, another Macumba-like festival. The earliest recording of African religious forms.

640 Guimarães, Reginaldo. "Contribuções bantus para o sincretismo fétichista." In *O Negro no Brasil*, compiled by E. Carneiro and A. do Couto Ferraz. Rio de Janeiro: Civilização Brasileira, 1940, pp. 129-37.
Candomble – funeral aspects.

641 Guimarães, Reginaldo. "A divinisação da musica negro-brasileira." *Seiva* (Bahia) 1, no. 4 (1939): 10-11.

642 Guimarães, Reginaldo. "Notas sobre o culto de Oxalá." *Revista Academica* (Rio de Janeiro), no. 17 (1937), 14-15.

643 Guimarães, Ruth. *Os filhos de Mêdo, atual conceito de demônio na tradição popular brasileira*. Pôrto Alegre: Editôra Globo, 1950, 231 pp.

644 Haggard, Phoebe. *The master's children*. London: John Lane, 1939, 310 pp., illus.
A sequel to *Red Macaw* (below), bringing the period story nearly to the present.

645 Haggard, Phoebe. *Red Macaw*. London: Jonathan Cape, 1934, 384 pp.
A novel by the niece of H. Rider Haggard, living on a farm in the interior of S. Paulo state, with an appealing account of the evolution of the Negro in the New World. Divided into ten-year epochs, from the capture of slaves on the west coast of Africa, through the voyage to the New World, their gradual assimilation into the life of the Brazilian plantation, their ill treatment in early days, and the fortitude with which they bore their sufferings. Vivid as background.

646 Hamilton, Russell G. "Afro-Brazilian cults in the novels of Jorge Amado." *Hispania* (Wichita, Kans.), May 1967, pp. 242-52.
Important account of Amado's developing relation to Afro-Brazilian religion, from interested observer to knowledgeable participant, holding certain offices in Candomble, and how he championed the poor and oppressed through his writings. Detailed comments on, with extracts from, many of the novels, showing both the sensual and the aesthetic aspects of Candomble.

647 Hamilton, Russell G. "The present state of African cults in Bahia." *Journal of Social History* (Berkeley) 3, no. 4 (1970): 357-73.
Bahia is increasingly proud of its African heritage and recognises its commercial and tourist value.

Brazil

648 Harris, Marvin. "Race relations in Minhas Velhas." In *Race and class in Brazil*, edited by C. Wagley. 2d ed. Paris: UNESCO, 1963, pp. 47-81.
Pp. 50-51, African elements in the folk Catholicism of Negroes in the central mountain region who lack their own cults.

649 Harris, Marvin. *Town and country in Brazil*. Columbia University Contributions to Anthropology, 37. New York: Columbia University Press, 1956, 302 pp.
Pp. 208-210, Spiritualism in Minhas Velhas; pp. 222-39, popular Catholicism; pp. 239-41, lay brotherhoods; pp. 242-73, folk belief, healings, magic, etc.

650 Hattem, Willem C. van. "Brazil '82." *Update* (Aarhus) 6, no. 4 (December 1982): 33-41.
A leader in the Evangelical Lutheran Church in Brazil, on Brazil accepting Umbanda, Rosicrucians, and Japanese new religions, but not those coming from North America and Europe.

651 Hemming, John. *Red gold: The conquest of the Brazilian Indians, 1500-1800*. London: Macmillan, 1978, 677 pp., illus.
Pp. 46-49, 55-64, Indian religion; pp. 143, 156-58, 174, 243, messianic and Santidade movements; pp. 157-58, "Pope" Antonio.

652 Herskovits, M[elville] J[ean]. "Deuses africanos e santos católicos nas crenças do novo mundo." In *O Negro no Brasil*, compiled by E. Carneiro and A. do Couto Ferraz. Rio de Janeiro: Civilização Brasileira, 1940, pp. 19-29.

653 Herskovits, M[elville] J[ean]. "Deuses africanos em Pôrto Alegre." *Província de São Pedro*, no. 11 (March-June 1948), 63-70.

654 Herskovits, Melville J[ean]. "Drums and drummers in Afro-Brazilian cult life." *Musical Quarterly* 30, no. 4 (1944): 477-92, illus. Reprinted in *The New World Negro*. Bloomington: Indiana University Press, 1966, pp. 183-97. Portuguese translation. "Tambores e tamborileiros no culto afro-brasileiro." *Boletim Latino-Americano de Música* (Rio de Janeiro), no. 41 [6, no. 1] (1946): 92-112.

655 Herskovits, Melville J[ean]. "Estrutura social do candomblé afrobrasileiro." *Boletim do Instituto Joaquim Nabuco* (Recife) 3 (1954): 13-32.
Sociological analysis of social patterns involved in Candomble cults and suggested further enquiries.

656 Herskovits, Melville J[ean]. "The Negro in Bahia, Brazil, a problem in method." *American Sociological Review* 8, no. 4 (1943): 394-404.

657 Herskovits, M[elville] J[ean]. *The New World Negro*. Bloomington: Indiana University Press, 1966, 370 pp.
      Chapter 6 (pp. 199-275), "Cult life in Brazil." See also entries 654, 658, 661, 662, 663, and 664.

658 Herskovits, M[elville] J[ean]. "The Panan, an Afro-Bahian religious rite in transition." *Les Afro-Américains*. Mémoires de l'Institut Français d'Afrique Noire, 27. Dakar: 1952, 133-40. Reprinted in *Carribbean Quarterly* 5, no. 4 (1959): 276-83. Reprinted in *The New World Negro*. Bloomington: Indiana University Press, 1966, pp. 217-26.
      Ketu sect of Candomble.

659 Herskovits, Melville J[ean]. *Pesquisas etnológicas na Bahia*. Conference of the Faculdade de Filosophia da Bahia, Bahia, 6 May 1942. *Afro-Asia* (Bahia) 4, no. 5 (1967): 89-105. Extracted as "Importancia social do candomblé." In *Antologia do Negro brasileiro*, compiled by E. Carneiro. Rio de Janeiro: Edições de Ouro, 1967, pp. 342-43.

660 Herskovits, M[elville] J[ean]. "The Social Organization of the Afro-Brazilian Candomblé." *Phylon* 17, no. 2 (1956): 147-66.

661 Herskovits, Melville J[ean]. "The social organization of the Candomblé." *Anais do XXXI Congresso Internacional de Americanistas, 1954*. Vol. 1. São Paulo: Editôra Anhembi, 1955, pp. 505-32. Reprinted in *The New World Negro*. Bloomington: Indiana University Press, 1966, pp. 226-47. Reprint. Nendeln, Lichtenstein: Kraus Reprints, 1976.
      On Macumba cults.

662 Herskovits, M[elville] J[ean]. "Some economic aspects of the Afrobahian Candomblé." *Miscellanea Paul Rivet. Octogenario Dictata*. Vol. 2. Mexico: Universidad Autónoma de Mexico, 1958, pp. 227-47. Reprinted in *The New World Negro*. Bloomington: Indiana University Press, 1966, pp. 248-66.

663 Herskovits, Melville J[ean]. "Some psychological implications of Afroamerican studies." In *Acculturation in the Americas. Proceedings, 29th International Congress of Americanists, 1949*, edited by S. Tax. Vol. 2. Chicago: University of Chicago Press, 1951, pp. 152-60. Reprinted in

Brazil

The New World Negro, edited by M. J. Herskovits. Bloomington: Indiana University Press, 1966, pp. 145-55.
Pp. 153-55, possession in Afro-Brazilian cults in Bahia as adjustment mechanisms.

664 Herskovits, Melville J[ean]. "The southernmost outpost of New World Africanism." *American Anthropologist* 45, no. 4 (1943): 495-510. Reprinted in *The New World Negro*. Bloomington: Indiana University Press, 1966, pp. 199-216. Portuguese translation. "Os pontos mais meridionais dos africanismos de Novo Mundo." *Revista do Arquivo Municipal* (São Paulo) 9 (1944): 81-99. Extracted as "Os Paras de Pôrto Alegre." In *Antologia do Negro brasileiro*, compiled by E. Carneiro. Rio de Janeiro: Edições de Ouro, 1967, pp. 368-72.

665 Herskovits, Melville J[ean], and Waterman, Richard A[lan]. "Musica de culto afrobahiana." *Revista de Estudios Musicales* (Mendoza) 1, no. 2 (1949): 65-127.
Pp. 65-70, general features.

666 Hertzberg, Jan S. "The African religious heritage in Bahia, Brazil." M.A. thesis (history), University of Illinois, 1977, 136 pp.
The reconstruction of Yoruba religious heritage in Bahia in the eighteenth and nineteenth centuries, largely based on travel accounts from the period, and on government correspondence and legislation.

667 Hess, David John. "Spiritism and science in Brazil: An anthropological interpretation of religion and ideology." Ph.D. thesis, Cornell University, 1987, 355 pp.

668 Hollanda, Guy de. "Mucambas do nordeste." *Boletim de Ariel* (Rio de Janeiro) 7, no. 2 (1936): 38-39.

669 Homage to Iemanjá. *Time*, 10 January 1972, p. 44, illus.
The New Year beach rites for the goddess of the sea (Iemanjá = Virgin Mary) as an example of the popular Spiritism and Afro-Brazilian cults; brief mention of Chico Xavier and Seu Sete as faith healers.

670 Hoornaert, E. "Pressupostos antropólogico para a comprensão do sincretismo." *Revista de Cultura Vozes* (Petrópolis) 7 (1971): 43-52.

671 Horeis, Martin Werner. "The Afro-Brazilian Candomblé cult: An anthropological study of cultural performances of good and evil." Ph.D. dissertation (anthropology), Cornell University, 1974, 242 pp.
   Based on cults in Cachoeira, State of Bahia. Focuses on the invocation and arrival of spirits, as "replacing" rather than "possessing" the devotees (i.e., especially the replacement of evil spirits causing illness). Seeks meaning and interpretation rather than historical development and sources, or psychological components, of the Candombles, which show how evil is made manifest and is dealt with.

672 Horsch, Hans. "Die Ausbreitung afro-brasilianischer Kulte als Herausforderung für die Evangelisation Brasilien." Doctoral dissertation (theology), Erlangen University, 1984.

673 Hrankowska, Teresa. "Afro-brazylijskie obrzedy 'candomble' w stanie Bahia." *Etnografia Polska* (Warsaw) 16, no. 2 (1972): 177-83.
   Afro-Brazilian Candomble rites in the state of Bahia.

674 Hutchinson, Harry W[illiam]. "Race relations in a rural community of the Bahian Recôncavo." In *Race and class in rural Brazil*, edited by C. Wagley. Paris: UNESCO, 1952, pp. 16-46.
   P. 42, Candomble in decline, and the derivative Janaina cult, in area around Salvador.

675 Hutchinson, Harry William. *Village and plantation life in northeastern Brazil.* American Ethnological Society Monograph. Seattle: University of Washington Press, 1957, 209 pp., illus., maps.
   The old plantation section of the Recôncavo of Bahia. Chap. 8, religion: pp. 156-66, Roman Catholic Church (and African cult influences); pp. 166-77, African cults; pp. 177-78, Spiritualism.

676 Instituto Histórico e Geográfico de Alagoas. "Catalogo ilustrado da coleção perseverança." Maceió, Brazil: Secretaria de Educação e Cultura de Alagoas, Depto. de Assuntos Culturais *em convênio com o*, Ministério de Educação e Cultura, 1974, 1 vol., (unpaged), illus., bib.
   Catalogue of Afro-Brazilian artifacts, mostly religious, with scholarly introductions.

677 Ireland, Rowan. "Getting it right: The everyday experience of Pentecostalism and Spiritualism in a northeast Brazilian town." In *Religious experience in world religions*, edited by V. E. Hayes. Bedford Park, South Australia: Australian Association for the Study of Religions, 1980, pp. 145-59.

Brazil

Two case studies in Campo Alegre, set in context of such movements being innovative and creative in relation to social change, rather than alienative, as some have thought.

678 Janzen, John M. *Lemba, 1650-1930: A drum of affliction in Africa and the New World*. New York: Garland, 1982, 383 pp., illus.
Pp. 273-77 on Kongo parallels with Afro-Brazilian religion.

679 Jarric, Pierre du. *Histoire des choses plus memorables advenues tant ez Inde Orientale, que autres païs des la descouverte des Portugais ... jusques à l'an 1600*. 3 parts. Bordeaux: 1608-14. Another ed. Bordeaux: 1610-14. Part 2 only. Arras: 1611.
Pt. 2, pp. 319-22, a Jesuit report on new semi-Christian, anti-Portuguese religion in 1583. See also entry 988.

680 [Jesuit Order]. *Cartas jesuiticas, avulsas, 1550-1568*. Rio de Janeiro: Publicação da Academia Brasileira de Letras, 1931.
See p. 100, note on Fr. Nobrega on "hommes-dieux" and p. 89, other Jesuits on same theme.

681 Jesus, Carolina Maria de. *Child of the dark*. Translated from the Portuguese by David St. Clair. New York: E. P. Dutton & Co., 1962.
A personal diary of life in the *favelas*, slums of rough shacks on outskirts of São Paulo, including religious dimensions.

682 Johnson, Harmon A[lden]. "Authority over the spirits: Brazilian spiritism and evangelical church growth." M.A. thesis (missions), School of World Mission, Fuller Theological Seminary, 1969, 136 pp.
Includes all forms of Afro-Brazilian and Spiritist cults; the attitudes thereto of Roman Catholicism, "traditional" Protestantism, and Pentecostal churches; evangelical church growth and Spiritism (pp. 113-28).

683 Jones, Bryn, and Jones, Betty. "West Amazon news: The strange appearance of a new priest-saint." *Light and Life* (London, Unevengelized Fields Mission), January-March 1973, pp. 18-19.
"Up-river" from riverside village of Jacare; a healer and wonder-worker operating "in the name of Jesus."

684 Kalverkamp, Desidéro, and Kloppenburg, Boaventura. *Ação pastoral parente o espiritismo: Orientação para sacerdotes*. Vozes em Defesa da Fé, Estudo 3. Petrópolis: Editôra Vozes, 1961, 301 pp.
Pastoral measures necessary in dealing with Spiritism.

685 Kasper, Elizabeth A. *Afrobrasilianische Religion. Der Mensch in der Beziehung zu Natur: Kosmos und Gemeinschaft in Candomble – eine tiefenpsychologische Studie.* Franfurt am Main: P. Lang, 1988, 147 pp.

686 Kemper, Werner. "Archaisch-ekstatische Massenbewegungen im heutigen Brasilien." In *Massenbewegugnen in Geschichte und Gegenwart: Ein tagungsbericht*, edited by W. Bitter. Stuttgart: 1965, pp. 133-50.

687 Kemper, Werner. "Gottheiten im Schmelzprozess: Erlebetes Brasilien." *Frankfurter Hefte*, 1964, pp. 797-98.
    On Umbanda and Macumba.

688 Kent, R. K. "African revolt in Bahia: 24-25 January 1835." *Journal of Social History* (Berkeley) 3, no. 4 (1970): 334-56.
    The Malê-led slave revolt.

689 Kloppenburg, Boaventura. "E alarmante o crescimento do baixo Espiritismo no Brasil." *Revista Eclesiástica Brasileira* (Petrópolis) 13 (1953): 416-20.

690 Kloppenburg, Boaventura. "Apelo aos que lidam com as vitimas do Espiritismo." *Revista Eclesiástica Brasileira* (Petrópolis) 12 (1952): 384-86.

691 Kloppenburg, Boaventura. "Atuação do demônio no Espiritismo." *Revista Eclesiástica Brasileira* (Petrópolis) 17 (1957): 301-20.

692 Kloppenburg, Boaventura. "Der brasilianische Spiritismus als religiöse Gefahr." *Social Compass* 5, nos. 5-6 (1957-58): 237-55.
    Brazilian Spiritism as a religious danger.

693 Kloppenburg, Boaventura. "Campanha Nacional contra a heresia espírita." *Revista Eclesiástica Brasileira* (Petrópolis) 13 (1953): 838-52.

694 Kloppenburg, Boaventura. "Começa a Campanha Nacional contra heresia espírita." *Revista Eclesiástica Brasileira* (Petrópolis) 13 (1953): 655-57.

695 Kloppenburg, Boaventura. "Contra a heresia espírita." *Revista Eclesiástica Brasileira* (Petrópolis) 12 (1952): 85-111.

Brazil

696 Kloppenburg, Boaventura. "Criminosa mistificação espírita." *Revista Eclesiástica Brasileira* (Petrópolis) 18 (1958): 471-73.

697 Kloppenburg, Boaventura. "A cristologia do espiritismo." *Revista Eclesiástica Brasileira* (Petrópolis) 13 (1953): 87-105.

698 Kloppenburg, Boaventura. "Cruzada de defesa da fé católica no I centenário do espiritismo." *Revista Eclesiástica Brasileira* (Petrópolis) 16 (1956): 825-31. Also in Supplemento do Fasciculo de Dezembro de 1956, pp. 1-44.

699 Kloppenburg, Boaventura. "Deus e a criação na doutrina espírita." *Revista Eclesiástica Brasileira* (Petrópolis) 12 (1952): 793-827.

700 Kloppenburg, Boaventura. "Ensaio de una nova posição pastoral perante a umbanda." *Revista Eclesiástica Brasileira* (Petrópolis) 28 (1968): 404-17.

701 Kloppenburg, Boaventura. "O espiritismo do Sr. Governador Jánio Quadros." *Revista Eclesiástica Brasileira* (Petrópolis) 16 (1956): 944-47.

702 Kloppenburg, Boaventura. "O espiritismo no Brasil." *Revista Eclesiástica Brasileira* (Petrópolis) 19 (1959): 842-71.

703 Kloppenburg, Boaventura. "Fragen der Theologie un des religiösen Lebens: Der Spiritismus in brasilien." *Herder-Korrespondenz* 13 (July 1959): 489-95.

704 Kloppenburg, Boaventura. "Fundamentos da doutrina espírita." *Revista Eclesiástica Brasileira* (Petrópolis) 12 (1952): 273-303.

705 Kloppenburg, Boaventura. "As heresias do espiritismo brasileiro." *Revista Eclesiástica Brasileira* (Petrópolis) 13 (1953): 395-414.

706 Kloppenburg, Boaventura. "Indicações bibliográficas sobre o espiritismo." *Revista Eclesiástica Brasileira* (Petrópolis) 13 (1953): 141-43.

707 Kloppenburg, Boaventura. "Juntos ICAB, maçonaria e espiritismo." *Revista Eclesiástica Brasileira* (Petrópolis) 21 (1961): 411-13.

708 Kloppenburg, Boaventura. *Material para instruções sobre a heresia espírita.* Petrópolis, 1953.

709 Kloppenburg, Boaventura. "Nossa atitude pastoral perante o espiritismo." *Revista Eclesiástica Brasileira* (Petrópolis) 17 (1957): 1-9.

710 Kloppenburg, Boaventura. *Nossas superstições*. Petrópolis, 1959.

711 Kloppenburg, Boaventura. "Pequenos casos pastorais: Juramento antiespírita." *Revista Eclesiástica Brasileira* (Petrópolis) 14 (1954): 142f.

712 Kloppenburg, Boaventura. *Porque a Igreja condenou o espiritismo*. Petrópolis, 1960.

713 Kloppenburg, Boaventura. "Posição perante a fenomenologia do espiritismo." *Revista Eclesiástica Brasileira* (Petrópolis) 16 (1956): 591-609.

714 Kloppenburg, Boaventura. "The prevalence of spiritism in Brazil." In *The religious dimension in the new Latin America*, edited by J. J. Considine. Notre Dame, Ind.: Fides, 1966, pp. 77-87.
A simple survey.

715 Kloppenburg, Boaventura. "O proximo centenario de espiritismo." *Revista Eclesiástica Brasileira* (Petrópolis) 16 (1956): 420-22.

716 Kloppenburg, Boaventura. "Quem é espirita?" *Revista Eclesiástica Brasileira* (Petrópolis) 15 (1955): 429-34.

717 Kloppenburg, Boaventura. *O reencarnacionismo no Brasil: Orientação para os católicos*. Vozes em Defesa da Fé, Estudos 4. Petrópolis: Editôra Vozes, 1961, 215 pp.
Why the Catholic Church rejects reincarnation, without criticism of any particular sections of Brazilians who so believe (i.e., Spiritists).

718 Kloppenburg, Boaventura. "Se on espiritismo é juridicamente uma seita católica." *Revista Eclesiástica Brasileira* (Petrópolis) 14 (1954): 126-30.

719 Kloppenburg, Boaventura. "A teoria espírita da reencarnação." *Revista Eclesiástica Brasileira* (Petrópolis) 13 (1953): 581-611.

720 Kloppenburg, Boaventura. "Visão espírita do cristianismo." *Revista Eclesiástica Brasileira* (Petrópolis) 12 (1952): 546-70.

Brazil

721 Kloppenburg, Boaventura, and Keller, Alfredo. *Saravá – Cultos afrobrasileiros*. Rio de Janeiro: Sonó-Viso do Brasil, 1969.
Includes estimate of ten to twenty million "spiritists" in Brazil.

722 Knobloch, Francis A. "The Baniwa Indians and their reaction against integration." *Mankind Quarterly* 15, no. 2 (1974): 83-91.
Inali River area (i.e., Rio Içana, N.W. Amazonia): outline description, including religion and the reaction to white contacts. Pp. 88-89, messianic movements with local "Christs" from 1858; pp. 89-91, the beginnings of an independent Baniwa church within the Baptist mission contact, in the 1960s.

723 Koch, Kurt E. *Welt Ohne Chance?* Baden: Evangelisations-Verlag 1971. English translation. *World Without Chance?* Grand Rapids, Mich.: Kregel Publications, 1974, 96 pp.
Pp. 49-64, "From Macumba to Christ" – a case history of a woman cult leader in Rio de Janeiro, from a viewpoint very hostile to Macumba.

724 Koch-Grünberg, Theodor. *Zwei Jahre unter den Indianern: Reisen in Nordwest-Brasilien, 1903-1905.* ... 2 vols. Berlin: E. Wasmuth; Stuttgart: Strecker & Schröder, 1909-10. Reprinted in *Klassiker der Ethnographie Südamerikas 2*. 2 vols. Graz: Akad. Druck und Verlagsanstalt, 1967, 769 pp., illus.
Vol. 1, pp. 39-41; vol. 2, p. 14, on various new religions in mid-nineteenth century in Northeast of South America, based on R. Avé-Lallemant. *Reise durch Nord-Brasilien im Jahre.* 1859. Leipzig: Brockhaus, 1860; "New Christs" or "Saints," antiwhite, and millennial, cease work and dance and drink holy drinks – the whites are to be expelled.

725 Kockmeyer, Thomas. "Candomblé." *Santo-Antônio. Provinzzeitschrift der Franziskaner in Nordbrasilien* (Bahia) 14, no. 1 (1936): 25-36; 14, no. 2 (1936): 123-39.

726 Kordon, Bernardo. *Candomblé: Contribucion al estudio de la raza negra en el Rio de la Plata.* Buenos Aires: Editorial Continente, 1938, 60 pp.
Especially pp. 3, 21-30, 53-55.

727 Krebs, Carlos Galvão. "Da Arabia para os terreiros de macumba." *Senhor* (Rio de Janeiro) 4, no. 3 (1962).

728 Krebs, Carlos Galvão. "Cavalo de Santo." *Provincia de São Pedro* (Pôrto Alegre) 21 (1957): 145-54.

729 Krebs, Carlos Galvão. "Por que cresce a macumba no Brasil?" *Monchete* (Rio de Janeiro), 4 April 1953.

730 Kroker, Valdemar. "Spiritism in Brazil." *Mission Focus* (Elkhart, Ind.) 15, no. 1 (1987): 1-6, bib.
   A Mennonite missionary's account.

731 Kubik, Gerhard. "Extensionen afrikanischer Kulturen in Brasilien." Part 2. *Weiner Ethnohistorische Blätter* 22 (1981): 3-77.
   Pp. 20-50, Afro-Brazilian as syncretist?; pp. 33-51, methodology of Afro-Brazilian research.

732 Landes, Ruth. *The city of women*. New York: Macmillan Co., 1947, 248 pp. Portuguese translation. *A cicade das mulheres*. Rio de Janeiro: Civilização Brasileira, 1967.
   Cultism in city of S. Salvador (i.e., Bahia) – Candomble, Oxala, and a variety of Yoruba-influenced temples; all described in narrative style without academic structures, theories, etc. – pp. 36-58, Candomble temples and their rites; pp. 160-69, Yemanja pilgrimage to the sea – an "informed traveller's" account, with much detail.

733 Landes, Ruth. "A cult matriarchate and male homosexuality." *Journal of Abnormal and Social Psychology* 3, no. 3 (1940): 386-97. Partially reprinted in *Antologia do negro brasileiro*, compiled by E. Carneiro. Rio de Janeiro: Edições de Ouro, 1967, pp. 346-48.
   The admission of "passive" male homosexuals from a position as outcastes to the highest roles in Candomble and the consequent changes in these cults.

734 Landes, Ruth. "Fetish worship in Brazil." *The Journal of American Folklore* 53 (October-December 1940): 261-70. Extract in Portuguese. "Os deuses africanos." In *Antologia do Negro brasileiro*, edited by E. Carneiro. Rio de Janeiro: Edições de Ouro, 1967, pp. 358-61.
   Her theory of homosexual "pai de santos" modeling themselves on creole matriarchate of women priestesses as cult leaders.

735 Langguth, A[rthur] J[ohn]. *Macumba: White and black magic in Brazil*. New York: Harper & Row; Toronto: Fitzhenry & Whiteside, 1975, 372 pp.

Brazil

By an American novelist, a participant in Candomble in rural Bahia, whose serious endeavors to receive the spirit failed; a somewhat discursive though sympathetic account, without any systematic framework.

736 Lapassade, Georges. "La macumba, une contre-culture en noir et rouge." *Homme et la Société* (Paris) 22 (1972): 147-70.

737 Lapassade, Georges, and Luz, M[arco] Aurélio. *O segredo da macumba*. Estudos Sobre o Brasil e a América Latina, 19. Rio de Janeiro: Editôra Paz e Terra, 1972, 101 pp., illus.
   Pp. xi-xxvii, Preface; pp. 5-48, "O ritual da Meia-Noite"; pp. 51-101, "Umbanda contra Quimbanda."

738 Lasebikan, E. L. "The Yoruba in Brazil." *West Africa* (London) 4 August 1962, p. 843, illus.
   The Candombles and Egungun cult in the state of Bahia and other examples of Yoruba influence–by the Yoruba who began instruction in Yoruba in the University of Bahia.

739 Laytano, Dante de. *Festa de Nossa Senhora dos navegantes*. Pôrto Alegre: Edicão da Comissão Estudual de Folclore, 1955.
   Afro-Brazilian Batuque cult festival in Pôrto Alegre, and Yemanja.

740 Laytano, Dante de. *A Igreja e os orixás*. Pôrto Alegre: Comissão Gaúcha de Folclore, 1969, 60 pp.
   On Batuque.

741 Leacock, Seth. "Ceremonial drinking in an Afro-Brazilian cult." *American Anthropologist* 66, no. 2 (1964): 344-54, bib.
   Urban cult in Belém city, calling itself Nagô, Mina, or Umbanda, with African, American Indian, and Spiritualist components, but more individualistic than the Candomble.

742 Leacock, Seth. "Fun-loving deities in an Afro-Brazilian cult." *Anthropological Quarterly* 37, no. 3 (1964): 94-109.
   Batuque in Belém as a greatly "Brazilianized" new religion, less conservative and formalized than Candombles in Bahia, and more akin to the festivals of folk-Catholicism.

743 Leacock, Seth, and Leacock, Ruth. *Spirits of the deep: A study of an Afro-Brazilian cult*. Garden City, N.Y.: Doubleday Natural History

Press for American Museum of Natural History, 1972, 404 pp., illus., bib.

Batuque, in Belém, in the early 1960s with sensitive case studies and good photographs.

744 Leahy, J. Gordon. "The presence of the gods among the mortals. The Candomblé dances." *Brazil* (New York) 29, no. 4 (1955): 4-5, 7-8, 10-13, illus., music text.

Candomble dances and music; Candomble foods; herbs, reasons for survival, table of the gods.

745 Lemos, Ubiratan de. "Os grandes orixás da umbanda e do candomblé." *O Jornal* (Rio de Janeiro), 13 November 1970.

746 Leo, Maximus, and Teixeira, Antonio Alves. *Nossos pretos velhos (desenhos e mensagens psicografadas).* Rio de Janeiro: Brasilart Editôres, 1968, 95 pp., illus.

747 Léonard, E[mile G.]. "Le problème du messianisme dans ses rapports avec le nationalisme chez les Nègres brèsiliens: Théorie sociologique." *Le Monde Non-chrétien*, n.s. 19 (July-September 1951): 316-26.

748 Lima, Estácio de. *Candomblé senegalês, commentários de uma viajem.* Salvador, 1967.

749 Lima, Estácio de. *O mundo místico dos Negros.* [Salvador: Empresa Gráfica da Bahia], 1975, 220 pp., illus.

750 Lima, José. *A festa de Egun e outros ensaios.* Salvador: Oficina Tipografica Manu, 1952, 66 pp. 3d ed. Rio de Janeiro: 1955, 128 pp.

751 Lima, José. *Folklore baiano: Tres ensaios.* Bahia: N.d., 136 pp. New ed. *A festa de Egun.* Bahia: 1952, 66 pp.

752 Lima, Vincente. *Xangô.* Recife, Pernambuco: Divulgação do Centro de Culturo Afro-Brasileira, 1937, 77 pp., illus.

Shows the interest of the rising bourgeois population of color in pantheistic nature-cults rather than in Afro-Brazilian Xango cults.

753 Lima, Vivaldo da Costa. "O conceito de nação nos candomblés da Bahia." *Afro-Asia* (Universidade Federal Bahia, Centro de Estudos Afro-Orientais) 12 (June 1976): 65-90.

How the concept of "nation" is used among Candomble groups.

Brazil

754 Lima, V[ivaldo] da Costa. *A família-de-santo nos candomblés. Jeje-nagôs da Bahia: Um estudo de relações intra-grupais.* Salvador: Universidad Federal da Bahia, 1977.

755 Linares, R. A., and Fernandes, Trinidade. *Oxun e Oriossa.* São Paulo: Triade, 1987, 79 pp.

756 Lindig, Wolfgang H. "Wanderungen der Tupí-Guaraní und Eschatologie der Apapocúva-Guaraní." In *Chiliasmus und Nativismus,* edited by W. E. Mühlmann. Berlin: D. Reimer, 1961, pp. 19-40, maps, bib. French translation. "Migrations des Tupi-Guarani et eschatologie des Apapocuve-Guarani." In *Messianismes révolutionnaires du tiers monde.* Paris: Gallimard, 1968, pp. 21-39.

757 Lody, Raul Giovanni da Motta. *Afoxé.* Cadernos de Folclore, n.s. 7. Rio de Janeiro: Ministério da Educação e Cultura, Departamento de Assuntos Culturais, Fundação Nacional de Arte, 1976, 36 pp., illus., bib.
  Afoxé is a street procession, related to Candomble, in Salvador, Fortaleza, and Rio, and with African origins.

758 Lody, Raul Giovanni da Motta. *Candomblé, religião e residencia cultural.* São Paulo: Ed. Alica, 1987, 85 pp.

759 Lody, Raul Giovanni da Motta. "Exu, o mensageiro dos orixas." In *O som do Adjá.* Salvador: Departamento de Cultura da SMEC, Prefeitura Municipal de Salvador, 1975, 101 pp., illus., music.
  Popular analysis of functions and attributes of some twenty-four African divinities with cults in Bahia. Pp. 85-88 present Candomble music.

760 Lody, Raul Giovanni da Motta. "Ritos populares – candomblé e umbanda." *Campanha de Defesa do Folclore Brasileiro.* Rio de Janeiro, 1975.

761 Lopes, Edmundo Correia. "Algo de novo sobre a introdução dos nagôs no Brasil." *Revista do Brasil* (Rio de Janeiro), n.s., no. 44 (February 1942), pp. 35-36.

762 Lopes, Edmundo Correia. "Candomblés." *Santo Antônio* (Bahia) 15, no. 1 (1937): 15-29.

763 Lopes, Edmundo Correia. "Exéquias no Bôgum do Salvador." *O Mundo Português* (Lisbon), no. 109 (1943), pp. 539-65.
On the Dahomeans (Gege).

764 Lopes, Edmundo Correia. "O Kpoli da Mãe Andresa." *O Mundo Português* (Lisbon), no. 99 [9] (1942): 139-44.
One of the earliest first-hand studies of black religion in Maranhão, but "to be used with caution" as confusing the Kpoli of the Dahomean people with a local Poli-Bogi or god of smallpox (Bastide).

765 Lopes, Edmundo Correia. "O pessoal gêge." *Revisto do Brasil* (Rio de Janeiro), n.s., no. 20 (February 1940), pp. 44-57.

766 Lopes, Edmundo Correia. "A proposito de 'A casa das Minas.'" *Atlantico Revista Luso-Brasileira* (Lisbon), n.s. 5 (1947): 78-82.

767 Macedo, Joaquim Manuel de. *As vítimas Algozes*. 2 vols. Rio de Janeiro: F. Briguiet, 1937.
Three antislavery novels. Vol. 1, pp. 127-28, describe a Macumba or Candomble ceremony, regarded as absurd. Selection reprinted in R. S. Sayers, *The Negro in Brazilian Literature*. New York: Hispanic Institute of the United States, 1956, pp. 177-78.

768 Macedo, Sérgio D[iogo] T[eixeira de]. *Crônica do negro no Brasil*. Rio de Janeiro and São Paulo: Distribuidora Record, 1974, 134 pp., illus.
Chap. 8 (pp. 99-108), "A religião africana": On African divinities and Catholic saints; on the Egun festival (based on J. Lima, *A festa de Egun e outros ensaios* [entry 750]) and saints' cults – popular accounts.

769 McGregor, Pedro, and Smith, T. Stratton. *The moon and two mountains: The myths, ritual, and magic of Brasilian spiritism*. London: Souvenir Press, 1966, 238 pp., illus. Reprinted as *Jesus of the spirits*. New York: Stein & Day, 1967, 238 pp., illus. French translation. *La lune et les deux montagnes*. Paris: A. Michel, 1971.
On Candomble, Umbanda (chaps. 9-10), Kardec and Spiritism, and the "Temple of Universal Religion" (chap. 12) of which McGregor, "one of Brazil's most expert spirit mediums," is founder and head.

770 Machado, Aires da Mata, Filho. "A procedência dos Negros Brasileiros e os arquivos eclesiásticos." *Afroamerica* 1, nos. 1-2 (1945): 67-70, illus.

771 Machado, Lourival Gomes. "Viagem a Ouro Preto." *Revista do Arquivo Municipal* (São Paulo) 124 (1949): 7-46.

Brazil

Pp. 25-27, Afro-Brazilian churches.

772 Machado, Paulo Pinto. *Joaquim Matheus – O feiticeiro*. São Paulo, 1930.

773 "Macumba: Brazil's devil worshippers." *Our Sunday Visitor* (Huntington, Ind.) 12 March 1972, pp. 8-9.
As an example of sensational reporting outside Brazil.

774 Maeyama, Takashi. "Ancestor, emperor, and immigrant: Religion and group identification of the Japanese in rural Brazil, 1908-1950." *Journal of Inter-American Studies and World Affairs* (Coral Gables, Fla.) 14, no. 2 (1972): 151-82.
Changes from emperor cult to ancestor cults and to religious movements, especially since World War II.

775 Magalhães, Basílio de. "O elemento religioso afro-brasileiro." *Cultura Política: Revista Mensal de Estudos Brasileiros* (Rio de Janeiro), no. 19 [2] (1942): 155-59.

776 Magalhães, Basílio de. "Folclore religioso afro-brasileiro." *Cultura Política: Revista Mensal de Estudos Brasileiros* (Rio de Janeiro), no. 20 [2] (1942): 136-40.
Reviews various authorities; concerned with Afro-Brazilian gods.

777 Magalhães, Elyette Guimarães de. *Orixás de Bahia*. 3d ed. Salvador, 1974, 161 pp., illus.

778 Maggie, Yvonne. "Afro-Brazilian cults." In *The Encyclopedia of Religion*, edited by M. Eliade. Vol. 1. New York: Macmillan, 1987, pp. 102-5.

779 Maia, Vasconalos. *ABC do candomblé*. Coleção do Autor, 3. Salvador: Carlito Ed., 1978, 93 pp., illus.

780 Maior, Mário Souto. "Aspectos particulares do devocionário dos sontos juninos." Recife: Empetur, 1976. Mimeo.

781 Major, Alfred Roy. "The origin and development of Spiritualism in Brazil." M.A. thesis, New Orleans Theological Seminary, 1957.

782 Manfroi, Olivio. "Religion d'attestation et créativité communautaire: L'immigration italienne au Rio Grande do Sul (1875-1914)." *Archives de Sciences Sociales des Religions* 41 [21, no. 1] (1976): 55-75.

Pp. 72-75, the close analogy between Italian religion and colonization and the Afro-Brazilian religions as interpreted by R. Bastide.

783 Marão, José Carlos, and Butsuem, Jorge. "Yakanam é em profeta." *Realidade* 2 (1967): 92-101.

784 Marcondes de Moura, Carlos Eugenio, ed. *Meu sinal esta no teu corpo: Escritos sobre a religião dos orixás*. São Paulo: Edicon, 1989, 269 pp.

785 Marques, Xavier. *O feiticeiro: Romance*. Rio de Janeiro: L. Ribeiro, 1922, 371 pp.
     A somewhat sympathetic novel on Bahian Negroes.

786 Marques, Xavier. "Tradições da Bahia." *A Tarde* (Bahia), 19 January 1929.
     A novelist's sympathetic account of Afro-Brazilian religion.

787 Mattos, Dalmo Belfort de. "As macumbas em São Paulo." *Revista do Arquivo Municipal* (São Paulo) 49 [5] (July-August 1938): 151-61, illus.
     A survey of the curious combination of African religion, Spiritualism, and Catholicism that sponsors the practice of the magic arts in the outlying districts of São Paulo.

788 Maust, John. "The land where spiritism thrives." *Latin America Evangelist*, October-December 1985, pp. 6-9, illus.
     A useful overview, including the four "varieties" (Candomble, Macumba, Quimbanda, Umbanda) – from an evangelical viewpoint, and using James Wiebe's and B. Kloppenburg's work.

789 Medeiros, José. *Candomblé*. Rio de Janeiro: Edições O Cruzeiro, 1957, 83 pp., illus.
     Photographs of aspects of Candomble rituals in Bahia, with brief notes.

790 Medeiros, José. "A purificação pelo sangue." *O Cruzeiro* (Rio de Janeiro), 15 December 1951, pp. 26-77, 104.

791 Meier, Johannes. "Berichte Symposion: 'Negro e Igreja no Brasil,' Salvador de Bahia." *Zeitschrift für Missionswissenschaft und Religionswissenschaft* 72, no. 1 (1988): 65.
     Includes report of papers on Afro-Brazilian religiosity and on the existence of an indigenous black theology in Brazil.

Brazil

792 Melatti, Julio Cesar. *Indios e criadores: A situação dos Kraho no área pastoril do Tocantins.* Monografias, 3. Rio de Janeiro: Universidade Federal, Instituto de Ciências Sociais, 1967, 166 pp., illus., maps, bib.
Pp. 152-66, the Kraho (Goiás) have retained tribal identity. A prophet, Ropkur, had visions leading to a millennial movement whereby the Kraho will be transformed into civilized people.

793 Melatti, Julio Cesar. *O messianismo krahó.* Coleção Antropologia e Sociologia. São Paulo: Editôra Herder (Universidade de São Paulo), 1972, 138 pp.
The 1951 messianic movement among the Kraho in central Brazil; pp. 73-77, comparison with Ramkokamekra movement, also among the Timbira.

794 Mélo, Veríssimo de. "Festa de N.S. do Rasário (dos Pretos) em jardim do Seridó." *Arquivos do Instituto de Antropologia* (Natal, Universidade do Rio Grande do Norte) 1, no. 1 (1964): 7-15, illus., music, bib.
Description of a festival with manifestations of totemism from the Negro past.

795 Mélo, Veríssimo de. "Banibelô: Sobrevivência negra no nordeste." *Arquivos do Instituto de Antropologia* (Natal, Universidade do Rio Grande do Norte) 2, nos. 1-2 (1966): 185-90, bib.; English summary.

796 Mélo, Veríssimo de. "As cofradias de Nossa Senhora do Rosario como reação contra-acculturation dos Negros no Brasil." *Afro-Asia* (Salvador, Bahia), no. 13 (1980).
Cofradias, men's and women's, as preserving African spirituality.

797 Melvin, Harold Wesley, Jr. "Religion in Brazil: A sociological approach to religion and its integrative function in rural urban migrant adjustment." Th.D. dissertation (religion), Boston University, 1970, 362 pp.
Includes history of Candomble, Umbanda, Spiritism, and Indian religion in this context.

798 Mendonça, Heitor Furtado de. *Primeira visitição do Santo Ofício às Partes do Brasil (confissões da Bahia 1591-1592).* 2 vols. São Paulo: Ed. Paulo Prado, 1923. Reprint. 1925. Reprint. Rio de Janeiro: Soc. Capistrano de Abreu, 1935.
Various references to the Inquisition and early syncretist Indian movements (e.g., vol. 1, p. 169, Antonio movement; also vol. 2, pp. 251-

54; vol. 2, pp. 254, 265, 267, 315, 437 on Santidade de Jaguaripe syncretist church of 1583).

799 Mendonça, João Hélio. "O crescimento e a localização dos terreiros e centros de xangó e de umbanda no Grande-Receife: Uma interpretação sociológica." *Ciência e Trópico* (Recife) 3, no. 1 (1975): 41-63, tables, bib.; Spanish, English, and French summaries.

800 Mendonça, Renata. *A influência africana no português do Brasil.* Biblioteca Pedagógia Brasileira, série V: Brasilians, vol. 45. São Paulo: Companhia Editora Nacional, 1933. 2d ed. 1935, 255 pp., plates, folded maps.

The major portion of this work is a linguistic study. The chapter entitled "O Negro no literatura brasileira" comments on a number of books, most of which are listed in this compilation. Contains a glossary of words of African origin.

801 Meneses, Heraldo. *Iára, a deusa do mar: iniciação, magía, ritual, ponto, fetiches.* Rio de Janeiro: Coleção Afro-Brasileira, 1946, 32 pp., illus.

802 Menezes, Bruno de. *Batuque: Poemas.* Belém do Pará, 1931. 4th ed. 1953, 94 pp.

803 Merriam, Alan P. "Songs of the Afro-Bahian cults: An ethno-musicological analysis." Ph.D. dissertation (music), Northwestern University, 1951, 464 pp., illus.

804 Merriam, Alan P. "Songs of the Ketu cult of Bahia, Brazil." *African Music* (Johannesburg) 1, no. 1 (1957): 53-67; 1, no. 2 (1957): 73-80.

805 Métraux, Alfred. "The Guaraní." In *Handbook of South American Indians,* edited by J. H. Steward. Vol. 3. Bureau of American Ethnology Bulletin 143. Washington, D.C.: Government Printing Office, 1948, pp. 69-94.

806 Métraux, Alfred. "Les hommes-dieux chez les Chiriguano et dans l'Amérique du Sud." *Revista del Instituto de Etnología de la Universidad Nacional de Tucumán* 2, no. 1a (1931): 61-91.

Early Indian messiahs and prophets, in Brazil especially, and among the Guaraní, as anti-European protests.

Brazil

807 Métraux, Alfred. "Les migrations historiques des Tupí-Guaraní." *Journal de la Société des Américanistes* (Paris), n.s. 19 (1927): 1-45, map, table, bib. Also same title: Paris: Maisonneuve Frères, 1927. Millennial movements.

808 Métraux, Alfred. *La religion des Tupinamba et ses rapports avec celle des autres tribus Tupi-Guarani.* Bibliothèque de l'E.P.H.E., "Sciences Religieuses," 45. Paris: Ernest Leroux, 1928, 262 pp. Portuguese translation. *A religião dos Topinambas e suas relações com a des demais tribus Tupí-Guaranís.* Translated by E. Pinto. São Paulo: Companhia Editora Nacional, 1950, 421 pp.
On the Tupi migrations.

809 Mischo, John. "Der Spiritismus in Brasilien." *Neue Wissenschaft. Zeitschrift für Grenzgebiete des Seelenlebens* 9 (1960-61): 17-30.

810 Monteiro, Duglas Teixeira. "Églises, sectes et agences: Aspects d'un oecuménisme populaire." *Diogène* (Paris), no. 100 (Winter 1977), pp. 53-86. English version. *Diogenes* (Florence), no. 100 (Winter 1977), pp. 48-78.
Open-air and radio healing and exorcism – the radio being a new form for conveying blessings, with commercial aspects; sale of pious objects, with magical overtones – as operated by Umbanda and Pentecostal centers.

811 Monteiro, Duglas Teixeira. "A macumba de Vitória." *Anais do XXXI Congresso Internacional de Americanistas, São Paulo, 1954.* Vol. 1. São Paulo: Editôra Anhembi, 1955, pp. 463-72.

812 Monteiro, Mario Ypiranga. "Festa dos cachorros." *Revista Brasileira de Folcore* (Rio de Janeiro) 1 (1961): 29-43.

813 Morais, Alexandre José de Mello, Filho. *Poèmes de l'esclavage et légendes des Indiens.* Rio de Janeiro: Garnier, 1884, 210 pp.
Includes a poem, "O candomblé," expressing his disgust at a frenzied Negro religious ceremony including dancing and feasting, but probably fairly accurate as a description.

814 Mörner, Magnus, ed. *Race and class in Latin America.* New York: Columbia University Press, 1970. Reprint. 1971, viii + 309 pp.
Pp. 156-69, religious cults in Brazil.

815 Moser, Bruno. *Die schwartze Mutter von São Paulo: Brazilien heute und morgen*. Cologne: Eugen Diederich's Verlag, 1966, 251 pp.

Brazilian Negroes have some Indian and some white "blood," and although nominally Catholic accept Spiritism and retain some African religious beliefs. A general survey and prediction of the future.

816 Motta, Roberto [M. C.]. *Os Afro-brasileiros*. Recife: Fundação Joaquin Nabuco, 1985.

817 Mo[t]ta, Roberto [M. C.]. "Bandeira de Alairá: A festa de Xangô-São João o es problemas do sincretismo afro-brasileiro." *Ciência e Trópico* (Recife) 3, no. 2 (1975): 191-203, bib.

Alairá Flag – a Shango festival of St. John; and the problems of Afro-Brazilian syncretism.

818 Motta, Roberto M. C. "Comida, família, dança e transe. (Sugestões para o estudo do xangô)." *Revista de Antropologia* (São Paulo) 25 (1982): 147-57.

819 Moura, Abdalazis de. "O pentecostalismo como fenômeno religioso popular no Brasil." *Revista Eclesiástica Brasileira* (Petrópolis), no. 121 [31] (March 1971): 78-94.

If one places this idea alongside the other kind of Spiritism it seems like Spiritism of a Christian or syncretistic kind.

820 Mourão, Fernando Augusto Albuquerque. "La contribution de l'Afrique bantoue à la formation de la société brésilienne: Une tentative de rédefinition méthodologique." *Africa* (São Paulo) 3 (1980): 1-17.

821 Mulvey, Patricia Ann. "The black lay brotherhoods of colonial Brazil: A history." Ph.D. dissertation (history: Latin America), City University of New York, 1976, 349 pp.

A comparative study of 165 lay brotherhoods of free blacks, mulattoes, and slaves, with their comprehensive and independent functions as against the parish priests. Attendance at a wide range of religious rites was mandatory. Most such brotherhoods were in the mining boom towns of eighteenth-century Minas Gerais, but many also in Salvador do Bahia, Rio de Janeiro, and Pernambuco. Pp. 285-303: Black Brotherhoods from the 1540s in Argentina (1), Colombia (1), Cuba (6), Peru (22), Uruguay (2), Venezuela (11), and Brazil [pp. 293-303] (165).

Brazil

822 Muniz, Junior J. *Do batuque à escola de samba.* São Paulo: Edições Simbolo, 1976.

823 Muzzi, Thomas Scotti. "Mitologia negra no Brasil." *Revista: Orgão Culturel dos Alunos do Colégio de Aplicação da Faculdade de Filosofia* (Belo Horizonte, Universidade de Minas Gerais) 2, no. 2 (1962): 51-59, illus., bib.
African rituals as basically Yoruba; lists African divinities still venerated along with Catholic figures.

824 Nabeji, Ogosse. *Xangô.* Preface by João da Goméia. Rio de Janeiro, 1949, 29 pp.

825 Nakamaki, Hirochika. "Religões japonesas no Brasil estratégias multinacionais." *Communicações do ISER* 5, no. 18 (1986): 16-23.
Describes the well-organized expansion of Japanese religions, forming a kind of "multinational" set of religions.

826 Negrão, Lisias Noquerira. "Kardecism." In *The Encyclopedia of Religion,* edited by M. Eliade. Vol. 8. New York: Macmillan, 1987, pp. 259-61.

827 Nery, D. João Correa. "A cabula." In *Antologia do Negro brasileiro,* compiled by E. Carneiro. Rio de Janeiro: Edições de Ouro, 1967, pp. 363-67.
A priest on the dangers of syncretism.

828 Nimuendajú, Kurt [Unkel]. "Apontamentos sôbre os Guaraní." Translated by E. Schaden. *Revista do Museu Paulista* (São Paulo), n.s. 8 (1954): 2-57.
Includes their millenarian travelings. "Unkel" was his original German surname, sometimes retained in publications.

829 Nimuendajú, Kurt Unkel. "Die Sagen von der Erschlaffung und Vernichtung der Welt als Grundlagen der Religion der Apapocuva-Guaraní." *Zeitschrift für Ethnologie* (Brunswick) 46 (1914): 284-403.
Especially pp. 287, 318-20, 327, and 399, on the search for Paradise by a band of Apapocuva Guarani led by a succession of prophets in the nineteenth and early twentieth centuries.

830 Nimuendajú, Kurt Unkel. "Sagen der Tembè-Indianer (Paráund Maranhão)." *Zeitschrift für Ethnologie* (Brunswick) 47 (1915): 281-305.
Pp. 287-88, a Tupi tribe of Brazil, and the "terre-sans-mal" theme.

831 Nimuendajú, Kurt Unkel. "The tropical forest tribes." In *Handbook of South American Indians*, edited by J. H. Steward. Vol. 3. Bureau of American Ethnology Bulletin 143. Washington, D.C.: Smithsonian Institution, 1948.
Pp. 724-25, Tukuna messianism.

832 Nimuendajú, Kurt [Unkel]. *The Tukuna*. University of California Publications in American Archaeology and Ethnology, vol. 45. Berkeley and Los Angeles: University of California Press, 1952, illus., maps.
Pp. 100-140, religion and magic; pp. 137-40, messianic movements.

833 Nina Rodrigues, Raymundo. *Os Africanos no Brasil*. São Paulo: Nacional, 1932, 409 pp. + plates. 3d rev. ed. 1945, 435 pp.
By the pioneer of modern Afro-Brazilian studies. Includes Muslims, pp. 89-112 (1st ed.)

834 Nina Rodrigues, Raymundo. *L'animisme fétichiste des Nègres de Bahia*. Bahia: Reis & Cia, 1900, 158 pp. Portuguese edition. *O animismo fetichista dos Negros bahianos*. Bibliotheca de Divulgação Scientifica, vol. 11. Rio de Janeiro: Civilização Brasileira, 1935, 199 pp.
A basic work, first published in Portuguese as various articles in *Revista Brasileira*, 1896-97.

835 Nina Rodrigues, Raymundo. *As collectividades anormaes*. Edited by Arthur Ramos. Rio de Janeiro: Civilização Brasileira, 1939, 332 pp.
A collection of his articles, especially on subjects in psychological medicine, but also dealing with Negroes.

836 Nóbrega, Manoel da. "Informação das terras do Brasil." *Revista do Instituto Histórico e Geográphico Brasileiro* (Rio de Janeiro) 6 (1844). Reprinted in Cartas Jesuíticas, *Cartas avulsas 1550-1568*. Rio de Janeiro: Publicações da Academia Brasileiro, 1931, pp. 393-94.
Pp. 90-92, on sixteenth-century messianic prophets; brief quotation in A. Métraux, *Religions et magies indiennes d'Amérique du Sud* (Paris: Gallimard, 1967).

837 Nunes, Maria Luisa. "The preservation of African culture in Brazilian literature: The novels of Jorge Amado." *Luso-Brazilian Review* 9, no. 1 (1972): 86-101.
A detailed survey of African religious forms in Amado's novels, and survey of some other fiction.

Brazil

838 Oberg, Kalvero. "Afro-Brazilian religious cults." *Sociología* (São Paulo) 21, no. 2 (1959): 134-41.
    Describes Nago or Yoruba Candomble as in Bahia.

839 O'Gorman, Frances. *Aluanda: A look at Afro-Brazilian Cults*. Rio de Janeiro: Livraria Francisco Alves Editora, 1977, 108 pp.
    Chap. 1, general survey; chap. 2, historical background; chap. 3, Candomble, Macumba, and Umbanda; chap. 4, "Looking beyond." A popular but useful survey, based on E. Carneiro, *Candomblés da Bahia* (entry 488), with his four characteristics: possession by a divinity, personal relation with the divinity, divination or oracles between the two parties, and Eshu as messenger (pp. 53-55).

840 Oliveira, Jota Alves de. *Candomblés, feitiços e orixás (obra intuitíva)*. Rio de Janeiro: Editora Eco, 1975, 159 pp., illus.

841 Oliveira, Pedro A. Ribeiro de. "Coexistência das religões no Brasil." *Vozes* 71, no. 1 (1977): 555-62.

842 Oro, Pedro Ari. "Negros e brancos nas religiões afro-brasileiras no Rio Grande do Sul." *Communições do ISER* 28 (1988): 33-54.

843 Ortiz Oderigo, Néstor [R.]. *Calunga: Croquis del candombe*. Buenos Aires: EUDEBA, 1969.

844 Ortiz Oderigo, Néstor R. . "Notas de etnografia afrobrasileña: El 'candomblé.'" *Ciencias Sociales* (Washington, D.C.), no. 36 [6] (December 1955): 310-19.
    Candomble in Bahia – a detailed survey.

845 Ortiz Oderigo, Néstor [R.]. *Macumba: Culturas africanas en el Brasil*. Colecçion Ensayos, 16. Buenos Aires: Editorial Plus Ultra, 1976, 240 pp., illus.
    By an anthropologist: pp. 75-104, Orixas; pp. 105-40, Candomble; pp. 141-67, Afro-Brazilian dances; pp. 178-212, Candomble music analyzed; pp. 213-31, Candomble musical instruments.

846 Ott, Carlos. "A transformação do culto da morte da igreja do bonfim em santuário de fertilidade." *Afro-Asia* (Bahia) 8-9 (June-December 1969): 35-39.
    The transference of the cult of Jesus of Bonfim (literally "good end," as euphemism for death) from Portugal to Bahia, and its nineteenth-century development into a fertility cult for Afro-Brazilian

Candomble members while continuing as a Catholic sanctuary of Christ, the Lord of death.

847 Paixão, Manoel Bernardino. "Ligeira explicação sobre a Nação Congo." In *O Negro no Brasil*, compiled by E. Carneiro and A. do Couto Ferraz. Rio de Janeiro: Civilização Brasileira, 1940, pp. 349-56.

848 Palmes, F[ernando Maria]. *Metapsíquica e espiritismo.* 2d rev. ed. Barcelona and Madrid: Editorial Labor, 1950, 630 pp.
On Spiritualism.

849 Pecorari, Giorgio. "La chiesa di fronte al candomble, religione der brasiliani neri." *Mondo e Missione* (Milan), no. 108 (1979), 549-53.

850 Pedemonte, Hugo Emilio. "El candomblé." *Revista de Cultura Brasileña* (Madrid), no. 16 [5] (March 1966): 76-79, illus.

851 Pereira, José. *Festa de Yemanjá.* Salvador: Col. Recôncavo, no. 7, 1951.

852 Pereira, Nunes. *A Casa das Minas: Contribuição ao estudo das sobrivivências daomeianas no Brasil.* Introduction by A. Ramos. Publicações da Sociedade Brasileira de Antropologia e Etnologia, 1. Rio de Janeiro: The Society, 1947, 67 pp.
An important study of Dahomean religious forms in Maranhão.

853 Pereira, Nuno Marques. *Compéndia narrativo do Peregrino da América.* [5 printings 1728 to 1765]. 6th ed. 2 vols. Rio de Janeiro: Academia Brasileira de Letras, 1939.
An eighteenth-century seminovel based on a trip to Brazil; vol. 1, pp. 123-26, describe African dance, the *calundu*, its music and leaders.

854 Pessar, Patricia R. "Unmasking the politics of religion: The case of Brazilian millenarianism." *Journal of Latin American Lore* 7, no. 2 (1981): 255-77.
Considers Canudos, Contestado, Joaseiro, and Santa Brigida (in Bahia, 1939–led by Pedro Batista). Although strictly not within this subject, useful for comparisons.

855 Picchia, Paulo Menotte del. *Salomé.* Rio de Janeiro: Editôra a Noite, n.d., 394 pp.
Afro-Brazilian rites in São Paulo, as featured in a novel.

Brazil

856 Pierson, Donald. "Os 'Africanos' da Bahia." *Revista do Arquivo Municipal* (São Paulo) 78 [7] (1941): 39-64.

Based on a protracted study of the customs and superstitions of the Negroes of Bahia; recounts specific instances showing a blind belief in werewolves and other creatures of fantasy.

857 Pierson, Donald. "'Almas' e a Santa Cruz numa communidade paulista." *Sociologia* 14, no. 3 (1952): 244-55.

Portuguese text of part of the material on religion in his study of 1951.

858 Pierson, Donald. *O candomblé de Bahia, gonache de Robolo Gonzales.* Curitiba: Editora Guáira, 1942, 65 pp.

Shows especially the reactions of the younger generation to the traditions.

859 Pierson, Donald. *Cruz das Almas: A Brazilian village.* Smithsonian Institution, Institute of Social Anthropology, Publication 12. Washington, D.C.: Government Printing Office, 1951, 226 pp., maps + 20 plates. Portuguese translation. *Cruz das Almas.* Coleção Documentos Brasileiros, 124. Rio de Janeiro: José Olympio Editôra, 1966, 458 pp., illus.

Pp. 143-84 (1951 ed.): ritual, ceremony, and belief–includes, pp. 147-52, *Santos*; pp. 167-71, the Cross and its *festas*; p. 182, Spiritualism (absent locally, but sometimes in the town of Boa Vista).

860 Pierson, Donald. "The Negro in Brazil." *American Sociological Review* 4, no. 4 (1938): 524-33. Portuguese translation. "O negro na Bahia." *Sociologia* 3, no. 4 (1941): 282-94.

The interrelations of ecological and cultural processes in the Bahian population of African descent.

861 Pierson, Donald. *Negroes in Brazil: A study of race contact in Bahia.* Chicago: University of Chicago Press, 1942, 392 pp. Reprint, with new introduction by R. E. Park. Carbondale: Southern Illinois University Press; London and Amsterdam: Feffer & Simons, 1967, xxxiii + 420 pp., bib. Portuguese translation. *Brancos e pretos na Bahia.* São Paulo: Ed. Nacional, 1945, 486 pp.

Cultism in the city of Salvador (i.e., Bahia). The first full study of the assimilated contemporary Negro in Brazilian society, and not only of groups remaining distinct; also recognizes that the special relation with Africa continued at Bahia, which maintains a certain segregation and racial solidarity expressed in the Candombles even though there is no color (racial) bar as in the United States. Part 5, "The African Heritage," is on Afro-Brazilian cults.

862 Pimenta, M. "Batuques em Belém." *Revista do Arquivo Municipal* (São Paulo), no. 178 [31] (1969).

863 Pinto, Estêvão. "A 'santidade.'" *Revista do Brasil* (São Paulo) 3d ser. 1 (May 1939): 37-40.
   On the continuance of Santidade to date.

864 Pinto, Estêvão. "Sincretismo religioso afro-brasileiro." *Muxarabis e Balcões e outros ensaios*. São Paulo: Cia. Editôra Nacional, 1958, pp. 59-63.
   Pp. 59-63, 78-88 (notes).

865 Pinto, Luis de Aguiar Costa. *O Negro no Rio de Janeiro: relações de raça numa sociedada em mudança*. São Paulo: Cia. Ed. Nacional, 1953.
   See especially chap. 7.

866 Pollak-Eltz, Angelina. *Afroamerikaanse Godsdiensten en culten*. Roemond: Romen & Zonen, 1970, 221 pp., illus. English translation by J. Jessop, July 1988. Spanish translation, rev. and enl. *Cultos afroamericanos*. Caracas: Instituto de Investigaciones Historicas, Universidad Catolica Andrés Bello, 1972, 168 pp., bib.
   Afro-American cults in Brazil (Candomble in Bahia, Batuque in Pôrto Alegre, Xango in Recife, Macumba in Rio de Janeiro, Afro-Indian cults, Catimbo, etc.).

867 Pollak-Eltz, Angelina. "Notizen über den Batuquekult der Neger in Porto Alegre (Brasilien)." *Mitteilungen der Anthropologischen Gesellschaft in Wien* (Vienna) 96-97 (1967): 138-46, bib.
   Comparison of Batuque cults in Pôrto Alegre and in Bahia, ritual, the pantheon, in relation to Yoruba and Christian influences – especially trance, festivals, and initiation of mediums. The cult has probably come with migration from Bahia, and the original background was in Dahomey and Nigeria.

868 Porta, E. M. la. *Estudo psicoanalîtico dos rituais afro-brasileiros*. Rio de Janeiro, 1979.

869 Posern-Zielinski, Aleksander. "Funkcje millenarystyeznego mitu w ruchach spoleczno–religijnych Tupí-Guaraní" [The functions of the millenarian myth in social-religious movements of Tupí-Guaraní

Brazil

Indians]. *Etnografia Polska* (Warsaw) 16, no. 2 (1972): 93-115; English
summary (pp. 115-16).

870 Price, Richard, ed. *Maroon societies: Rebel slave communities in the
Americas.* Garden City, N.Y.: Doubleday, Anchor Books, 1973, 429 pp.
Pp. 194-201, *quilombos* of Indians and blacks in Brazil from the
eigthteenth century, and their syncretist religious features.

871 Prince, Howard Melvin. "Slave rebellions in Bahia, 1807-1835." Ph.D.
dissertation (history), Columbia University, 1972, 274 pp.
Includes the Islamic Negro (Malês) revolts with millenarian
overtones.

872 Prost, Tadeu H. "Thirty years in the Amazon Valley." *Worldmission* 24,
no. 4 (1973-74).
Interview with a Catholic bishop with a sympathetic attitude to
the search for healing, etc., through Spiritism.

873 Queiroz, Maria Isaura Pereira de. "Les années brésiliennes de Roger
Bastide." *Archives de Sciences Sociales des Religions*, no. 40 [20, no. 2]
(1975): 79-87.
Includes the contribution of his study of Afro-Brazilian cults to
his understanding of Brazilian culture, and his overcoming his
European ethnocentrism, especially when he came to regard these
movements, as well as messianisms in the interior, as normal rather
than pathological. This intellectual change is also outlined by Bastide in
the preface to his *Estudos afro-brasileiros* (entry 416); by one of his
former students.

874 Queiroz, Maria Isaura Pereira de. "Autour du messianisme." *Présence
Africaine*, n.s. 20 (June-July 1958): 72-76. Rev. ed. "Les noirs du Brésil
et les mouvements messianiques." *Sondeos*, no. 87. Mexico: CIDOC,
1972, pp. 6/1-6/14.
Reasons for lack of messianism in coastal Negroes, but it does
occur in white populations.

875 Queiroz, Maria Isaura Pereira de. "Brazilian messianic movements: A
help or hindrance to 'participation'?" *Bulletin, International Institute for
Labour Studies* 7 (1970): 93-121.
Theoretical introduction; Padre Cicero movement as a case-study
(pp. 97-102); the only urban movement (of Yokaanam in Rio de
Janeiro, 1949) (pp. 110-17).

876 Queiroz, Maria Isaura Pereira de. "Classifications des messianismes brésiliens." *Archives de Sociologie des Religions*, no. 5 [3] (January-June 1958): 11-120. Reprinted in *Sondeos*, no. 87. Mexico: CIDOC, 1972, pp. 1/1-1/10.

Similar to her *O messianismo – no Brasil e no mundo* (entry 882).

877 Queiroz, Maria Isaura Pereira de. "L'étude ethno-sociologique des faits religieux au Brésil." *Archives de Sociologie des Religions*, no. 9 [5] (January-June 1960): 145-52.

A survey of religious forms and the main studies for each group: pp. 149-50, research into Afro-Brazilian cults.

878 Queiroz, Maria Isaura Pereira de. "Evolution et création religieuses: Les cultes Afro-brésiliens." *Diogène* (Paris), no. 115 (Fall 1982), pp. 1-21, bib. Portuguese translation. "Evolução religiosa e criação: Os cultos sincreticos brasileiros." *Cristianismo y Sociedad* (Buenos Aires) 24, no. 2 (1986): 7-25.

Candomble, Macumba, and Umbanda as three successive forms.

879 Queiroz, M[aria] I[saura] Pereira de. "Images messianiques du Brésil." *Sondeos*, no. 87. Mexico: CIDOC, 1972, pp. 7/1-7/25; 8/1-8/23.

Pp. 7/6-7/7, Indian messianisms in very small remote groups, and African messianism is absent; otherwise on rural messianic movements in the white or mestizo population.

880 Queiroz, Maria Isaura Pereira de. "Indianische Messiasbewegungen in Brasilien." *Staden-Jahrbuch* (São Paulo) 11-12, (1963-64): 31-44, plates, bib.

Movements since the fifteenth century classified as (1) precontact millennial migrations to a mythical promised land; (2) postcontact syncretisms (or neoprimal movements) as under Yaguacaporo and under Guiravera; (3) syncretistic movements among detribalized Indians, with "new Christs" (i.e., Santidade movements such as those of [p. 37] Aniceto, Venantius, Alexander, Vincente and Obera). Indian religious elements remain more basic than borrowed Christian forms.

881 Queiroz, Maria Isaura Pereira de. "L'influence du milieu social interne sur les mouvements messianiques brésilens." *Archives de Sociologie des Religions*, no. 5 [3] (January-June 1958): 3-30, bib. Reprinted in *Sondeos*, no. 87. Mexico: CIDOC, 1972, pp. 3/1-3/28.

Pp. 3-8, Indian movements; pp. 9-16, rural messianisms; pp. 16-30, theoretical discussions.

Brazil

882 Queiroz, Maria Isaura Pereira de. *O messianismo—no Brasil e no mundo*. Ciencias Sociais, Dominus 5. São Paulo: Dominus Editôra. Editora da Universidade de São Paulo, 1965, 373 pp., bib. + footnotes. 2d rev. and enl. ed. São Paulo: Editora Alfa-Omega, 1977, 441 pp.
   Pp. 161-64 (1965 ed., pp. 139-42), introduction; pp. 164-216 (pp. 142-94), movements in Indian tribes—a comprehensive study with abundant references.

883 Queiroz, Maria Isaura Pereira de. "A participação do Negro brasileiro em movimentos messianicos e o problema da marginalização." *Revista do Instituto de Estudios Brasileiros* (São Paulo), no. 10 (1971), pp. 111-21, bib.

884 Queiroz, Maria Isaura Pereira de. *Reforme et révolution dans les sociétés traditionelles: Histoire et ethnologie des mouvements messianiques*. Paris: Éditions Anthropos, 1968, 394 pp., illus., bib. Spanish translation. *Historia y ethnologia de los movimientos mesianicos*. Mexico City: Siglo XXI Editores, 1969, 355 pp. German translation. *Reform und Revolution in traditionalen Gesellschaften*. Geissen: A. Achenback, 1974.
   Pp. 136-38 (1968 ed.), absence of messianism in Brazilian Negroes; pp. 193-206, Indian movements (mainly on the Guarani); pp. 206-15, acculturated Indian movements since the 1570s. See also entry e:.

885 Queiróz, Maurício Vinhas de. "'Cargo-cult' na Amazônia. Observações sobre o milenarismo Tukuna." *América Latina* (Rio de Janeiro) 6, no. 4 (1963): 43-61; Spanish, French, and English summaries. Russian translation. "K boprosu o nporoceskikh bidenijakh (messianstve) sredi Tukunov." *Sovetskaja Etnografÿa* (Moscow) 1 (1965): 72-79; English summary.
   Concerning Tukuna messianism: on Solimoes River, north Peru/Columbia borders. The 1946 movement, in contrast to earlier movements, brought better socioeconomic conditions and elimination of exploitation by *civilizados*. Cargo cults are compared.

886 Querino, Manoel [Raymundo]. *Costumes africanos no Brasil*. Bibliotheca de Divulgação Scientifica, vol. 15. Rio de Janeiro: Civilização Brasileira, 1938, 351 pp., illus., music.
   Collected and arranged by A. Ramos as reprints from earlier works. Pt. 1, cult customs; part 4, Negro folklore; pp. 125-27, "Candomblé de caboclo," covers festivals, rites, divinities, songs; also defines a number of terms.

887 Querino, Manoel Raymundo. "A raça africana e os seus costumes na Bahia." *Annaes do Quinto Congresso Brasileiro de Geographia* (Salvador) 1 (1916): 617-75. Reprint. *Revista Academia Brasileira de Letras* (Rio de Janeiro) 18, no. 4 (1927): 126-99. Reprinted separately. 2d ed. Salvador: Progresso, 1955, 174 pp.

The Africans imported into Bahia, with emphasis on their religion, based on participant observation by an able Bahian Negro.

888 Rabassa, Gregory. *O Negro na ficção brasileira.* Biblioteca de Estudos Literários, 4. Rio de Janeiro: Edições Tempo Brasileiro, 1965, 461 pp., bib. (pp. 447-61).

Especially chap. 3 (pp. 108-21), on Cohelo Neto; chap. 4 (pp. 165-325), José Luis do Rego; chap. 7 (pp. 263-321), on Jorge Amado and the sociological significance of many of his works.

889 Raffauf, Ildefonso. "Candomblé." *Santo Antônio. Provinzzeitschrift der Franziskaner in Nordbrasilien* (Bahia) 15, no. 2 (1937): 61-70; 16, no. 1 (1938): 10-19.

See the second article signed "P. Ildefonso."

890 Ramos [de Arauja Pereira], Arthur. "Acculturation among the Brazilian Negroes." *Journal of Negro History* 26, no. 2 (1941): 244-50.

Theoretical considerations based on a study of the Negro Macumbas and Candombles of Bahia, also the Islamic Malês, together with the original African and later Catholic influences – a compact account.

891 Ramos [de Arauja Pereira], Arthur. *As culturas negras no Novo Mundo.* Bibliotheca de Divulgação Scientifica, vol. 12. Rio de Janeiro: Civilização Brasileira, 1937, 399 pp., illus., maps. 2d ed. São Paulo, 1946, 373 pp. Spanish translation. *Las culturas negras en el Nuevo Mundo.* Mexico, D.F.: Fondo de Cultura Económica, 1943. German translation. *Die Negerkulturen in der Neuen Welt.* Erlangen and Zurich, 1947.

Part V, "As culturas negras na America do Sul: Brasil," on the persistence of African languages, institutions, ritual, belief, folklore, music, musical instruments, dances, dress, cuisine, sculpture; on cultural conflict and cultural fusion.

892 Ramos [de Arauja Pereira], Arthur. "O espirito associativo do Negro brasileiro." *Revista do Arquivo Municipal* (São Paulo) 47 (May 1938): 105-26.

Brazil

Negro collective behavior as seen in the religious brotherhoods like the Irmandades of Nossa Senhora do Rosario and São Benedicto, the ceremonies known as *congos* and *reisados*, the *cordoes* of Carnival, the *escolas de samba* of the *morros* of Rio de Janeiro, the work groups like the *cantos* of Bahia and the *bandeiras* of Rio de Janeiro, the *quilombos* of fugitive slaves, "slave insurrections" at Bahia and elsewhere, recent organizations set up in certain parts of Brazil by race-conscious Negroes.

893 Ramos [de Arauja Pereira], Arthur. *O folklore negro do Brasil: Demopsychologia e psychanalyse*. Bibliotheca de Divulgação Scientifica, vol. 4. Rio de Janeiro: Civilização Brasileira, 1935, 279 pp., illus. 2d ed., rev. and illustrated. Rio de Janeiro: Livraria Caso do Estudante do Brasil, 1954, 264 pp.

When one religion, considered superior, tends to supplant another, the elements of the inferior religion do not disappear but become hidden and secret. They form the "superstition" in the midst of the myth and ritual of the new faith. African folklore, animal myths, the superstitious belief in werewolves, the cult of the water sprite, Yemanja, etc., in today's descendants of Africans who long had professed their ancient cults. Pp. 13-17 (1st ed.), syncretism; pp. 86-93, cofradias.

894 Ramos [de Arauja Pereira], Arthur. "Os horizontes mythicos do Negro da Bahia." *Archivos do Instituto Nina Rodrigues* (Bahia) 1, no. 1 (1932): 47-95.

Afro-Brazilian witchcraft "orgies," instruments, and rhythms.

895 Ramos [de Arauja Pereira], Arthur. "Os instrumentos musicais dos candomblés da Bahia." *Bahia Médica* 3 (July 1932): 191-95.

896 Ramos [de Arauja Pereira], Arthur. *Introdução à antropologia brasileira*. 2 vols. Rio de Janeiro: Guanabara, 1943-47, 534, 631 pp. Reprint. 2 vols in 3. Vol. 2, *As culturas indigenas*. Rio de Janeiro: Livraria Editora da Casa do Estudante do Brasil, 1972, 316 pp. Vol. 3, *As culturas negras*. Rio de Janeiro: Livraria Editora da Casa do Estudante do Brasil, 1972, 222 pp.

Vol. 2, chap. 2, Tupi-Guarani, includes migrations; chap. 4, myths and modern forms. Selections from vol. 3 reprinted in *Antologia do Negro brasileiro*, compiled by E. Carneiro (Rio de Janeiro: Edições de Ouro, 1967): pp. 344-45, "Liturgia Malé"; pp. 354-56, "Linha de Umbanda."

897 Ramos [de Arauja Pereira], Arthur. "Magia e folclore." *Revista do Arquivo Municipal* (São Paulo) 16 [2] (1935): 155-57.
Brief notes on superstition and the magic arts, with special reference to Negro influences.

898 Ramos [de Arauja Pereira], Arthur. "O mytho de Yemanjá e suas raízes inconscientes." *Bahia Médica* 3 (August 1932): 209-12.

899 Ramos [de Arauja Pereira], Arthur. "Os mythos de Xangô e sua degradação no Brasil." *Estudos Afro-Brasileiros* (Rio de Janeiro) 1 (1935): 49-54.
A paper presented to the 1st Congresso Afro-Brasileiro ... Recife, 1934.

900 Ramos [de Arauja Pereira], Arthur. *O Negro brasileira.* Rio de Janeiro: Civilização Brasileira, 1934, 303 pp. 2d enl. ed. São Paulo: Editôra Nacional 1940, 434 pp., illus. 3d ed. 1951. English translation. *The Negro in Brazil.* Washington, D.C.: Associated Publishers, 1939. Reprint. 1951, 210 pp., bib. Partially reprinted in *Brazil: A portrait of half a continent,* edited by T. L. Smith and A. Marchant. New York: Dryden Press, 1951, chap. 5.
Part 1, African cultural forms extant in Brazil, with chapters on religious syncretism, especially Candomble and possession; also on Gege-Nago cults. Part 2 uses psychoanalytic theory to explain this persistence.

901 Ramos [de Arauja Pereira], Arthur. "O Negro e o folclore cristão do Brasil." *Revista do Arquivo Municipal* (São Paulo) 47 [4] (1938): 47-78, illus.; French summary (p. 78).
Folk syncretistic Catholicism from the Iberian peninsula combined with African elements in popular Catholicism in Brazil.

902 Ramos [de Arauja Pereira], Arthur. "A possessão fétichista na Bahia. Psychopathologia dos chamados 'estados de santo.'" *Archivos do Instituto Nina Rodrigues* (Bahia) 1, no. 2 (1932). Reprint. Rio de Janeiro: Bibliotheca Nacional, 1932, 32 pp.
Afro-Brazilian "religious mania" and its psychopathology.

903 Ramos [de Arauja Pereira], Arthur. "As prácticas de feitiçaria entre os Negros e Nestiços brasileiros." *Archivos do Instituto de Medicina Legal e Identificação* (Rio de Janeiro) 5, no. 11 (1935), 31-45.

Brazil

904 Ratz, Erhard. "Afrika als neues Ziel brasiliansicher Kulte." *Zeitschrift für Missions* 3, no. 4 (1977): 245-46.

905 Read, William R. *New patterns of church growth in Brazil.* Grand Rapids, Mich.: William B. Eerdmans, 1965. Reprint. 1968, 240 pp., illus.
Pp. 208f., sources of rapid growth; outline of factors leading to rapid Pentecostal growth; includes section on Spiritism and African cults.

906 Read, William R., and Ineson, Frank A. *Brazil 1980: The Protestant handbook.* Monrovia, Calif.: MARC, 1973, 405 pp.
Pp. 15-16, Spiritism (based on W. R. Read, V. M. Monterroso, and H. A. Johnson (entry 907).

907 Read, William R.; Monterroso, V[ictor] M.; and Johnson, H[armon] A[lden]. *Latin American church growth.* Grand Rapids, Mich.: William B. Eerdmans, 1969, 421 pp.
Pp. 248-52, syncretistic Christianity, Spiritism (including Umbanda), lessons for church growth.

908 Real, Katarina. *O folclore no Carnaval do Recife.* Rio de Janeiro: Ministerio da Educação e Cultura, 1967.
An American ethnographer's study of 12 types of carnival associations, embracing over 180 individual groups, in the Recife street carnival. Includes the macaratú (a Yoruba Xango group, p. 70), the *Caboclos de Pena* (a society of Amerindian origin, p. 90), and the Macumba of another Indian group (p. 119).

909 "Receitas de quitutes afro-brasileiros." *Estudos Afro-Brasileiros* (Rio de Janeiro) 1 (1935): 259-60.

910 Rêgo, José Lins do. *O moleque Ricardo.* Rio de Janeiro: Livraria José Olympio, 1936, 282 pp.
A novel on the northeast with sympathetic reference to Xango.

911 Reichert, Rolf. "El ocaso del Islam entre los Negros brasileños." *Actas y Memorias XXXVI Congreso Internacional de Americanistas, España, 1964.* Vol. 3. Seville: Editorial Catolica Española, 1966, pp. 621-25.
Includes references to syncretism between Islam and African-Brazilian religions.

912 Rémy, Jean-Marie. "Le candomblé du Bresil." In *Encyclopaedia Universalis: Le grand atlas des religions*. Paris: Encyclopaedia Universalis France, 1988, p. 133, illus.

Neither Candomble nor the Black Brotherhoods that preceded it in the churches represent a real syncretism – in contrast to Umbanda, which does; the sacred places, pantheons, priesthoods, rites and forms of possession in Candomble.

913 Ribeiro, Joaquim. *Os Brasileiros*. Rio de Janeiro: Editora Pallas for Instituto Nacional do Livro, Brasília, 1977, 593 pp.

Major social types in various cultural regions of Brazil. Final section examines Brazilian mysticism and messianism.

914 Ribeiro, José. *As festas dos Eguns*. Rio de Janeiro: Editôra Eco, [1969], 117 pp.

915 Ribeiro, José. *Candomblé no Brasil: Feitichismo religioso afro-amerindio*. Rio de Janeiro: Editôra Espiritualista, 1957. 4th ed. 1972, 216 pp., illus.

Candomble, Xango, Pajelanca, Catimbo, Umbanda. Cerimônias, cânticos, rituais preceitos. Vocabulary: Gege-Nago-Angola.

916 Ribeiro, José. *O ritual africano e sens misterios: Grupos e figuras, orixas, e voduns, lendos, provérbios, etc.* Rio de Janeiro: Editôra Espiritualista, 1969, 156 pp.

917 Ribeiro, Júlio. *A carne*. Rio de Janeiro: Livraria Imperio, n.d., 107 pp. Many later eds. 23d ed. Rio de Janeiro: F. Alves, 1953.

A novel with negative attitudes to Afro-Brazilians (e.g., barbarous rituals and heinous cult activities of a witchdoctor).

918 Ribeiro, Leonidio, and Campos, Murillo de. *O espiritismo no Brasil*. Contribução ao seu estudo clinico e medico-legal. São Paulo: Companhia Editora Nacional, 1931, 199 pp., illus.

919 Ribeiro, René. "The Afrobrazilian cults-groups of Recife – A study of social adjustment." M.A. thesis (anthropology), Northwestern University, 1949. Published in Portuguese. *Os cultos afrobrasileiros. . . .* Recife: Gráfico Editora do Recife, 1952. Part of chap. 6 of the thesis amplified in Portuguese translation as "O individuo e os cultos afrobrasileiros do Recife." (Parts 1, 2). *Sociologia* (São Paulo) 13, no. 3 (1951): 195-208; 13, no. 4 (1951): 325-40.

Brazil

Part 1, a Portuguese version of a chapter in his 1949 M.A. thesis (Northwestern University)–on initiation of new cult members; Part 2, a general account of cult rites.

920 Ribeiro, René. "Análise sócio-psicológica da possessão nos cultos afro-brasileiros." *Neurobiologia* 19 (1956): 188-211. Spanish translation. "Análises socio-psicológico de la posesión en los cultos afro-brasileños." *Acta Neuropsiquiatrica Argentina* (Buenos Aires) 5 (1959): 249-62.
Emphasizes the psychological features.

921 Ribeiro, René. "Brazilian messianic movements." In *Millennial Dreams in Action*, edited by S. L. Thrupp. The Hague: Mouton, 1962, pp. 55-69. Reprint. New York: Schocken Books, 1970.
Three classes: nativistic; messianic/millenarian under Western influence; salvation, under Christian inspiration; differs from Pereira de Queiroz's interpretations and classification.

922 Ribeiro, René. "Cultos afrobrasileiros do Recife: 'Liminaridade' e 'communitas.'" *Revista de Antropologia* (São Paulo) 29 (1986): 145-54.

923 Ribeiro, René. *Os cultos afrobrasileiros no Recifé: Um estudo de adjustamento social*. Boletím do Instituto Joaquim Nabuco, número especial–1952. Recife: Gráfica Editora do Recife, 1952, 150 pp., illus., bib.
A detailed study of the organization, economic aspects, divinities, rites, festivals, and divination practices of Afro-Brazilian cults, set against their African inheritance; the admission of individuals and the obligations of membership; the nature of the soul and of the individual's place in the universe. Good full-page photos, many by Pierre Verger.

924 Ribeiro, René. "As estruturas de apoio e as reacções do Negro ao cristianismo na América portuguesa: Bases instrumentais numa revisão de valôres." *Boletim do Instituto Joaquim Nabuco de Pesquisas Sociais* (Recife) 6 (1957): 59-80.

925 Ribeiro, René. "Male homosexuality and Afro-Brasilian religions: A preliminary report. Environmental influence on genetic expression." *Transactions in Psychical Research* (Bethesda, Md., National Institute of Mental Health) 9 (1969): 148-49.

926 Ribeiro, René. "Novos aspectos do processo de reinterpretação nos cultos afro-brazileiros do Recife." *Anais do XXXI Congresso Internacional de Americanistas, São Paulo, 1954.* São Paulo: Editôra Anhembi, 1955, pp. 473-92. Reprint. Nendeln, Lichtenstein: Kraus Reprints, 1976.

927 Ribeiro, René. "Pai Rosendo faz uma Ialorixa." *O Cruzeiro* (Rio de Janeiro), 19 November 1949, pp. 51-54.

928 Ribeiro, René. "Personality and the psychosexual adjustment of Afro-Brazilian cult members." *Journal de la Société des Américanistes* (Paris) 58 (1969): 109-20.
    The sexual problems of individuals in Recife were found to derive from primary-group relationships rather than from any connection with Afro-Brazilian cults.

929 Ribeiro, René. "Possessão – problema de etnopsicologia." *Boletim do Instituto Joaquim Nebuco de Pesquisas Sociais* (Recife) 5 (1956): 5-44.

930 Ribeiro, René. "Problemática pessoal e interpretação divinatória nos cultos afro-brasileiros do Recife." *Revista do Museu Paulista* (São Paulo), n.s. 10 (1956-58): 225-242; English summary.

931 Ribeiro, René. "Projective mechanism and the structuralization of perception in Afro-Brazilian divination." *Revue Internationale d'Ethnopsychiatrie Normale et Pathologique* 1, no. 2 (1956): 161-81.
    The Rorschach test responses of a cult priestess in Brazil.

932 Ribeiro, René. "Relations of the Negro with Christianity in Portuguese America." *Americas* 14 (April 1958): 454-84.
    Pp. 470-71, Negro Brotherhoods; pp. 475-80, independent clandestine African cults – Shango, Orisha, Caboclo, etc.; pp. 480-82, newer Pentecostal churches replacing Spiritism.

933 Ribeiro, René. *Religião e relações raciais.* Preface by Gilberto Freyre. Rio de Janeiro: Ministério da Educação e Cultura, 1956, 241 pp.

934 Ribeiro, René. "Significado sóciocultural das ceremônias de Ibeji." *Revista de Antropologia* (São Paulo), 1951, pp. 129-44. Reprinted in *Homen, cultura e sociedade no Brasil*, edited by E. Schaden. Petrópolis: Ed. Vozes, 1972, pp. 269-89.

Brazil

935 Ribeiro, René. "Significado sócio-psicológico de la posesión en los cultos afro-brasileños." *Acta Neuropsiquiátrica Argentina* 5 (1959): 49-62.

936 Ribeiro, René. "O teste de Rorschach no estudo da 'aculturação' e da 'possessão fetichista' dos Negros do Brasil." *Boletim do Instituto Joaquim Nabuco de Pesquisas Socials* (Recife) 1, no. 1 (1952): 44-50.
   On possible uses of the Rorschach test in study of Afro-Brazilian cults.

937 Rio, João do [Barreto, Paulo]. *As religiões no Rio*. Rio de Janeiro and Paris: Garnier, 1906, 245 pp. New ed. 1950, 214 pp. Extracted as "O dia de dar o nome." In *Antologia do negro brasileiro*, compiled by E. Carneiro. Rio de Janeiro: Edições de Ouro, 1967, pp. 374-75.
   On the religions of the African population of Rio de Janeiro, including Afro-Brazilian cults, Spiritualism, and the positivist "church."

938 Rodman, Seldon. "African Brazil and its cults: *Batuque, Candomblé*, and *Umbanda*." *Americas* 27, no. 6 (1975): 6-13, illus.
   A popular overview–a useful introduction.

939 Russell-Wood, A[nthony] J[ohn] [Russell]. "Black and mulatto brotherhoods in colonial Brazil: A study in collective behaviour." *Hispanic American Historical Review* 54, no. 4 (1974): 567-602.
   An important study of these semi-independent socioreligious lay societies, including their religious activities, from the seventeenth to the twentieth centuries. The question is raised as to whether they exhibited syncretistic or African features, but evidence is lacking so far.

940 Russell-Wood, A[nthony] J[ohn] R[ussell]. *The black man in slavery and freedom in colonial Brazil*. London: Macmillan; St. Antony's College, Oxford, 1982, 295 pp.
   Pp. 98-99, African cults in Brazil; chap. 8 (pp. 128-60) the brotherhoods.

941 Russell-Wood, A[nthony] J[ohn] R[ussell]. "Colonial Brazil." In *Neither slave nor free: The freeman of African descent in the slave societies of the new world*, edited by D. W. Cohen and J. P. Greene. Baltimore: Johns Hopkins University Press, 1972, 344 pp.
   Pp. 92, 108, 122, on the Black Brotherhoods or Irmandades, limited to Yoruba and Gege-speaking blacks.

942 Rust, Frances M. "The Afro-Brazilian religious cults." *SSRC Project Report*. HR 1951-52, December 1972, pp. 1-10.

From the Social Science Research Council, London. On Macumba/Umbanda and one Candomble assembly in Rio, and Candomble in Bahia (also Festa de Omolu – St. Lazarus' Day syncretist open-air ceremony) – how these flourish in an industrializing society, which theory says should also be secularizing.

943 Rust, Frances M. "Brazil: Spirit-possession cults." *Contemporary Review* (London), no. 1307 [225] (1974): 299-306.

Historical, sociological, and psychological examination of Candomble (Bahia), Macumba and Umbanda (Rio de Janeiro) and Batuque (Rio Grande do Sol).

944 Sa', Victor de. "Origem e fixação dos cultos afro-subano." *Illustração Brasileira* (Rio de Janeiro) no. 213 [44] (January 1953), 16-17, illus.

945 St. Clair, David. *Drum and candle: First-hand experiences and accounts of voodoo and spiritism*. New York: Tower Publications, 1971. Reprint, with subtitle *Exploration of Brazilian spiritism*. London: Macdonald & Co., 1971, 304 pp., illus. French translation. *Macumba: Enigmes et mystères du Brésil*. Paris, 1972.

An American professional journalist's detailed accounts of Candomble initiation as "Daughter of the Saint," of Umbanda and Quimbanda sessions, and of spirit-healers, the untrained surgeon "Arigo," and other leading practitioners; the European and Brazilian development of upper-class Spiritism; Chap. 12, Fr. Kloppenburg's antispiritist campaign and post-Vatican II retraction; the author's own experience of and belief in Spiritism – popular in form and theoretically simplistic, but valuable information.

946 Sales, Nívio Ramos. "Pousando para retrato." *Religião e Sociedade* 1, no. 2 (1977): 157-72.

By a "pai de santo" in Rio de Janeiro with a degree in social science; extracts in *Religião e Sociedade* (São Paulo) no. 2 (November 1977), 157-72, with introduction by Yvonne Maggie.

947 Santos, Deoscóredes Maximiliano dos. *Axé Opô Afonjá: Noticia historica de um térreiro de santo da Bahia*. Rio de Janeiro: Instituto Brasileiro de Estudos Afro-Asíaticos, 1962, 109 pp.

948 Santos, Deoscóredes Maximiliano dos. *Contos de Nagô*. Capa e ilus, de Carybê. Rio de Janeiro, 1963, 113 pp., illus.

Brazil

Latin America documents on microcards.

949 Santos, Deoscóredes Maximiliano dos. "Festa da Mâe d'Agua em Ponta de Areia, Itaparica, Bahia." *Revista Brasileira de Folclore* (Rio de Janeiro), no. 14 [6] (1966): 65-74, illus.
A renowned Candomble leader in Bahia describes the annual festival at Itaparica.

950 Santos, Deoscóredes Maximiliano dos. "Yemanjá e o culto dos antepassados." *Yemanjá e Suas Lendas*. Rio de Janeiro: Editora Record, 1967.

951 Santos, Deoscóredes Maximiliano dos, and Santos, Juana Elbein dos. "La religion *nago* génératrice et réserve de valeurs culturelles au Brésil." In *Les religions africaines comme source de valeurs de civilisation*. Colloque de Cotonou. Paris: Présence Africaine, 1972, pp. 156-71.

952 Santos, Juana Elbein dos. "Les Nago et la mort." Doctoral thesis (anthropology), University of Paris (Sorbonne). Portuguese translation. *Os Nagô e a morte: Pàde, Asèsè o culto Egun na Bahia*. Petrópolis: Vozes, 1977, 240 pp., bib.
On the Egun (Yoruba) cult in Bahia.

953 Santos, Juana Elbein dos. "A percepão ideológica dos fenômenos religiosos: Sistema nagô no Brasil; Negritude versus sincretismo." *Revista de Cultura Vozes* (Petrópolis) 71, no. 1 (1977): 543-54; English summary.

954 Santos, Juana Elbein dos. "Résistance et cohésion de groupe: Perception idéologique de la religion négro-africaine au Brésil." *Archives de Sciences Sociales des Religions*, no. 47 [24, no. 1] (1979): 123-34.
Reformulated terminology is needed to express the profound content of Afro-American religion; analysis of its multiple variants can reveal the characteristics of this cultural and religious system that has aided resistance to oppressive political power.

955 Santos, Juana Elbein dos, and Santos, Deoscóredes Maximiliano dos. "Ancestor worship in Bahia: The Egun cult." *Journal de la Société des Américanistes* (Paris) 58 (1969): 79-108.
Afro-Brazilian cult centers with souls of the dead, rather than Orixas, as the supernatural focus.

956 Santos, Manuel Victorino dos [Manuel da Formiga, pseud.]. "O mundo religioso do Negro na Bahia." In *O Negro no Brasil*, compiled by E. Carneiro and A. do Couto Ferraz. Rio de Janeiro: Civilização Brasileira, 1940, pp. 343-47.

957 Sayers, Raymond S. *The Negro in Brazilian literature*. New York: Hispanic Institute in the United States, 1956, 240 pp., illus., bib. (pp. 225-34).

   Pp. 177-78, comment on (and extract from) J. M. de Macedo, *As vítimas Algozes* (entry 767), on a Macumba rite. Pp. 198-200, comment on (and extract from) T. A. Araripe, Jr., *O reino encantado* (entry 386).

958 Scarano, Julita. "Black brotherhoods: Integration or contradiction." *Luso-Brazilian Review* 16, no. 1 (1979): 1-17.

959 Scarano, Julita. *Devoção e escravidão*. São Paulo: Companhia Editora Nacional, 1976, 171 pp.
   Useful history of an Afro-Brazilian cofradia.

960 Schaden, Egon. "Aculturação de Alemães et Japoneses no Brasil." *Revista de Antropologia* (São Paulo) 4 (1956): 41-46.

961 Schaden, Egon. "Aculturação e assimilação dos indios do Brasil." *Revista do Instituto de Estudos Brasileiros* (São Paulo), no. 2 (1967), pp. 7-14, bib.
   Acculturation and assimilation as different processes; messianic movements oppose the latter by attempting their own new forms.

962 Schaden, Egon. "Aculturação indígena: Ensaio sôbre fatôres entendências da mundança cultural de tribos índias em contacto com o mundo dos brancos." *Revista de Antropologia* (São Paulo) 13, nos. 1-2 (1965): 3-351, illus., bib. (pp. 303-15).
   Tupi-Guarani, Tukuna, and Rio Negro area nativistic messianisms, with some Christian elements; a landmark in the comparative study of acculturation in Brazil's Indians.

963 Schaden, Egon. "Aspectos fundamentais da cultura guarani." *Boletim de Faculdade de Filosofia, Ciências e Letras da Universidade de São Paulo* 188 (1954): 216 pp., illus. 2d ed. São Paulo: Difusão Européia da Livro, 1962, 290 pp., illus.
   Chap. 8, religion, including acculturation; chap. 10, the myth of Paradise.

South America

Brazil

964 Schaden, Egon. "A assimilação dos Indios do Brasil." *Actas y Memorias XXXVII Congreso Internacional de Americanistas, Argentina, 1966.* Vol. 3. Buenos Aires: Librart, 1968, pp. 105-9.
P. 108, messianism, with reference to the Tukuna, Canela, etc.

965 Schaden, Egon. "Ensaio etno-sociológico sôbre a mitología heróica de algumas tribos indígenas do Brasil." *Boletim de Faculdade de Filosofia, Ciências e Letras da Universidade de São Paulo* 61 (1946). New ed. *A mitología heróica de tribos indígenas do Brazil: Ensaio etno-sociológico.* Coleção "Vida Brasileira," 115. Rio de Janeiro: Ministério de Educação e Cultura, Serviço de Documentação, 1959, pp. 37-59; English summary.
Indigenous millennialism, preparing for the advent of a Golden Age with the help of a god or hero among the Tupi-Guarani and Apapokuva-Guarani; an outstanding work.

966 Schaden, Egon. "Kulturwandel und Nativismus bei den Indianern Brasiliens." *Verhandlungen des XXXVIII Internationalen Amerikanistenkongresses, Stuttgart-München, 1968.* Vol. 3. Stuttgart and Munich: Klaus Renner, 1971, pp. 35-42, bib.
Survey of the comparatively few millennial movements among Brazilian Indians–the Baniwa, Tucano, Tukina, Canela (Ramkokamekra), and Kraho are included; why the Guarani are immune.

967 Schaden, Egon. "Le messianisme en Amérique du Sud (la région du Rio Negro); les Tukuna; les Ramkokamekra." In *Histoire des Religions,* edited by H. C. Puech. Vol. 3. Paris: Gallimard, 1976, pp. 1081-93.

968 Schaden, Egon. "Der Paradiesmythos im Leben der Guarani-Indianer." *Staden-Jahrbuch* (São Paulo) 3 (1955): 179-86.
"Terre-sans-mal" movements from 1515.

969 Scherer, V. "Carta pastoral coletiva do episcopado riograndense sobre o espiritismo." *Revista Eclesiástica Brasileira* (Petrópolis) 14 (1954): 489-91.

970 Schwartz, Stuart B. "Buraco de Tatú: The destruction of a Bahian Quilombo." *Verhandlungen des XXXVIII Internationalen Amerikanistenkongresses, Stuttgart-München, 1968.* Vol. 3. Stuttgart and Munich: Klaus Renner, 1971, pp. 429-38.
P. 430, sixteenth-century Santidade religious cult of escaped slaves–Indian, Catholic, and African elements.

971 Segato de Carvalho, Rita L. "A folk theory of personality types: Gods and their symbolic representation by members of the Sango cult in Recife, Brazil." Ph.D. thesis, The Queen's University of Belfast, 1984.

972 Seljam, Zora. *The story of Oxala: The feast of Bonfim. A play in the Afro-Brazilian tradition.* London: R. Collings; Rio de Janeiro: Sel Editora, 1978, 52 pp., illus.
    English translation from Portuguese: the feast of Bonfim is regarded as an example of the syncretism involving Catholic saints and African Orixas. Oxala is the mythical figure often syncretized with Jesus because of his patient endurance of painful suffering and his forgiveness of his opponents.

973 Sepilli, Tulio. "Il sincretismo religioso afro-cattólico in Brasile." *Studi e Materiali di Storia delle Religioni* (Bologna) 24-25 (1953-54): 1-49.

974 Sette, Mário. *Maxambombas e maracatús.* 2d ed. Recife: Rodolpho & Periera: Livraria Universal, 1938, 306 pp., illus.

975 Shah, Diane K., and Rohter, William. "Brazil's bizarre cults." *Newsweek (International)* (New York and London) 91, no. 9 (1978): 39, illus.
    Report of a self-crucifixion by Eliana Barbosa, with photo; general account of the popularity, and growing respectability and size, of Macumba and Umbanda.

976 Silva, Antonio Viera de. "The development of the traditional African religions in modern Brazil." Paper presented at 44th International Congress of Americanists, Manchester, 1982. Digest in *Abstracts of the Congress*, p. 394.
    From African religions, through Candomble to Umbanda–the "Brazilianization" of African religions.

977 Silva, Edson Nunes da. *Fontes da cultura popular afro-brasileira: Yemanjá, um símbolo cosmogênico.* Salvador, Bahia: Centro de Etudos Etnográficos, 1958, 16 pp.

978 Silva, Edson Nunes da. *Clotun e oduduwa.* Salvador, Bahia: Publicação do Centro de Estudos Etnográficos da Bahia, 1959, 36 pp.

979 Silva, José Amaro Santos. *O fascínio do candomblé.* Recife: Secretaria de Educação e Cultura, 1977, 60 pp., illus.
    On the songs of two cult centers in Pernambuco, with music texts.

Brazil

980 Silva, Woodrow Wilson da Matta e. *Macumbas e candomblés na umbanda*. Rio de Janeiro and São Paulo: Freitas Bastos, 1970, 193 pp.

981 Silversteirn, Leni M. "The search for tradition: Candomblé classes in the Umbanda tradition." Paper presented at 44th International Congress of Americanists, Manchester, 1982. Digest in *Abstracts of the Congress*, pp. 304-95.

982 Simpson, George Eaton. *Black religions in the New World*. New York: Columbia University Press, 1978, 415 pp.
   Pp. 158-63, Spiritism, especially Umbanda (notes, pp. 348-49); pp. 177-204, Afro-Brazilian cults in Maranhão (pp. 177-84), in Bahia (Candomble, pp. 185-90), in Recife (Xango, pp. 190-92), in Pôrto Alegre (pp. 192-95), in Belém (Batuque, pp. 195-203, and Macumba, pp. 203-4, notes pp. 350-53); pp. 290-94, Batuque and Umbanda (notes pp. 368-69).

983 Smith, T[homas] Lynn. *Brazil: People and institution*. Baton Rouge: Louisiana State University Press, 1947. 4th enl. ed. 1972, 778 pp., illus., bib.
   Pp. 528-46, Afro-Brazilian religions; pp. 546-57, "fanaticism and schisms" – Sebastianism, João Santos, Antonio Conselheiro, Cicero.

984 "Une soirée candomblé." *Peuples du Monde* (Paris) 190 (February 1986): 14-15.

985 Sometti, J. *O espiritismo moderno: Bases históricos e bases científicas*. São Paulo: 1981.

986 Sommer, Cecilio. "Musica e danso no candomblé." *Santo Antonio. Revista dos Franciscanos do Nordeste* (Bahia) 20 (1942): 24-30.

987 Sorio, Ezio. "Figli di nessuno." *Nigrizia* 82, no. 2 (1964): 23-26, illus.
   Spiritism, Umbanda, Candomble de Caboclo, etc.

988 Southey, Robert. *History of Brazil*. 3 vols. London: Longman, Hurst, Rees, Orme & Brown, 1810-17. 2d. ed. 1822. Reprint of 2d ed. 3 vols. New York: Greenwood Press, 1969. Portuguese translation. *História do Brasil*. 6 vols. Coleção Historia do Brasil. Paris and Rio de Janeiro: Livraria de B. L. Garnier, 1862. Reprint. 6 vols. Bahia: Aguir & Souza, 1949-54. Reprint. 6 vols. São Paulo: Obelisco, 1965.
   Vol. 1, pp. 371-73 (1969 reprint), an anti-Portuguese new religion of 1583 (based on P. Jarric, *Histoire des choses plus mémorables*

advenues tant ez Inde Orientale, ... *jusques à l'an 1600* [Bordeaux: 1608-1604]); p. 411, a new religion founded in 1603.

989 Souza, José Ribeiro de. *Candomblé no Brasil: Feitichismo religioso afro-ameríndio.* Rio de Janeiro: Editôra Espiritualista, 2d ed., 1957.

990 Souza, José Ribeiro de. *Ceremonias da umbanda e do candomblé.* Rio de Janeiro: Editora Eco, 1970.

991 Souza, José Ribeiro de. *Comidas de santo e oferenda*s. Rio de Janeiro: Folha Carioca Editora, 1962, 116 pp.

992 Souza, José Ribeiro de. *400 pontos riscados e cantados na umbanda e candomblé.* Rio de Janeiro, 1962.

993 Sparta, Francisco. *A dança dos orixás: As relíquias brasileiras da Afro-Asia pré-biblica.* São Paulo: Editôra Herder, 1970, 289 pp., illus., bib. (pp. 281-89).
   An anthropological study of Spiritist practices of Candomble, especially the Orixas, or saints, and their ceremonies.

994 Staden, Hans. *Wahraftige Historia.* Marburg, 1557. Reprint. *Zwei Reisen nach Brasilien, 1548-1555.* Marburg: Trauvetter & Fischer, 1970, 198 pp., illus., maps. Portuguese translation. *Aventuras de Hans Staden.* ... São Paulo: Companhia Editora Nacional, 1927. 6th ed. 1944. New Portuguese translation. *Viagem ao Brasil.* São Paulo: Officina Industria Graphica, 1930, 273 pp., illus. Reprint, under the same title. Rio de Janeiro: Ed. de Ouro, 1968, 294 pp., illus.
   By a sixteenth-century traveler. Chap. 22 on "hommes-dieux."

995 Stainbrook, Edward. "Some characteristics of the psychopathology of schizophrenic behavior in Bahian society." *American Journal of Psychiatry* 109 (1952): 330-35.

996 Stamato, Jorge. "A influencia negra na religião do Brazil." *Planalto* (São Paulo) 1, no. 4 (1941): 7-8, illus. with drawings of Mario Carréno.

997 Stoutjesdijk, Harriett (text), and Glaser, George W. (photos). *About spirits and Macumba.* Rio de Janeiro: The authors, 1960, 71 pp.

998 Sturm, Fred Gillette. "Afro-Brazilian cults." In *African religions: A symposium,* edited by N. S. Booth, Jr. New York: Nok Publishers, 1977, pp. 217-39.

Brazil

Pp. 219-22, the variety of cult names, and their origins; pp. 222-33, typical form of a cult, with emphasis on its special terminology.

999 Süss, Günter Paulo. *Volkskatholizismus in Brasilien: Sür Typologia und Strategie gelebter Religiosität.* Systematische Beitrage, 14. Munich: Kaiser; Mainz: Grünwald, 1978, 200 pp.
Pp. 85-86, African and Indian forms; pp. 100-102, the place of these forms in socioreligious typologies; otherwise on folk Catholicism.

1000 Tabor, D. C. "Some anthropological approaches to the study of Afro-Brazilian cults." B. Litt. thesis (social anthropology), University of Oxford, 1976.

1001 Talvares, Claudio T. "20 horas de candomblé." *A Garota* (Salvador) 1, no. 2 (1947): 1-23.

1002 Tiller, Ann Q. "The Brazilian cult as a healing alternative." *Journal of Latin American Lore* 5, no. 2 (1979): 255-72.
The healing aspects of all varieties of cult; also Z. Arigo (pp. 265-66) and other individual healers.

1003 *Times* (London), 3 August 1874, p. 12, col. C.
On the bishop of Pará and the prophet Moures.

1004 Timmermans, W. *De religie van de Braziliaanse neger in de veranderende samenleving.* Dokt. scriptie [i.e., approx. M.A.], Catholic University, Nijmegen. Roermond: Center Orientation Latin America, 1974, 126 pp.
On "Brazilian Negro religion in changing society."

1005 "Toades de xangô do Recife." *Estudos Afro-Brasileiros* (Rio de Janeiro) 1 (1935): 265-68.

1006 Toop, Walter R. "Organized religious groups in a village of Northeastern Brazil." *Luso-Brazilian Review* (Madison, Wis.) 9, no. 2 (1972): 58-77.
A town in Ceará state: pp. 62-67, Catholic, African, and Amerindian syncretism; pp. 68-71, Spiritualism; pp. 71-77, two Umbanda groups, established in 1964 and 1966: descriptive accounts.

1007 Torres, Guerra G. "Un elemento ritual: El 'osun.'" *Etnologia Folklore* (Havana) 3 (1967): 65-80, illus., bib.

South America

Brazil

1008 Tórres, João Camilo de Oliveira. *História das idéias religiosas no Brasil*. A Igreja e a sociedade Brasileira. São Paulo: Editorial Grijalba, 1968, 324 pp.

Chap. 3 (pp. 57-104), "A face oculta do Cristo": includes messianism (Canudos, etc.) (pp. 63-71); brotherhoods (pp. 71-77) including Afro-Brazilian acculturation, Macumba, and Umbanda (pp. 75f.); Sebastianism (pp. 94-104); chap. 7 (pp. 218-95) on forms of Spiritism, including details of its historical development, and Oriental connections: pp. 296-302, Néo-Pitagorismo.

1009 Tupinambá, Pedro. *Batuques de Belém*. Belém: Imprensa Oficial do Estado, 1973, 46 pp., bib.

1010 United States Government, Department of the Army. *Area handbook for Brazil*, edited by T. E. Weil, et al. Foreign Area Studies, the American University. DA Pam 550-20. Washington, D.C.: Government Printing Office, 1975.

Pp. 124-27, Spiritualism, Afro-Brazilian cults, messianic movements, and others.

1011 [United States Government, Department of the Army.] *U.S. Army area handbook for Brazil*, edited by B. C. Maday, et al. Foreign Area Studies Division, American University. DA Pam 550-20. Washington, D.C.: Government Printing Office, 1964, 725 pp.

Chap. 10 on religion: pp. 221-22, Catholic lay brotherhoods, but Negro ones not specified; pp. 224-25, Spiritualism and Umbanda; pp. 225-28, Gege-Nago cults, etc. Folk religion.

1012 Valente, Waldemar. *Etnografia religiosa afro-brasileira, curso*. Recife: Instituto Joaquim Nabuco de Pesquisas Sociais, 1961.

1013 Valente, Waldemar. *Influencias islamicas nos grupos de culto afro-brasileiros de Pernambuco*. Recife: Instituto Joaquim Nabico de Pesquisas Sociais, 1957.

1014 Valente, Waldemar. *Marcas muçulmanas nos xangös de Pernambuco*. Faculdade de Filosofia de Pernambuco, 1954.

1015 Valente, Waldemar. *Sincretismo com elementos não africanos*. Recife: IJNPS, 1961.

1016 Valente, Waldemar. *Sincretismo intertribal na Africa no Brasil*. Recife: 1961.

153

Brazil

1017 Valente, Waldemar. *O sincretismo religioso*. Recife: IJNPS, 1961.

1018 Valente, Waldemar. *Sincretismo religioso afro-brasileiro*. Brasiliana: Biblioteca Pedagogíca Brasileira, 5th ser., vol. 280. São Paulo: Companhia Editôra Nacional, 1955, 173 pp. 2d ed. 1976, xxiv + 117 pp., bib.
Pp. 1-9 (1955 ed.), Negro cultures in Brazil; pp. 10-23, religious syncretism; pp. 24-25, intertribal syncretism; pp. 46-52, with Islam; pp. 53-67, with Bantu culture; pp. 68-106, with Christianity.

1019 Valente, Waldemar. *Sobrevivências Daomeanas nos grupos-de-culto afronordestinos*. Recife: Instituto Joaquim Nabuco de Pesquisas Socias, Ministério de Educação e Cultura, 1964, 46 pp., illus., bib. French translation. *Survivances dahoméennes dans les groupes-de-culte africains du nord-est du Brésil*. Its, 9. Dakar: Centre d'Hautes Études Afro-Ibéro-Américaines de l'Université de Dakar, 1969, 36 leaves, bib.

1020 Vasconcelos, Salomão de. *Mariana e seus templos*. Belo Horizonte: Graphica Queiroz Breyner, 1938, 116 pp.
P. 107, a Candomble avoiding persecution.

1021 Vega, M. Moreno. "African religious traditions in Brazil." *Caribe* 3, no. 2 (1979): 3-4.

1022 Velho, Yvonne M[aggie] A[lves]. *Guerra de orixa: Um estudo de ritual e conflito*. Rio de Janeiro: Zahar Editores, 1975. Reprint. 1977, 170 pp.
On the formation of new groups through schism and conflict.

1023 Verger, Pierre. "Afro-Catholic syncretisms in South America." *Nigeria Magazine* (Lagos) 78 (September 1963): 211-16.
On the Afro-American cults, their equation of African divinities with Catholic saints, and their festivals, especially in Bahia; p. 215, Yemanja festival of Virgin of Regla in Havana, Cuba.

1024 Verger, Pierre. "Le culte des vodoun d'Abomey, aurait-il été apporté à Saint-Louis de Maranhon par la Mère du Roi Ghezo?" In *Les Afro-Américains*. Mémoires de l'IFAN, no. 27. Dakar: Institut Français de l'Afrique Noire, 1952, pp. 157-60.

1025 Verger, P[ierre]. *Flux et reflux de la traite des Nègres entre le golfe de Bénin et Bahia de todos os Santos du dix-septième au dix-neuvième siècle*. Paris and The Hague: Mouton, 1968, 720 pp., illus.

Pp. 527-28, African religious brotherhoods ("confrères"); pp. 533-36, Candombles.

1026 Verger, Pierre. "Influence du Brésil au Golfe du Bénin." In *Les Afro-Américains*. Mémoires de l'IFAN, no. 27. Dakar: Institut Français de l'Afrique Noire, 1952, pp. 11-101.

1027 Verger, Pierre. "Notes sur le culte des orisa et vodum, à Bahia, la Baie de tous les Saints, au Brésil et à l'ancienne Côte des Esclaves en Afrique." *Mémoires de l'Institut Français d'Afrique Noire* (Dakar) 51 (1957): 609 pp., illus., map.
Bib. (pp. 571-75), more on Africa than on Brazil.

1028 Verger, Pierre. "Première cérémonie d'initiation au culte des orishas nagô à Bahia au Brésil." *Revista do Museu Paulista* (São Paulo), n.s. 9 (1955): 269-91.

1029 Verger, Pierre. "Raisons de la survie des religions africaines au Brésil." *Les religions africaines comme source de valeurs de civilisation.* Colloque de Cotonou. Paris: Présence Africaine, 1972, pp. 172-85.

1030 Verger, Pierre. "Rôle joué par l'état d'hébétude au cours de l'initiation des novices aux cultes des orisha et vodun." *Bulletin de l'Institut Français d'Afrique Noire* (Dakar), Ser. B, 16, nos. 3-4 (1954): 322-40.

1031 Verger, Pierre. "Syncrétisme." *Recherche, Pédagogie et Culture* (Paris) 64 (1983): 40-45, illus.
African gods and Catholic saints as fused in various Candomble and similar cults.

1032 Verger, Pierre. "Yoruba influences in Brazil." *Odú: Journal of Yoruba and Related Studies* (Ibadan) 1, no. 1 (1955): 3-11.

1033 Vergolino e Silva, Anaíza. *Alguns elementos para o estudo do Negro na Amazônia*. Publicaões Avulsas, 8. Belém: Museu Paraense Emílio Goeldi, 1968, 20 pp.

1034 Vergolino e Silva, Anaíza. "O tambór das flores: Uma análise da Federação Espírita Umbandista e dos cultos afro-brasileiros do Pará (1965-1975)." M.A. dissertation (social anthropology), State University of Campinhas (Campinhas, São Paulo), 1976.

Brazil

1035 Vidale, Maria. "Rodici: Culti afro-brasiliani." *Nigrizia* 97, no. 14 (1979): 55-58, illus.
A general survey; the growing problem for the Catholic Church.

1036 Villela, Lavinia Costa. "Festa do Divino em São Luiz do Paraitinga em 27 à 29 maio 1944." *Sociologia* (São Paulo) no. 1 (1946), p. 115, 4 charts, p. 123.

1037 Wagley, Charles. *Amazon Town: A study of man in the tropics.* New York: Macmillan, 1953, 305 pp.
Itá town (fictitious name) on lower Amazon, below Negro River junction, with about 500 population; pp. 232-33, 262-64, "Spiritualism."

1038 Wagley, Charles. *An introduction to Brazil.* New York: Columbia University Press, 1963, 322 pp. Rev. ed. 1974, 341 pp., illus.
Rev. ed. pp. 214-44, Afro-Brazilian cults; pp. 244-47, Spiritism and other movements.

1039 Wagley, Charles, ed. *Race and class in rural Brazil.* Paris: UNESCO, 1952. 2d ed. 1963, 158 pp., illus., map.
See M. Harris (entry 648), H. W. Hutchinson (entry 674), and B. Zimmerman (entry 1070).

1040 Walker, Sheila S[uzanne]. "The Bahian Carnival." *Black Art* (Los Angeles) 5, no. 4 (1983): 23-27, illus.
Candomble.

1041 Walker, Sheila S[uzanne]. "Candomblé: A spiritual microcosm of Africa." *Black Art* (Los Angeles) 5, no. 4 (1983): 10-22, illus.
A comprehensive, well-illustrated survey of history, forms, and relation to Catholicism, based on Bahia.

1042 Walker, Sheila S[uzanne]. "The Feast of Good Death: An Afro-Catholic emancipation celebration in Brazil." *Sage: A Scholarly Journal on Black Women* (Atlanta) 3, no. 2 (1986): 27-31.
A case study of the cofradias arising within Catholicism: the Festa da Boa Morte of the Sisterhood of Good Death (created within the Catholic Church early in the nineteenth century) celebrated in Cachoeira in Bahia state to rejoice in the Assumption of the Virgin Mary, but rooted in the Candomble tradition from which it derives.

1043 Walker, Sheila S[uzanne]. "Master Didi." *Black Art* (Los Angeles) 5, no. 4 (1983): 4-9, illus.

On Deoscóredes dos Santos, Afro-Brazilian artist, Egun priest, Candomble official, cultural historian, author of a Yoruba-Portuguese dictionary, and his discovery of his roots on a visit to Benin. See also his own publications above.

1044 Warren, Donald, Jr. "The Negro and religion in Brazil." *Race* (London) 6, no. 3 (1965): 199-216; references.
   A fine historical treatment, especially on the attitudes of the whites and elites to the Negro and his religious life; the latter is treated in terms of the earlier lay brotherhoods of the Catholic Church (especially Our Lady of the Rosary of Black Men) and of the Afro-Brazilian cults.

1045 Warren, Donald, Jr. "Portuguese roots of Brazilian spiritism." *Luso-Brazilian Review* (Madison) 5, no. 2 (1968): 3-33.
   Sebastianism and folk Spiritism: their Portuguese background, and their forms in folk-culture in Portugal.

1046 Watson, James B. "Cayuá culture change: A study in acculturation and methodology." American Anthropological Association Memoir 73. *American Anthropologist* 54, no. 2:2 (1952): 1-144 + plates.
   Southern Matto Grosso: pp. 50-54, "religiously" inspired migrations, 1832 to 1850; pp. 42-43, shamans and messianic tendencies.

1047 Watson, Peter. "An experience of voodoo." *Illustrated London News*, October 1971, pp. 32-33, illus.
   Eyewitness account of a Macumba sacrifice in Rio de Janeiro.

1048 Wellington, R. A. *The Brazilians – how they live and work.* London: David & Charles, 1974, 175 pp.
   Pp. 37-41, religion (including African cults, and Yemanja); pp. 108-9, spiritual leaders.

1049 Westra, Allard D. Willemier. "Uncertainty reduction in the Candomblé religion of Brazil." In *Popular religion, liberation, and contextual theology: Papers from a Congress, Nijmegen, January 1990, in honour of Arnulf Camps*, edited by J. van Nieuwenhove and B. K. Goldewijk. Forthcoming, 1991.

1050 Wiebe, James Peter. "Persistence of spiritism in Brazil." D. Missiology thesis, School of World Mission, Fuller Theological Seminary, 1979, 191 pp.

Brazil

Interprets "spiritism" as "animism" and has no differentiation of varieties of Afro-Brazilian, etc., cults, or of forms of "spiritism."

1051 Willeke, Venantius. "Kirche und Negersklaven im Brasilien, 1550-1888." *Neue Zeitschrift für Missionswissenschaft* 32, no. 1 (1976): 15-26.

Catholic efforts on behalf of Negro slaves; "racial segregation in cult was ... practised in order to avoid friction, but it had an unexpected result: the Negro churches, left alone, fell prey to syncretism."

1052 Willems, Emílio. "Religious mass movements and social change in Brazil." In *New Perspectives of Brazil*, edited by E. N. Baklanoff. Nashville, Tenn.: Vanderbilt University Press, 1966, pp. 205-32. Reprinted in *Contemporary Anthropology*, edited by D. G. Bates and S. H. Lees. New York: A. A. Knopf, 1981, pp. 273-91.

Includes Spiritism in three groups: Assemblies of God (Christian Congregation), Spiritualism (Society for Spiritualist Studies of the Confucius Group, 1873-), and Umbanda (from Macumba in 1930): interpreted as reflecting the changing needs of the masses.

1053 Willems, Emílio. *Uma vila Brasileira: Tradição e transição*. São Paulo: Difusão Européia do Livro, 1961, 222 pp.

Includes religious practices in an interior village of the Vale do Paraíba.

1054 Williams, Paul V. A. "Curandeirismo in the Recôncavo of Bahia: A study in cultural syncretism based on the fusion of African indigenous and European curing practices." Ph.D. dissertation, University of St. Andrews, 1976, 367 pp., illus.

In the context of Candomble de Caboclo. Chap. 2, the religious bases underlying *curandeirismo:* pp. 41-43, Spiritism; pp. 44-46, African religions in Brazil; pp. 47-56, Candomble (traditional African); pp. 57-61, Candomble de Caboclo; pp. 62-64, functions of priests in both Candombles; pp. 297-310, conclusions on the syncretism of European, African, and Amerindian elements.

1055 Williams, Paul V. A. "Exú: The master and the slave in Afro-Brazilian religion." In *The fool and the trickster*, edited by P. V. A. Williams. Ipswich: D. S. Brewer, 1979, pp. 109-19, illus., + notes (pp. 137-39).

1056 Williams, Paul V. A. "Notes on Exú." In *The Trickster*, edited by D. Gifford. Working Papers, 3. St. Andrews, Fife: Centre for Latin America Linguistic Studies, University of St. Andrews, 1975, pp. 1-11.

On the "most respected and most feared" *orishá* in Candomble cults, and his dual nature.

1057 Williams, Paul V. A. *Primitive religion and healing—A study of folk medicine in North East Brazil.* Totowa, N.J.: Rowman & Littlefield; Cambridge: Brewer, for the Folk Society, 1979, 212 pp., illus.
Chaps. 2-3 (pp. 4-21), the African background of many cults. Based on his doctoral dissertation (entry 1054).

1058 Williams, Paul V. A. "Some recent developments in an Afro-Brazilian religion." *Anthropos* 74, nos. 1-2 (1979): 47-54.
Candomble de Caboclo as a movement away from Candomble and Africa, towards Europe through Kardecist (Spiritist) influence, and so becoming more socially acceptable; the essential features are described.

1059 Wilson, Bryan R[onald]. *Magic and the millennium: A sociological study of religious movements of protest among tribal and third-world peoples.* London: Heinemann Educational Books; New York: Harper & Row, 1973, 547 pp. Reprint. Frogmore, St. Albans: Granada Publishing, Paladin Books, 1975.
Pp. 106-20, Catholic background, possession cults, Umbanda (pp. 112-14), Spiritualism and Spiritism; pp. 206-14, Tupi-Guarani.

1060 Winters, Clyde-Ahmad. "The African Ummah al-Musulmin of Brazil." *Islam and the Modern Age* 10, no. 4 (1979): 1-12, bib.
P. 9, Islam as found in Macumba, Shango, and Candomble cults—the latter being seen by some as social clubs rather than religions.

1061 Winz, Antônio Pimental. "Notas históricas sobre Nossa Senhora de Copacabana." *Anais do Museu Histórico Nacional* (Rio de Janeiro) 15 (1965): 87-220, illus., bib.
Well-documented account of a Bolivian cult that spread to the Iberian Peninsula, then to Brazil; its history in Rio de Janeiro since colonial times.

1062 Wöhlcke, Manfred. "Analyse der afro-brasilianischen Kulte unter dem Aspekt interethnischer Marginalität." Doctoral dissertation (Phil. Fakultät), Erlangen-Nürnberg University, 1969, 238 pp. + 16 pp. not paginated, illus.
Pp. 23-53, Candomble cults; pp. 54-77, Umbanda cults; pp. 78-93, Macumba cults; otherwise on the theory of marginality.

Brazil

1063 Wöhlcke, Manfred. "Unterschichtreligiosität in Brasilien." *Berichte zür Entwicklung in Spanien, Portugal, Lateinamerika* (Munich) 1, no. 4 (1976): 18-26.

Of rural population in Brazil, 90% practice their own form of folk Catholicism under considerable influence from Afro-Brazilian cults, magic, and primal religious beliefs.

1064 Woodward, Ruth E. "Patron Saint of the Brazilian Negroes." *Travel* 85 (May 1945): 28-29, 34, illus.

St. Benedict's festival in the town of Pocos de Caldas, Minais Gerais state, intermingling Iberian, Amerindian, and African elements, and in celebration of abolition of slavery on 13 May 1888.

1065 Wright, Robin M., and Hill, Jonathan D. "History, ritual, and myth: Nineteenth century millenarian movements in the northwest Amazon." *Ethnohistory* 33, no. 1 (1986): 31-54, map.

Documentation and interpretation of the life of Venancio Kamiko and his politico-religious movement of the late 1850s in the Upper Rio Negro region in Arawakan culture–"redefining the indigenous ancestor cult into a cult of historical oppostion to external domination."

1066 Wulfhorst, Ingo. *Der "spiritualistische-christliche Orden." Ursprung und Erscheinungsformen einer neureligiösen Bewegung in Brasilien*. Erlangen: Verlag der Ev.-Luth. Mission, 1985, 440 pp., illus., maps.

Chap. 2 (pp. 21-43), Kardecist Spiritualism; chap. 3 (pp. 44-71), Umbanda; chaps. 4-8 (pp. 72-242), detailed study of Ordem Espiritualista Crista in Brasilia; chaps. 9-10 (pp. 243-312), relation to the church, and missiological reflections; pp. 395-432, bibliography, especially valuable for Umbanda and Kardecist publications as primary sources.

1067 X [pseud.]. "Candomblé." *Santo Antonio* 15, no. 1 (1937): 15-29.

The Catholic Church doctrine in relation to Candombles and analysis of the bishop of Bahia's pastorals threatening and disciplining Catholics connected with them.

1068 Yai, Olabiyi Babalola. "On the future of candomblé in Brazil." Paper presented at 44th International Congress of Americanists, Manchester, 1982. Digest in *Abstracts of the Congress*, p. 392.

1069 Zanichelli, Nicola. *Il sincretismo religioso afro-cattolico in Brasile*. 2 parts. Bologna: N. Zanichelli, 1955.

1070 Zimmerman, Ben. "Race relations in the arid Sertão." In *Race and class in rural Brazil*, edited by C. Wagley. 2d ed. Paris: UNESCO, 1963, pp. 82-115.

Pp. 90-93, African elements and popular religion in the southern Sertão (Monte Serrat area) – cult of the saints, and Candomble (local term = "terreiro").

Chile

There is no black segment of the population and the 5% who are Indians are in the north (Aymara and Quechua) or the south (Mapuche).

There are only the two items. E. Bello is on a festival representing Indian folk Catholicism in the north. R. C. Padden is on an early political revolt with religious dimensions which was influenced by the white contact, and is somewhat typical of such responses among Indians in Latin America in general.

As in Bolivia there are many small independent Indian churches, both Pentecostal and non-Pentecostal, but no available literature on them.

1071 Bello, Enrique. "Danza y circunstancia en la Fiesta de la Tirana." *Boletín de la Universidad de Chile* (Santiago), nos. 61-62 (October-November 1965), pp. 94-118.

Describes a northern Chile festival of a Virgen del Carmen who is identified with an Inca princess who opposed the Spanish.

1072 Padden, Robert C. "Cultural change and military resistance in Araucanian Chile, 1550-1730." *Southwestern Journal of Anthropology* 13 (1957): 103-27.

Pp. 117-18, maintenance of primal religion, and late conversion to Christianity, probably to be seen as a negative instance.

Colombia

Although about a fifth of the population is mulatto and some 5% is black, there is little available literature on religious movements. The single item, I. Castellanos, is on festivals. There could be much more on the various emphases between cults of the ancestors and cults of the Catholic saints in the black population.

The Indian movements produce important studies on the significant early reactions against the Spanish. One of these, a movement in 1546 in the Quimbaya area, would appear to be among the first recorded movements in modern times of the type with which we are concerned (i.e., since Columbus,

Columbia

or the European peoples' expansion). On this and other early movements see G. Eckert (entries 1075 and 1076). Also see G. Guariglia (entry 1080) on movements from 1546 to 1603, and J. Friede (entry 1078); also A. Posern-Zielinski (entry 295, p. 154).

For two messianic movements among Páez Indians in the south in 1707 and 1833 see J. Rappoport (entry 1082).

On more recent movements see I. Goldman (entry 1079) for the late nineteenth century, and G. and A. Reichel-Dolmatoff (entry 1084) for a millennial and healing movement in the 1960s.

Pentecostal forms have developed among the marginal peoples, including blacks and Indians, but no literature has been available, other than the item by C. B. Flora (entry 1077).

1073 Calasan Vela, José. *Desde Villavicencio hasta San Fernando de Atabapo*. Cartagena: Editorial "Seminario Popular," 1936.

On the millennial movement of Luis Mea among the Tama tribe of the Puinave Indians on the Guaviare River, in 1887, until he was imprisoned.

1074 Castellanos, Isabel, and Atencio, Jaime. "Raices hispanas en las fiestas religiosas de los Negros del norte del Cauca, Colombia." *Latin American Research Review* 19, no. 3 (1984): 118-42.

Two festivals: Adoration of the Three Wise Men (Reyes Magos), and Adoration of the Infant God (Niño Dios).

1075 Eckert, Georg. "Prophetentum und Freiheitsbewegungen im Caucatal." *Zeitschrift für Ethnologie* (Brunswick) 76 (1951): 115-25.

Three movements: Quimbaya, 1546; Sobce's, in Antioquia, 1576; Quimbaya, 1603.

1076 Eckert, Georg. "Zum Kult des Buciraco in Cartagena." *Zeitschrift für Ethnologie* (Brunswick) 79, no. 1 (1954): 118-20.

The traditional god, Buciraco, appeared to Pedro Simon in 1613.

1077 Flora, Cornelia Butler. "Pentecostalism and development: The Colombian case." In *Perspectives in Pentecostalism: Case studies from the Caribbean and Latin America*, edited by S. D. Glazier. Washington, D.C.: University Press of America, 1980, pp. 81-93.

The capacity of Pentecostalism for indigenization among marginal sectors of the population, which distinguishes the local Pentecostal church from its sponsoring North American Pentecostal Church.

1078 Friede, Juan. "Los quimbayas: Aportacion documental al estudio de la demografia precolombina." *Revista Colombiana de Antropologia* 9 (1962): 301-18.

Pp. 309-11, description of two brief uprisings by the indigenous population against the Spanish in 1542 and 1557, as well as the curious appearance of a "Messiah" in 1557 advising the Indians to die rather than serve the Christian invaders.

1079 Goldman, Irving. *The Cubeo Indians of the Northwest Amazon.* Illinois Studies in Anthropology, 2. Urbana: University of Illinois Press, 1963, 305 pp., illus.

P. 16, messianic movements in the Vaupes area (Colombia), 1875-1900 (Anizetto's and Vicente Christo's movements mentioned); only slight evidence of such movements in the Cuduiari river area in 1940.

1080 Guariglia, Guglielmo. *Prophetismus und Heilserwartungs-Bewegungen als völkerkundliches und religionsgeschichtliches Problem.* Vienna: F. Berger, 1959, xvi + 232 pp., maps, bib.

Pp. 177-79, movements in 1546 and 1603 in Quimbaya, and in 1576 in Antioquia.

1081 Price, Thomas James, Jr. "Saints and spirits: A study of differential acculturation in Colombian Negro communities." Ph.D. dissertation (anthropology), Northwestern University, 1955, 243 pp.

Two aspects of African religions – the cults of the dead and of the divinities – have been syncretized with the Catholic rites for the dead and cults of the saints; in el Manzillo (on the Caribbean coast) the cult of the ancestors surpasses that of the saints; in Tumaco (Pacific coast) the cult of the saints has the greater individual and public importance, and the wake for the dead is of less significance.

1082 Rappoport, Joanne. "Mesianismo y las transformaciones de símbolos mesiánicos en Tierradentro." *Revista Colombiana de Antropologia* (Bogota) 23 (1980-81): 365-413.

Messianic movements among the Páez in southern Colombia: in 1706 under Francisco Undachi, in 1727 under Pedro Chuvis, in 1883 at Suin; also on relation of the biblical symbols to those of local primal religion. An important detailed article.

1083 Reichel-Dolmatoff, Gerardo. *Diario de viaje entre los Indios y Negros de la Provincia de Cartagena en el Nuevo Reino de Granada, 1781-1788.* Bogota: Editorial ABC, 1955.

Columbia

Pp. 86-88, a religious movement among Negroes in the Majagual area.

1084 Reichel-Dolmatoff, G[erardo], and Reichel-Dolmatoff, A. "Notas sobre un movimiento apocaliptico en el Choco, Colombia." *Folklore Americano* (Lima) 14 (1966): 110-45, bib., map, photos.
A millenarian healing movement in the 1960s among Indians.

Ecuador

As with Colombia and some other areas, there is more literature available on the earliest Indian movements than on those in recent times; see the items of U. Oberem on the sixteenth century. Otherwise there is only the brief survey from the United States Army Handbook, despite the fact that over 40% of the population is Indian. This includes the large Quechua population of several million, among whom there has been substantial growth of a Christian community since about 1970; in due course one would expect some independent developments in this context.

The black population amounts to somewhere between 5% and 10%, but no literature has been available. Nor is there information about possible Pentecostal developments among blacks or Indians, although this form is well established in the country.

1085 Oberem, Udo. "Die Aufstandsbewegung der Pende bei den Quijo Ost-Ekuadors in Jahre 1578." In *Chiliasmus und Nativismus*, edited by W. E. Mühlmann. Berlin: D. Reimer, 1961. Reprint. 1964, pp. 75-80.

1086 Oberem, Udo. "Diego de Ortegón's Beschreibung der 'Gobernación de los Quijos, Zumaco y la Canela': Ein ethnographischer Bericht aus dem Jahre 1577." *Zeitschrift für Ethnologie* (Brunswick) 83 (1958): 230-51.
The Pende revolt.

1087 Oberem, Udo. "Los Quijos: Historia de la transculturación de un grupo-indigena en el Oriente Ecuatoriano (1538-1956)." *Memorias de Departamento de Antropologia y Etnologia de America* (Madrid) 1 (1971).

1088 United States Goverment, Department of the Army. *Area handbook for Ecuador*, edited by E. E. Erickson. American University, Foreign Area Studies Division. DA PAM 550-52. Washington, D.C.: Government Printing Office, 1966.

Pp. 216-17, Indian syncretisms.

Paraguay

This country is unusual in that some 90% of the population is mestizo (Guarani-Spanish) and mostly bilingual in these two languages, and therefore homogenous.

Most of the following items concern the Guarani Indians during the early Spanish period when the Jesuits were responsible for an enlightened and successful mission and settlement policy. There were, however, Indian revolts with a religious aspect, but the special nature of Guarani millennialism seems to have provided a pre-existing alternative to the development of many new movements. Most discussion is incidental to the many and substantial histories of the period. On the Jesuit era (1558 to 1767, when they were expelled) and on the early "man-gods," see F. Jarque (entry 1100); similarly P. Lozano (entry 1101).

On Guarani messianism itself see J. C. Espinola (entry 1092, with English summary), who distinguishes "endogenous" from "external" messianism; M. Haubert (entry 1096) supports this distinction by discussing messianism in the Europe of the period and hence of the missionaries also, as distinct from Guarani messianism. See also W. Regehr (entry 1103) on the Indians of the Paraguayan Chaco.

Other items are the general survey in the United States Army Handbook (entry 1108); G. Guariglia (entry 1093); J. Guevara (entry 1094); and R. J. Hunt (entry 1098) on a cult among the Lengua people influenced by the English Anglican mission. There is a review article by E. E. Benitez (entry 1090) on H. Hack (entry 1095) on Mennonites and Indians.

The black population is under 1% and no literature is available.

1089 Bareiro Saguier, Rubén, and Clastres, Hélène. "Aculturación y mestizaje en las misiones jesuíticas del Paraguay." *Aportes* (Paris), no. 14 (October 1969), pp. 6-27; separate bib. (pp. 62-66.)

The early Jesuit settlements among the Guarani, whose messianic expectations had prepared them for the changes involved; but there were also revolts led by the *pagé*, or shamans.

1090 Bénitez, Ebelio Espínola. "Algunas anotaciones en torno a 'Indios y mennonitas en el Chaco paraguayo' de Henk Hack." *Suplemento Antropológico* (Asunción) 16, no. 2 (1981): 213-26.

A review of entry 1095.

Paraguay

1091 Cadógan, León. "Curuzú Yeguá: Apostilla a la interpretación psicoanalítica del Culto a la Cruz en el folklore paraguayo." *Revista de Antropologia* (Faculdade de Filosofia ..., University of São Paulo) 9, nos. 1-2 (1961): 39-50, bib.
Shows that the Paraguayan rite of the Cult of the Cross is Iberian and not Guarani in origin as had been thought; by an expert on Guarani culture.

1092 Espíndola, Julio César. "A propósito del messianismo primitivo en las tribus Guaraní." *América Indígena* 21 (1961): 307-25; English summary (p. 307).
Distinguishes "endogenous" from "external" messianism; pp. 317-18, text of letter of 1556 reporting a "Son of God" movement in Paraguay; pp. 318 ff., comment on this "external" messianism.

1093 Guariglia, Guglielmo. *Prophetismus und Heilserwartungs-Bewegungen als völkerkindliches und religionsgeschichtliches Problem.* Vienna: F. Berger, 1959, xvi + 332 pp., maps, bib.
Pp. 188-89, Santiago, Mazavi, and Apiawaiki movements.

1094 Guevara, José. *Historia del Paraguay, Rio de la Plata y Jucumán.* Colección de Obras y Documentos Relativos á la Historia Pratigua y Moderna de las Provincias del Rio de la Plata. Por Pedro de Angelis. Buenos Aires, 1910.
Vol. 2, pp. 50-51 on Indian *pagé* cult at San Ignacio de Guayra.

1095 Hack, Henk. "Indios y menonitas en el Chaco paraguayo." *Suplemento Antropológico* (Asunción) 13, nos. 1-2 (1978): 207-60, illus., maps; 14, nos. 1-2 (1979): 210-48, illus.; 15, nos. 1-2 (1980): 45-137, bib.
See review article by E. E. Bénitez (entry 1090).

1096 Haubert, Maxime. "Indiens et jésuites au Paraguay: Rencontre de deux messianismes." *Archives de Sociologie des Religions* 27 (January-June 1969): 119-33; references in notes.
On the millennialism of the sixteenth century in Europe and among missionaries; pp. 125ff. on the beliefs in the quick conversion of the Americas; pp. 125 ff., 132, Guarani "terre-sans-mal," and "hommes-dieux"; pp. 127-30, Jesuit treatment of "hommes-dieux"; pp. 129-30, Guiravera; pp. 127-28, 130, Guaira (Guiravera's centre).

1097 Haubert, Maxime. "L'oeuvre missionnaire des jésuites au Paraguay, 1585-1768, genèse d'un 'paradis'. ..." 2 vols. Thèse de doctorat de 3e

Cycle, Université de Paris, École Pratique des Hautes Études, 6e Section, 1966, 382 pp. Mimeo.
Includes messianic movements.

1098 Hunt, R[ichard] J[ames]. *The Livingstone of South America: The life and adventures of W. Barbrooke Grubb.* . . . London: Seeley Service, 1933, xvi + 347 pp., illus., maps.
Pp. 299-301, "Among the Suhin of the Monte Lindo"; the "Short Blanket" or "Our Father" cult, among the Lengua, and the reaction to it by visiting Tobas.

1099 Jarque, Francisco. *Insignes misioneros de la Compañia de Jesus en la Provincia del Paraguay.* . . . Pampelona: J. Micon, 1687, 432 pp.
"Man-gods," etc.,–references on pp. 41, 46, 56, 63, 70, 138, 141, 152, 156.

1100 Jarque, Francisco. *Ruiz Montoya en Indias, 1608-1652.* Saragosse, 1664. Reprint. 4 vols. Colección de Libros que Tratan de América, raros e curiosos. Madrid: V. Suárez, 1900.
Vol. 2, pp. 285-86, 302, 326, on Guiravera "man-god" in Paraguay; vol. 3, pp. 56-59, 98-105, 113-21, 262-63; vol. 3, pp. 288-89.

1101 Lozano, Pedro. *Historia de la conquista del Paraguay, Rio de la Plata y Jucumán.* 4 vols. Buenos Aires: Imprinta Popular, 1873-75.
A Jesuit account. Vol. 1, pp. 403-5, on prophets; vol. 3, pp. 210-29, on Obera; pp. 332-63 on Rodrigo Yaguariguay cult.

1102 Queiroz, Maria Isaura Pereira de. "O mito da Terra sem Males: Uma utopia Guarani?" *Revista de Cultura Vozes* (Petrópolis) 67, no. 1 (1973): 41-50, bib.

1103 Regehr, Walter. "Movimientos messiánicos entre los grupos etnicos del Chaco paraguayo." *Suplemento Antropológico* (Asunción, Universidad Catolica) 16, no. 2 (1981): 105-17.

1104 Ruiz de Montoya, A. *Conquista espiritual hecha por los religiosos de la Compania de Iesus, en las Provincias del Paraguay, Parana, Uruguay, y Tapé.* Madrid, 1639.
Pp. 12, 15-17, 29, 36-38, 44-45, 53-54, 71, 74-78, 89-90, "Man-gods." By a Jesuit.

1105 Service, Elman R[ogers]. "The encomienda in Paraguay." *Hispanic American Historical Review* 31, no. 2 (1951): 230-52.

Paraguay

Summarizes part of his doctoral dissertation on Spanish-Guarani acculturation in early colonial Paraguay, dealing with the rapid racial and cultural fusion between the two groups. Useful background.

1106 Service, Elman R[ogers]. *Spanish-Guaraní relations in early colonial Paraguay.* University of Michigan, Museum of Anthropology, Anthropological Papers, 9. Ann Arbor: University of Michigan, 1954, 106 pp., map.
Discusses acculturation process between 1537 and 1620.

1107 Techo, Nicolás del. *Historia Provinciae Paraquariae Societatis Iesu.* Liège, 1673. Spanish translation. *Historia de la Provincia del Paraguay de la Compania de Jesus.* Madrid, 1897.
"Man-gods" in an early Jesuit history. Spanish translation, vol. 1, pp. 30, 108-9, 130, 154, 190, 220-26, 249-50, 311; vol. 2, p. 222; vol. 3, pp. 179-80, 303; vol. 4, p. 370; vol. 6, p. 76.

1108 United States Government, Department of the Army. *Area handbook for Paraguay,* edited by T. E. Weil. Foreign Area Studies Division, the American University. DA PAM 550-156. Washington, D.C.: Government Printing Office, 1972, 315 pp.
Pp. 29-32, ethnic groups–their languages and religions; the Mennonite settlements.

1109 Velásquez, Rafael Eladio. *La rebelión de los Indios de Arecayá, en 1660: Reacció indígena contra los excesos de la encomienda en el Paraguay.* Asuncion: Centro Paraguay de Estudios Sociológicos, 1965, 42 pp.
Resistance in which prophet figures played a part; well documented.

Peru

There is extensive literature on Peruvian movements. This is due firstly to a comparatively large population of some 16 million in which Indians form a major sector (some 46%, with Quechuas and Aymaras as the two largest groups). It also reflects the fact that Peru was the center of the great Inca civilization, the only such society in South America, which led to substantial and prolonged resistance to the Spanish colonizers. The resultant revolts from the mid-sixteenth to the late eighteenth century exhibited a religious dimension that included a strong millennial hope for the restoration of the Inca empire, and something of this feature may still be found.

There is little evidence in the nineteenth century of the phenomena with which we are concerned, but a new range of forms appears in the present century as a result of independent responses to the advent and success of Protestant missions, which arrived late in the previous century, and to the more recent Pentecostal developments. At the same time secessions from the Catholic Church are known to have occurred in recent years, especially under Catholic charismatic and other Pentecostal influences, but documentation has not been available. See K. D. Scott (entry 1222) for an overview of the history and movements in Peru.

For general surveys, see H. E. Dobyns et al. (entry 1142); D. W. Gade (entry 1152) for further on the earthquake cults; and J. I. Tellechea Idigoras (entry 1229) on popular religion. For background to the millenarian aspects and to movements expressing these, see M. Lopez-Baralt (entry 1187), D. D. Gow (entry 1157) on the Inkarri figure in relation to Christ, F. Hardy (entry 1161) in a review article. On messianism as a potential for movements rather than as overt mass movements, see L. Millones (entry 1195), J. H. Rowe (entry 1217), H. O. Urbano (entry 1232), also N. Wachtel (entries 17, 46, and (1239).

On the earliest notable revolt, Taqui Onqoy (or Ongo), Dance of Saint Guy, or Huaca cult of Tupac Amaru, 1565-72, see the depth study by M. Curatola (entries 1137 and 1139), P. Duviols (entry 1146), G. Kubler (entry 1182), F. de Armas Medina (entry 1116), the many items of L. Millones (entry 1195 for background), C. de Molina's contemporary account and its English translation (entry 1199), and R. T. Zuidema (entry 1242).

For other Indian revolts see W. Espinoza Soriano (entry 1150) on a Yanhuara movement in 1586, and F. Fuenzalida (entry 1151) on Santiago movements. On Juan Santos Atahualpa as Apo Inca or "Son of God" in 1742 see M. Castro Arenas (entry 1130) with comparison to Amazonian shamanism, new texts, and especially his conclusions on pp. 153-58; also A. Métraux (entry 1192).

For later Indian revolts see J. L. Klaiber (entries 1179 and 1180) for the eighteenth century onward, F. Pease (entry 1207) for the Lircay 1811 movement, B. Roedl (entry 1216) for a survey to 1952, K. Spalding (entry 1226), W. W. Stein (entry 1227) on the 1885 Atusparia rising. Of special interest is D. Menzel (entry 1190) on the nativistic reaction of the Ica people in the mid-sixteenth century against their imperial Inca overlords when the latter were weakened by the advent of the Spanish; this has important theoretical implications.

For recent movements see M. Sarkisyanz (entry 1218) on movements in 1915 and 1923 in comparison with popular movements in the Philippines, M. Vasallo (entry 1238) on the Rumi Maqui of 1915, and especially K. D. Scott (entry 1222) for the Lima area.

Peru

On the 1780-81 revolt of José Gabriel Condorcanqui, known as Tupac Amaru II, together with that of Tupac Tomás Catari, there is extensive literature which concentrates on the political and military aspects and says little about the religious dimensions or implications. No attempt has been made to include this material here, except for J. Hidalgo (entry 1165, with English summary) which is specifically on the messianic aspects. Otherwise there are incidental references in some of the other items here included.

There are two movements, among others, emerging from a Seventh Day Adventist mission milieu. Among the Campa people a movement emerged in 1928 after the S.D.A. Mission with its eschatological emphasis had been there about seven years; this movement rejected local culture in favor of forms associated with Western Christianity; see J. H. Bodley (entry 1118), also W. R. Read et al. (entry 1210) on two other ex-S.D.A. groups.

The largest movement from an S.D.A. background is the Israelitas del Nuevo Pacto Universal since the mid-1950s; this may well be the third largest non-Catholic group in Peru. See A. Cordoba (entry 1134) for a systematic account and theological interpretation based on direct experience, K. D. Scott (entries 1220, 1222, and 1224) for the most thorough recent study. The Israelitas themselves have published a good deal; see under Israelitas (entries 1172, and 1174 with English translation) for their rules, hymns, constitution, etc.

On folk Catholicism see A. M. M. Gorlitz (entry 1155) on forms that are somewhat equivalent to the new movements we survey.

The black population of Peru is very small and items concentrate on the cofradias among Afro-Peruvians, where the African elements seem to be submerged and of minor importance. See D. Cuche (entry 1135), C. Junquera (entry 1177), Z. Mendoza (entry 1189). For Indian equivalents see R. Vargas Ugarte (entry 1236, pp. 314-17) and R. Varon (entry 1237).

1110 Abad[lujan], Jesús. "Secta recluta esclavos en la Selva." *Crítica* (Lima, Miercoles) 1, no. 41 (1980): 10-11, illus.

   A Communist paper on the alleged exploitation of members of the Israelitas del Nuevo Pacto Universal in its "jungle" communities.

1111 Aguero, O. "El mileno en la Amazonia peruana: Los hermanos cruzados de Francisco de la Cruz." *Amazonia Peruana* (Lima) 6, no. 12 (1985): 133-45.

1112 Alvarido, Elisa. "Pastor descarriado." *Si* (Lima), 25 May 1987, pp. 60-62, illus.

1113 Ambrosio, Abel B. Paucar. "Associacion Evangelica de la Mision Israelita del Nuevo Pacto Universal." M.Th. thesis, Seminario Adventista Latinoamericano de Teologia (Peru), 1985, ca. 330 pp.

   History, beliefs, rites and attitudes of the churches.

1114 America [pseud.]. "Buscan al 'Rasputín' peruano que dijo ser 'enviado de Dios' y violó a una de sus creyentes." *Testigo* (Lima) 5 (16 December 1980): 4-5, 9, 16, illus.

   On the Israelita del Nuevo Pacto Universal.

1115 Aponte, Manuel Jesús Granados. "El movimiento religioso de los Israelitas del Nuevo Pacto Universal." Master's thesis (anthropology), Pontificia Universidad Católica del Perú (Lima), 1986, 80 pp.

   Includes founder, organization, religious content, relation to social situation and socioeconomic features.

1116 Armas Medina, Fernando de. "Christianización del Perú (1532-1600)." Seville: Escuela de Estudios Hispano-Americanos de Sevilla, 1953, 635 pp., illus.

   Chap. 19, "Reaccíon indígena"–including Manco Inca (pp. 567-70), the attack on idolatry (pp. 570-76), its survival (pp. 586-93); syncretism (pp. 593-99).

1117 Bodley, John H. *Development of an inter-tribal mission station in the Peruvian Amazon.* M.A. thesis, University of Oregon, 1967, 137 pp.

   Contains a fuller account of the Campa movement than his *Anthropos* article.

1118 Bodley, John H. "A transformative movement among the Campa of Eastern Peru." *Anthropos* 67, nos. 1-2 (1972): 220-28.

   Arawak-speaking Amazonian Indians' religious movement from 1928, rejecting traditional culture in favor of Christianity, after three centuries of resistance to Western influence; prompted by a new Seventh Day Adventist mission from 1921, with an eschatological advent emphasis.

1119 Campbell, Leon G. "Church and state in colonial Peru: The Bishop of Cuzco, and the Túpac Amaru rebellion of 1780." *Journal of Church and State* 22, no. 2 (Spring 1980): 251-70.

   The creole bishop Moscoso, with ties with Tupac Amaru, caught between all parties, and deported to Spain in 1784 to be tried for treason.

Peru

1120 Campos, Soledad. "Asomandonos al raro de la 'Misión Israelita Nuevo Pacto Universal.' Los 'enganchadores' de Jehova." *Unidad* (Lima), no. 692 (28 June 1979), pp. 6-7.

1121 Campos, Soledad. "La congregación de los Hijos de Israel." *El Comercio*, 27 July 1979, p. 10.
On the Israelitas del Nuevo Pacto Universal.

1122 Campos, Soledad. "Mas 'destapes' en la secta de los 'Israelitas.'" *Unidad* (Lima), no. 693 (5 July 1979), p. 6, illus.
More "revelations" concerning the Israelitas.

1123 Campos, Soledad. "'Enviado de Dios' era un maniático sexual." *La Crónica* (Lima), 29 August 1980, p. 14.
On founder of the Israelitas del Nuevo Pacto Universal.

1124 Campos, Soledad. "Estafa en Barridas." *Ultima Hora* (Lima) 19 (18 February 1969): 1, 3.
On the Israelitas del Nuevo Pacto Universal.

1125 Campos, Soledad. "No lea esto." *Testigo* (Lima) 7 (16 February 1981): 14-19.
Israelitas del Nuevo Pacto Universal.

1126 Campos, Soledad. "El pecado se boraa consangre." *Caretas* (Lima), no. 565 (13 August 1979), p. 5.
On sacrifice in the Israelitas del Nuevo Pacto Universal.

1127 Campos, Soledad. "Sacerdotes tienen prontuario policial: 'Mision Israelita.'" *Unidad* (Lima), no. 694 (13 July 1979), p. 10.

1128 Campos, Soledad. "El testimonio de Emiliano Quispe." *Unidad* (Lima), no. 706 (27 September 1979), p. 10.
On the Israelitas del Nuevo Pacto Universal.

1129 Carrion, Mario. "Fugitivo de la Tierra Prometida." *Pueblo Indio* 2, no. 8 (1986): 28-29, illus.
The testimony by an Israelitas ex-member, of exploitation by the movement.

1130 Castro Arenas, Mario. *La rebelíon de Juan Santos*. Lima: Carlos Milla Batres Editores, 1973, 167 pp. + 35 pp. of appended documents.

Treated as a messianic movement with a leader similar in some respects to Amazonian shamans; appendix with nine texts (one in facsimile) representing new materials. See especially pp. 153-58 (conclusion).

1131 Celestino, Olinda, and Meyers, Albert. *Las cofradias en el Perú: Región central*. Frankfort: Editorial Klaus D. Vervuert, 1981, 352 pp.
    Andean region – indigenous peoples' cofradias.

1132 CENCIRA. *Diagnóstico socio-económico, de las Cuencas de los Rios Palcazu Pichis*. Lima: Centro Nacional de Capitación e Investigación para la Reforma Agraria [CENCIRA], 1973.
    Pp. 64-69 report on the religious factor as explaining the success of a colonizing project (i.e., interior rural development) of the Israelites of the New Universal Covenant. See extract in K. D. Scott (entry 1222), pp. 51-52.

1133 Chaves, Julio César. *Tupac Amaru*. Buenos Aires: Editorial Asuncion, 1973 [1972 on cover], 318 pp., illus., bib.
    Part 3 (pp. 119-83), ideology; especially chap. 19 (pp. 143-49), "Ante la religion."

1134 Cordoba, Armando. "Asociacíon o Iglesia Evangélica de la Misíon Israelita del Nuevo Pacto Universal." Lima, [ca. 1978], 8 pp. Typescript.
    By the general secretary of Iglesia Evangélica Peruana, a graduate of Lima Evangelical Seminary: systematic account of Israelites of the New Universal Covenant, set in a theological framework, based on firsthand experience.

1135 Cuche, Denys. "La mort des dieux africains et les religions noires au Pérou." *Archives de Sciences des Religions*, no. 43 (1) [22] (January-March 1977): 77-91.
    On the reinterpretations of Catholicism by Africans in Peru, and their use of fraternities and associations; argues that African religious concepts have been submerged through syncretism, and survive only as minor magical notions.

1136 Cuche, Denys. *Poder blanco y resistencia negra en el Peru*. Lima: Ed. Instituto Nacional de Cultura, 1975.
    Includes cofradias among Afro-Peruvians.

Peru

1137 Curatola, Marco. "El culto de crisis del 'Moro Oncoy.'" *Scientia et Praxis. Revista de la Universidad de Lima*, no. 12 (June 1977), p. 54-62, illus.

1138 Curatola, Marco. *Introduzione allo studio di un culto di crisi: Taqui Ongo*. Doctoral dissertation, Universitá degli Studi di Genoa, Instituto de Etnologia, 1975.
Depth analysis of the 1560-70 movement: historical reconstruction of events, and the inner logic of this "crisis cult," with its specific religious aspects.

1139 Curatola, Marco. "Nito y milenarismo en los Andes: Del Taki Onqoy a Inkarrí. La vision de un pueblo invicto." *Allpanchis* (Cuzco) 10 (1977): 65-92.

1140 Davies, Thomas M[ockett], Jr. *Indian integration in Peru: A half century of experience, 1900-1948*. Lincoln: University of Nebraska Press, 1974, 204 pp.
Pp. 30-31, the 1866 Altiplano revolt, "nativistic, with millenarian overtones," as cited by D. D. Gow (entry 1156), p. 126.

1141 Directorio Evangelico. *Directorio evangélico, 1981-1982*. Lima: Consejo Latinamericano de Iglesias, 1982.
See pp. 34-35, 47-58, 66-68 for independent churches.

1142 Dobyns, Henry E., and Doughty, Paul L. *Peru: A cultural history*. Latin American Histories. New York: Oxford University Press, 1976, 336 pp., bib. (pp. 274-95).
Pp. 105-13, Peruvian Catholic saints and the cults, festivals, and brotherhoods that developed among mestizos, Indians, and blacks; pp. 133-34, Tupac Amaru II's millenarian movement; pp. 135-37, peasant and millenarian leaders as later important popular symbols.

1143 Duviols, Pierre. *La destruccíon de las religiones andinas (Durante la conquita y la colonia)*. Serie de Historia General, 9. Mexico: Universidad Nacional Autónoma de México, 1977.
Includes Taqui Onqoy.

1144 Duviols, Pierre. "L'Inca Garcilaso de la Vega, interprète humaniste de la religion incaïque." *Diogène* (Paris) 47 (1964): 39-54. English version. "The Inca Garcilaso de la Vega, humanist interpreter of the Inca religion." *Diogenes* 47 (1964): 36ff.

An Inca's attempts to redeem Inca institutions allied to Spanish humanism – thus suggesting that Inca religion was a "higher" religion rather than primal. This is significant for D. Menzel's article (entry 1190) on the Ica reaction to the Inca. Garcilaso de la Vega was half royal Inca, half Spanish, and a notable sixteenth-century historian of the Inca. See also entry 1145.

1145 Duviols, Pierre. "Un inédit de Cristóbal de Albornoz: La instrucción paradescubir todas las guacas del Pirú y sus camayos y haziendas." *Journal de la Société des Américanistes* (Paris) 56, no. 1 (1967): 7-39.
Good documentary information on Inca religion by the suppressor of the Taqui Onqoy movement, although little on the latter.

1146 Duviols, Pierre. *La lutte contre les religions autochtones dans le Pérou colonial: "L'extirpation de l'idolatrie" entre 1532 et 1660.* Travaux de l'Institut Français d'Études Andines, 13. Lima: The Institute, 1971, 428 pp., bib., ethnic map.
Pp. 112-22, 346-7, a nativistic messianic revolt, Taqui Onqoy, against the Spanish and Catholicism in central Peru, 1565-72, with ecstatic dancing and possession.

1147 Duviols, Pierre. "Sur le système religieux des *Comentarios reales de los Incas.*" *Annales de la Faculté de Lettres d'Aix* (Aix-en-Provence) 37 [1966?]: 227-41.
Fuller development of 1964 article presenting Inca religion as a "higher" form superseding earlier primal cults.

1148 Duviols, Pierre. "Un symbolisme de l'occupation, de l'aménagement et de l'exploitation de l'espace: Le monolithe *'huanca'* et sa fonction dans les Andes pre-Hispaniques." *Homme* (Paris) 19, no. 2 (1979): 7-31, bib.; English summary.
The continuation of the *huanca* cult (distinguished from *huaca*) in Peru in the seventeenth century; functions of the monoliths.

1149 Espinoza, Enrique. "La secta Israel del Nuevo Pacto Universal, un movimiento mesiánico peruano." *Revista Teológica Limensa* 18, no. 1 (1984): 47-81.
An anthropological enquiry.

1150 Espinoza Soriano, Waldemar. "Un movimiento religioso de libertad y salvación nativista Yanhuara – 1596." In *Ideologia mesiánico del mundo andino*, edited by Juan Ossio A.. Lima: Ignacio Prado Pastor, 1973, pp. 85-101, bib. (pp. 143-52).

Peru

1151 Fuenzalida, Fernando. "Santiago y el Wamani: Aspectos de un culto pagano." *Cuadernos de Antropología* (Lima) 5, no. 8 (1966) [i.e., 1968]: 118-65.

1152 Gade, Daniel W. "Coping with cosmic terror: The earthquake cult in Cuzco, Peru." *American Benedictine Review* 21, no. 2 (1970): 218-23.
    The "Lord-of-the-Earthquake" cult beginning in a major quake in 1650, revived in similar crises in 1707, 1834, and 1950, and contributing an annual procession to the Holy Week rites.

1153 Gamonal-Ataucusi, Ezechiel. "Carta de Misión Israelita." *Unidad* (Lima), no. 692 (28 June 1979), p. 6.
    A letter from the founder of Israelitas del Nuevo Pacto Universal.

1154 Gavelan, Luis Castro, and Rengifo, Rousseau Paredes. [Series of six illustrated articles on the Israelitas]. *Diario La Republica* (Lima), 21 April 1986, pp. 14-15; 22 April 1986, pp. 18-19; 23 April 1986, pp. 20-21; 24 April 1986, pp. 20-21; 25 April 1986, pp. 18-19; 26 April 1986, Epilogue.
    Charges the movement with enslaving Indian peasants, growing marijuana, harboring false prophets, etc.

1155 Gorlitz, A. M. Mariscotti de. "Der Kult der Pachamama und die autochthone Religiosität in den Zentral und Nördlichen Süd-Anden." *Zeitschrift für Missionswissenschaft und Religionswissenschaft* 62, no. 2 (1978): 81-100; English summary.
    The earth-goddess cult, its sanctuaries, rituals, festivals, and shamanistic officiants; other autochthonous cults and the assimilation of all such cults to the cult of Mary and Catholic Christianity without losing their religious structures and dualistic world view. Not "new movements" but serve as the local equivalent.

1156 Gow, David Drummond. *The gods and social change in the High Andes.* Ph.D. dissertation (anthropology), University of Wisconsin (Madison), 1976, 309 pp., maps.
    On the ideological support for peasant resistance to tyranny provided by primal religion, and especially by a christianized version of the cult of Inkarri, Andean messianic culture hero. (chap. 6, pp. 112-37). Peasant movements in Andean history–includes Taqui Onqoy (pp. 114-17), Juan Santos Atahualpa (pp. 117-20), Tupac Amaru (pp. 120-26); chap. 8 (pp. 177ff.), Andean history through myth–especially Andean concept of time: includes Andean Joachism (pp. 187-92) on

the myths of Inkarri; chap. 10, the Pilgrimage of El Senor de Qoyllur Rit'i (pp. 214-38) as a syncretism.

1157 Gow, David D[rummond]. "The roles of Christ and Inkarrí in Andean religion." *Journal of Latin American Lore* 6, no. 2 (1980): 279-96, bib.

1158 Gow, David D[rummond]. "Simbolo y protesta: Movimientos redentores en Chiapas y en los Andes Peruanos." *América Indígena* 39, no. 1 (1979): 47-80.
    Mexican and Peruvian Indian movements compared.

1159 Grandos, Manuel, and Gonzalez Del Rio, Miguel. "Sinaipicchu: Entre oriente y occidente, el arco iris incaico." *Caretas* (Lima), 8 September 1986, illus. pp. 57-60, 72.
    On the Israelitas del Nuevo Pacto Universal, based on an anthropologist's information.

1160 Guariglia, Guglielmo. *Prophetismus und Heilserwartungs-Bewegungen als Völkerkundliches und religionsgeschichtliches Problem.* Vienna: F. Berger, 1959, xvi + 332 pp., maps, bib.
    Pp. 189-90, Atahualpa; p. 190, Condorcanqui.

1161 Hardy, Friedhelm. "Despair and hope of the defeated–Andean messianism." *Religious Studies* 11, no. 2 (1975): 257-64.
    Review article on J. Ossio A., *Ideología mesiánica del mundo andino* (entry 1203). Suggests Andean movements have a "messianic potential" rather than explicit messianic expectations, which have not been developed under Christian influence.

1162 Harner, M. J. "Inca is coming: A messianistic religion among the Conibo-Shipibo Indians." *Proceedings, 36th International Congress of Americanists, 1964 (Barcelona, etc.).* Seville, 1966.
    Summary of paper on a movement with "cargo" hopes, on the Ucalayi River.

1163 Hemani, Enrique Sanchez. "Queman becerro en homenaje a Jehová: Israelitas del Nuevo Pacto Universal celebran Pascua como en Sagradas Escrituras." *Diario La Republica* (Lima), 24 April 1984, pp. 15, 17, illus.

1164 Hemming, John. *The conquest of the Incas.* London: Macmillan, 1970, 641 pp., illus., bib.

Peru

P. 310, Taqui Onqoy, pp. 592-93, references; table of Tupac
Amaru Inca and descendants; a classic study of the period.

1165 Hidalgo [Lehuede], Jorge A. "Amarus y cataris: Aspectos mesiánicos
de la rebelión indígena de 1781 en Cusco, Chayanta, La Paz y Arica."
Revista Chungara (Arica, Universidad de Tarapaca Instituto de
Antropologia) 10 (March 1983): 117-38; English summary.
Nativistic expectations in the General Rebellion of 1781, hoping
for reversal of the cosmological order introduced by the Spaniards, but
with European doctrinal elements in the millenarian prophecies and
symbols.

1166 Hoggarth, Leslie. "Primal religion in relation to Romans 1." *Bulletin of
the Evangelical Fellowship for Missionary Studies* (London), 1969, p. 1.
On the Inca imperial high god religion imposed on conquered
peoples along with their existing cults, citing John Rowe (entry 1217)
as authority.

1167 Huaman, Santiago A. *La primeria historia del movimiento pentecostal
en el Perú*. Lima: Editorial e Imprenta "El Gallo de Oro," 1982.
Names at least fifteen independent Pentecostal churches, and
refers to others.

1168 Huertas V[allejos], L[orenzo]. "Los sacerdotes indigenas de Canta,
Chancay, y Cajatambo en el siglo XVII." *Campesion: Revista
Cuatrimestral de Estudios Sociales* (Lima) 2, no. 3 (1970): 57-69.
The *camaquenas* worshippers movement of the later seventeenth
century and earlier eighteenth century.

1169 Huertas Vallejos, Lorenzo. "Testimonios referentes al movimiento de
Túpac Amaru II: 1784-1812." *Allpanchis Phuturinga* (Cuzco) 11-12
(1978): 7-16.
The spread and persistence of Tupac Amaru's message.

1170 Israelitas del Nuevo Pacto Universal. [Hymns.] Lima: The Church,
n.d., 2 pp.

1171 Israelitas del Nuevo Pacto Universal. *Lucero de la mañana* (Lima) 1,
no. 1- (December 1985-). [Irregular, approx. 20 pp.]
A sophisticated, well-produced magazine of general interest that
presents the teachings of the movement; with color cover.

1172 Israelitas del Nuevo Pacto Universal. "Reglamento interno de las Iglesias de Lima Metropolitana y a nivel nacional de la Asociación." Lima: Israelitas del Nuevo Pacto Universal, [1978?], 4 pp. Mimeo.
Constitution and rules drawn up in January 1978.

1173 Israelitas del Nuevo Pacto Universal. *Los Diez Mandamientos de la Ley de Dios, por Ezequiel Atacusi Gamonal.* Lima: Edit. Asencias, 1980, 36 pp., illus., map.

1174 Israelitas del Nuevo Pacto Universal. *Mandamientos y Salmos.* Lima: Asociacion Evangelica de la Mision Israelita del Nuevo Pacto Universal, 1980, 22 pp. English version. *Psalms and Commandments, Israel Congregation of Jehovah.* Lima: Edit. Asencios, n.d., 30 pp.
Some Psalms, and the Ten Commandments as elaborated and given biblical support by the founder, Ezequiel Ataucusi Gamonal.

1175 Israelitas del Nuevo Pacto Universal. *Santos Salmos: Himnos coros del alto monte de Israel.* Lima: Asociacion Evangelica de la Mision Israelita del Nuevo Pacto Universal, n.d. [1984?], 168 pp.
Hymn-book of the Israelites of the New Universal Covenant.

1176 "'Israelitas' sadicos y pologamos: Santones son el mismo Diablo." *Selva Central* (La Merced, Junín) 1, no. 6 (November-December 1979): 10.
On the Israelitas del Nuevo Pacto Universal.

1177 Junquera, Carlos. "Pervivencia de las religiones africanas en Peru." *Ibero-Amerikanisches Archiv*, n.s. 10, no. 2 (1984): 175-88; English summary.
Cofradias as the means for Africans to reinterpret Catholicism and establish their own identity; contemporary peasant religion, a syncretism defined as black rather than African.

1178 Kapsoli E., Wilfredo. *Los movimientos campesinos en el Perú, 1879-1965.* Lima: Delva Editores, 1977, 308 pp.

1179 Klaiber, Jeffrey L. "Religion y revolucion en los Andes en siglio XIX." *Historica* 1, no. 1 (1977): 93-111.

1180 Klaiber, Jeffrey L. *Religion and revolution in Peru, 1824-1976.* Notre Dame: University of Notre Dame Press, 1977, 259 pp.
Pp. 50-69 (and notes pp. 210-15), Indian uprisings from the eighteenth century; pp. 87-91, popular religiosity, with example of a

Peru

movement created around a young girl, and the churches' response. By a Jesuit.

1181 Klumpp, Kathleen M. "El retorno del Inca: Una expressión ecuatoriana de la ideología mesiánica andina." *Cuadernos de Historia y Arqueología* (Guayaquil, Casa de la Cultura Ecuatoriana, Núcleo del Guayas) 44 (1976): 99-135, bib.
Messianism in the Andes region includes belief in the return of the Inca, and this was involved in the incipient revolt of 1666.

1182 Kubler, G. "The Quechua in the colonial world." In *Handbook of South American Indians,* edited by J. H. Steward. Vol. 2. Bureau of American Ethnology Bulletin 143. Washington, D.C.: Smithsonian Institution, 1946, pp. 331-410.
Pp. 406-7, Tupac Amaru's *huaca* cult, or Taqui Onqoy.

1183 Lassegue-Moleres, Juan Bautista. "Fundación laical y movimiento del Taki-Onkoy: Parinacochas, diocesis del Cusco, 1567." Paper presented at 44th International Congress of Americanists, Manchester, 1982. Digest in *Abstracts of the Congress,* pp. 309-10.

1184 Lehnertz, Jay. "Juan Santos: Primitive rebel on the Campa frontier, 1742-1752." In *Actas y Memorias del XXXIX Congreso Internacional de Americanistas, Lima, 1970.* Vol. 4. Lima: Instituto de Estudios Peruanos, 1972, pp. 111-26, bib.
The Campa revolt, although not a nativistic revival, led to reversion to a pre-Spanish situation, in spite of its outward basic Catholicism; mostly on the personal history and military campaigns of Juan Santos.

1185 Lewin, Boléslao. *La rebelión de Túpac Amaru y los orígines de la independencia de Hispanoamérica.* Buenos Aires: Editorial Claridat, 1943. 2d ed. Librería Hachette, 1957. 3d ed. Sociedad Editora Latino Americana, 1967, 963 pp., illus., bib.
An important, detailed study, including the repercussions in Argentina, Ecuador, Venezuela, and Panama; pp. 717-902, extracts from unpublished sources.

1186 Loayza, Francisco A. *Juan Santos, el invincible.* Lima: Editorial D. Miranda, 1942, xv + 246 pp.

1187 Lopez-Baralt, Mercedes. "Millenarism as liminality: An interpretation of the Andean myth of Inkarri." *Point of Contact* (New York) 2, no. 2 (Spring 1979): 65-82, bib.

Reproduces several versions of the myth of the return of the Inca, embodying millenarian hopes as found in Andean messianic movements.

1188 Mar, José Matos, et al. *Proyecto de estudio de los movimientos campesinas en el Peru desde fines del siglo xviii hasta nuestros dias*. Lima: Instituto de Estudios Peruanos, 1967.

P. 20 on the 1866 Altiplano nativistic revolt, cited by D. D. Gow, *The Gods and social change in the High Andes* (entry 1156), p. 127.

1189 Mendoza, Zoila. "Las cofradías en el Perú." *Allpanchis Phuturinga* (Cuzco) 17, no. 20 (1982): 291-94.

Indian Brotherhoods used as a pastoral strategy within the Catholic Church.

1190 Menzel, Dorothy. "Archaism and revival on the south coast of Peru." In *Men and Cultures*, edited by A. F. C. Wallace. Philadelphia: University of Pennsylvania Press, 1960, pp. 596-600.

Pp. 597-600, the Ica revival of pottery styles (late Ica pottery in early Colonial period) as chief manifestation of a "nativistic" reaction to the Inca occupation. An example of the use of archaeology in discovering cultural history, including religious movements. Note that the revival emanated from an encounter with a much more sophisticated Indian imperialist culture (Inca), and took advantage of the collapse of the Inca empire *after* the advent of the Spanish in 1540, and *before* effective Spanish control was established in 1570.

1191 Métraux, Alfred. *Les Incas*. Paris: Éditions du Seuil, 1962. English translation. *The Incas*. London: Studio Vista, 1965, 192 pp., illus.

Pp. 172-74, the Tupac Amaru revolt of 1780 in Peru, a general popular account, with brief mention of its messianic features; also other similar earlier and later revolts to 1815.

1192 Métraux, Alfred. "A Quechua messiah in eastern Peru." *American Anthropologist* 44, no. 4 (1942): 721-25.

Santos Atahualpa, 1742.

1193 Millones [Santa Gadea], Luis. "La 'idolatría de Santiago': Un nuevo documento para el estudio de la evangelizacíon del Perú." *Cuadernos*

Peru

del Seminario de Historia (Lima, Instituto Riva-Agüero), no. 7 (1964), pp. 31-33.

Reproduces a short section of a 1656 letter from the bishop of Huamanga to the king, mentioning the preaching of a native prophet claiming to be Santiago; together with notes on acculturation among the Indians.

1194 Millones [Santa Gadea], Luis. *Las informaciones de Cristóbal de Albornoz: Documentos para el estudio del Taki Onqoy.* CIDOC: Sondeos, 79. Cuernavaca, Mexico: Centro Intercultural de Documentacion, 1971, unpaged.

The documents on which his studies of Taqui Onqoy have been based.

1195 Millones [Santa Gadea], Luis. "Introducción al estudio de las idolatrías." *Aportes* (Paris), no. 4 (April 1967), pp. 47-82.

Describes the religious situation in which movements like Taqui Onqoy emerged – both the kind of Christianity and the current forms of Inca religion involved; a paper at the XXXVII Congreso de Americanistas, 1966, summarizing his doctoral dissertation.

1196 Millones [Santa Gadea], Luis. "Un movimiento nativista del siglo XVI: El Taki Onqoy." *Revista Peruana de Cultura* (Lima) 3 (1964): 134-140. Reprinted in *Ideología mesiánico del mundo andino*, edited by J. M. Ossio A. Lima: Edicion de Ignacio Prado Pastor, 1973, pp. 83-94, bib.

Refers to the discovery of documents by Cristóbal de Albornoz, who suppressed the Taqui Onqoy movement. See entry 1194.

1197 Millones [Santa Gadea], Luis. "Observaciones sobre el Taqui Onqoy." *Historia y Cultura* (Lima) 1, no. 1 (1965): 137-40. Reprint. "Nuevas aspectos del Taki Onqoy." In *Ideología mesiánica del mundo andino*, edited by J. M. Ossio A. Lima: Ignacio Prado Pastor, 1973, pp. 97-101, bib., notes.

The messianic anti-Spanish movement, 1565-72, repressed by Cristóbal de Albornoz, but with continuing influence into the seventeenth century.

1198 Millones [Santa Gadea], Luis. "Las religiones nativas del Perú: Recuento y evaluacíon de su estudio." *Bulletin de l'Institut Français d'Études Andines* (Lima) 8, nos. 1-2 (1978): 35-48, bib.

Annotated bibliography on Andean religion 1900-1977, in English, Spanish, French, or German, as a guide to Andean studies.

1199 Molina (of Cuzco), Christobal de. *Relación de las fabulas y ritos de los Incas*. 1573. Reprint. Edited by H. H. Urteaga and C. A. Romero. Coll. Libr. Doc. Ref. Hist. Perú, vol. 1. Lima: Sanmarti, 1916, pp. 93-103. Reprint. Buenos Aires, 1959. English translation. *The Fables and Rites of the Incas*. Translated by C. R. Markham. Cambridge: Hakluyt Society, 1st series, vol. 48, 1873, 220 pp.

Pp. 93-103 (1916), revival of *huaca* worship, 1565-72, by Incas-Quechuas, under Juan Santos Atuahalpa; pp. 59-64 (1873 volume), Taqui Onqoy Inca cult of 1565-72 – a contemporary account.

1200 Ortiz Rescaniere, Alejandro. *De Adaneva a Inkarrí: Una visión indígena del Perú*. Lima: Instituto Nacional de Investigación y Desarollo de la Educación (INIDE), Subdireción de Publicaciones y Material Didáctico, 1973, 189 pp.

Mythic themes with original texts on Peruvian native cosmology, revealing syncretism with Christian elements and messianic features.

1201 Ossio, Juan M. "Myth and history: The seventeenth century chronicle of Guaman Poma de Ayala." In *Text and context: The social anthropology of tradition*, edited by R. K. Jain. Philadelphia: Institute for the Study of Human Issues, 1977, pp. 51-93.

P. 80, Taqui Onqoy movement as similar to the aims of Guaman Parma, a Peruvian Indian who also sought a return to order after the cataclysm of the Spaniard's arrival, by total separation from them.

1202 Ossio, Juan M. "Rural society and the roots of insurgency." Paper presented at Pontificia Universidad Católica del Peru, [1987?], 22 pp. Mimeo.

Messianism as ideological framework for most peasant movements in Peruvian history, with Partido Comunista Peruano (or "Sendero Luminoso") and Israelitas del Nuevo Pacto Universal as representative examples.

1203 Ossio A., Juan M., ed. *Ideología mesiánica del mundo andino*. Lima: Edicion de Ignacio Prado Pastor, 1973, xiv + 476 pp.

See under L. Millones [Santa Gadea] (entry 1197) and N. Wachtel (entry 1239). Other articles related in a broad way to messianism and using the concepts of M. Eliade and C. Lévi-Strauss suggest that this is derived more from cyclical ideas in Andean primal religions than from Christian influences.

1204 Pallermo, Ernesto "¿Cual Camino? Una orientacion evangelica sobre las sectas falsas." *El Heraldo del Ando* 1, no. 1 (1984): 1, 7-9, 12-13.

Peru

A study of the Israelites of the New Universal Covenant by a pastor of the Peruvian Evangelical Church, with theological criticism.

1205 Paredes, M. A. "El levantamiento campesino del 'Rumi Maqui' (Azángaro 1915)." *Campesino. Revista Cuatrimestrial de Estudios Sociales* (Lima) 2, no. 3 (1970): 43-51.

1206 Pax y Guini, Melchor de. *Guerva separatista. Rebeliones de Indios en Sur América. La sublevación de Túpac Amaru, cronica. Con Apostillas a la obra. . . . por Luis Antonio Equiguren.* 2 vols. Lima, 1952.
By the viceregal secretary, in the 1780s, giving the Spanish viewpoints and much documentation–a basic source.

1207 Pease G[arcia] Y., Franklin. "Un movimiento mesíanico en Lircay, Huancavelica (1811)." *Revista del Museo Nacional* (Lima) 40 (1974): 221-52.
A peasant movement centred upon Inkarri, linked with St. James in a messianic way.

1208 Perez Huayta, Florentino. *Israelitas del Nuevo Pacto, una ficcion.* N.p.: n.d., 91 pp.
By an Assemblies of God pastor.

1209 Piel, Jean. "À propos d'un soulèvement rural péruvien au début du vingtième siècle: Tocroyoc (1921)." *Revue d'Histoire Moderne et Contemporaine* 14, no. 4 (1967): 375-405.
Pp. 396, 403, the Rumi Maqui movement of 1913-25, and messianism in Indian culture evident again in 1921.

1210 Read, William R., and Johnson, Harmon A. *Latin American church growth.* Grand Rapids, Mich.: W. E. Eerdman, 1969, 421 pp.
P. 114, two groups separated from the Seventh Day Adventist missions in Peru–the Israelitas in department of Junin, and the Reformed Adventists; pp. 249-52, various forms of Spiritism, especially in Brazil.

1211 Reina Loli, M. S. "Causas del movimiento campesino de 1885." *Campesino Revista Cuatrimestral de Estudios Sociales* (Lima) 1, no. 2 (1969): 31-39.
The rising under Pedro Atusparia, with messianic aspects.

1212 Rengifo, Antonio. "Esbozo biographico de Ezequiel Urviola y Rivero." In *Los movimientos campesinos en el Perú, 1879-1965: Ensayos*, edited by Wilfredo Kapsoli E. Lima: Delva Editores, 1977, pp. 179-209.

And see editor's identification of 1919-30 as a period of millenarian movements – pp. 179, 186-87, 190-209 are the most relevant.

1213 Rodriguez, Antonio. "Una justicia que no llego." *Unidad* (Lima), no. 705 (September 1979), p. 10.

On the Israelitas del Nuevo Pacto Universal.

1214 Rodriguez, Antonio. "Una poderosa secta explotadora." *Unidad* (Lima), no. 688 (31 May 1979), p. 8.

On the Israelitas del Nuevo Pacto Universal.

1215 Rodriguez, Antonio. "Tres 'Hermanos' en espera de justicia." *Unidad* (Lima), no. 695 (18 July 1979), p. 5.

On the Israelitas del Nuevo Pacto Universal.

1216 Roedl, Bohumír. "Indiánská povstani v andské oblasti Jizní Ameriky" [Indian rebellions in the Andes region of South America]. *Ceskoslovenská Etnografie* 10, no. 1 (1962): 57-65; German summary, pp. 64-65.

Rebellions from the sixteenth century, and the four stages in the movements from 1885 to 1952.

1217 Rowe, John H[owland]. "El movimiento nacional Inca del siglo XVIII." *Revista Universitaria del Cuzco*, no. 107 (2d semester 1954), pp. 17-47. English translation. "The Incas under Spanish colonial institutions." *Hispanic American Historical Review* 37 (1957): 155-99, bib. (pp. 191-99).

Pp. 183-86, Inca religion (and Pachkuti's state cult), the Taqui Onqoy revolt (p. 184) and other revolts; pp. 186-91, the reasons conversion to Christianity failed.

1218 Sarkisyanz, Manuel. "Longing for lost primeval bliss as revolutionary expectation on both sides of the Pacific: Millennialism in crisis in Peru and the Philippines." Paper presented at European Regional Conference, New Ecumenical Research Association, 21-25 June 1984, in Switzerland, at Weggis. 16 pp. Computer printout.

Pp. 6-8: Peru ("Rumi Maqui" of 1915; 1923 "Incaic Republic" millennialism; 1928-29 revolution similarly interpreted); pp. 9-13:

Peru

Philippines (Bonifacio, Rizalistas, Colorums and Katipunan, and Folk-Marxists).

1219 Sarkisyanz, Manuel. *Von Beben in den Anden: Propheten des undianseken Aufbruchs in Peru*. Munich: Dianus-Trikont Verlag, 1985, pp. 6-14, 206-7.

Includes the Peruvian part of his paper on millennialism in the Philippines and in Peru (entry 1218).

1220 Scott, Kenneth David. *Israelitas del Nuevo Pacto*. Lima: N.p., 1980, [13 pp.] Also in *Ensayos Ocasionales* (Lima, Seminario Evangélico de Lima), no. 806 (1980), pp. 7-13.

Pp. 1-9, an outline of the origin; the founder, Ezequiel; and the beliefs of the Israelites of the New Universal Covenant; pp. 9-13, characteristics of false sects – not specially related to this movement.

1221 Scott, Kenneth D[avid]. *Israelites of the New Universal Covenant – Peru*. M. Litt. dissertation (religion in primal societies), University of Aberdeen, 1981, 162 pp., illus. Spanish translation. *Israelitas del Nuevo Pacto Uneversalis*. Translated by Lida Perales Sáenz. Asociacion Evangelica de la Mision Israelita del Nuevo Pacto Universal, 1984, 96 pp., illus.

1222 Scott, Kenneth D[avid]. "Latin America: Peruvian new religious movements." *Missiology* 13, no. 1 (1985): 45-59.

An up-to-date survey of Peruvian movements, especially in the post-Protestant missions period, and around Lima, with Israelitas del Nuevo Pacto Universal as the case study.

1223 Scott, Kenneth D[avid]. "New religious movements in Peru." *Latin American Evangelist*, January-March 1987, pp. 14-15, illus.

Includes Crusada Cristiana para Naciones from 1979; the Israelitas; Yo Soy ("I Am") – ex-Catholic charismatics; and recommended Christian attitudes towards such new movements.

1224 Scott, Kenneth David. *Privileged Peru: The Israelites of the New Universal Covenant*. Ph.D. dissertation (religious studies), University of Aberdeen, 1989, 462 pp., illus., maps.

The major study of an important group, with good illustrations. By a missionary-lecturer in the Evangelical Seminary of Lima.

1225 Sharon, Douglas Gregory. *The symbol system of a north Peruvian Shaman*. Ph.D. dissertation (anthropology), University of California, Los Angeles, 1974, 363 pp.

A *curandero*, or folkhealer, Eduardo Calderón Palomino, with a functional syncretism of Indian and Christian religious beliefs that is also representative of shamanist practices and cosmologies widely distributed in Latin America; also use of a hallucinogenic cactus.

1226 Spalding, Karen. "The colonial Indian: Past and future research perspectives." *Latin American Research Review* 7, no. 1 (Spring 1972): 47-76.

Pp. 62-65 (and notes pp. 71-72) on the religious aspect of revolts against the Spanish.

1227 Stein, William W. "Myth and ideology in a nineteenth century Peruvian peasant uprising." *Ethnohistory* 29, no. 4 (1982): 237-61, bib.

On the Atusparia rising in 1885 – under Pedro Atusparia, in a deteriorating economic situation; presents the peasant view of the event and of society and history as expressed in myths, with messianic and redemptive elements, especially pp. 250-56.

1228 Stern, Steve J. "El Taki Onqoy: La sociedad andina (Huamanga, siglo XVI)." *Allpanchis Phuturinga* (Cuzco) 16, no. 19 (1982): 49-77.

1229 Tellechea Idigoras, José Ignacio. "Lord of the Miracles: Popular religion in Peru." *LADOC* (Lima) 8, no. 5 (1978): 38-49.

A religious procession, the cult of Lord of the Miracles – its form, and various interpretations of the cult; its future is evaluated, as an example of popular culture under threat from secularization.

1230 "El testimonio del Emiliano Quispe." *Unidad* (Lima), no. 706 (27 September 1979), p. 10.

On the Israelitas del Nuevo Pacto Universal.

1231 Tineo, Segunda Miguel de. "NERMS: Los Israelitas del Nuevo Pacto Universal." Monograph for Licentiate in Missiology, Seminario Evangelico de Lima, Escuela Superior de Teologia, 1986, 26 pp.

1232 Urbano, Henrique Osvaldo. "Millénarisme et trinité chrétienne. Quelques notes sur le discours millénariste dans les Andes." *Les Cahiers du Centre de Recherche en Sociologie Religieuse* (Quebec) 1, no. 1 (1977): 133-44.

Peru

1233 Urbano, Henrique Osvaldo. "Simbología religiosa y conflictos sociales en el Sur Andino." *Allpanchis Phuturinga* (Cuzco) 6 (April 1974): 161-77.
Part 1 on early Christian-Andean contacts; pp. 171-72, Taqui Onqoy, pp. 173-76, the role of *Pago* in passive resistance.

1234 Urquiga, José. "Indios: Puno 1916." Lima: Universidad Nacional Mayor de San Marcos, Seminario de Historia Rural Andina, 1916. Mimeo reprint. 1977, 60 pp.
The Puno revolt of 1915, and the Rumi Maqui movement.

1235 Valcarcel [Esparza], Carlos Daniel. *Tupac Amaru, precursor de la independencia*. Lima: Universidad Mayor de San Marcos, Dirección Universitaria de Biblioteca y Publicaciones, 1977, 201 pp., bib., illus.
His views restated – on the rebellion as mainly a social upheaval seeking justice for Indians rather than independence, although it contributed to the latter.

1236 Vargas Ugarte, Rubén. *Historia de la Iglesia en el Perú (1511-1568)*. Lima: Imprenta Santa Maria, 1953, 422 pp.
Vol. 1 of a Jesuit history: pp. 114-19, Taqui Onqoy, and the destruction of Inca "idols"; pp. 314-17, cofradias.

1237 Varon, Rafael. "Cofradías de indios y poder local en el Perú colonial: Huaraz, siglo XVII." *Allpanchis Phuturinga* (Cuzco) 17, no. 20 (1982): 127-46.

1238 Vasallo, Manuel. "Rumi Maqui y la nacionalidad quechua." *Allpanchis Phuturinga* (Cuzco) 11-12 (1978): 123-27.
The Rumi Maqui ("Hand of Stone") movement of 1915, seeking to restore the ancient Inca state through a crisis cult in the Puno region. Presents signed documents suggesting avoidance of publicity by local people.

1239 Wachtel, Nathan. "Rebeliones y Milenarismo." In *Ideología mesiánica del mundo andino*, edited by J. M. Ossio A. Lima: Edicion de Ignacio Prado Pastor, 1973, pp. 105-42, bib., extensive source notes.

1240 Wachtel, Nathan. "Structuralisme et histoire: À propos del l'organisation sociale de Cuzco." *Annales: Economies, Sociétés, Civilisations* (Paris) 21, no. 1 (1966): 71-94, diagrams.
Background for the revolt of Taqui Onqoy, 1565-72, which used traditional concepts in a new way, with a new meaning. For a long

extract from p. 89, see P. Duviols (entry 1146) p. 117, also quotation from p. 92, where the new or millennial features are explicitly discussed.

1241 Wistrand, Lila. "Desorganización y revitalización de los Cashibo." *América Indígena* 23, no. 3 (1968): 611-18.
 The Cashibo in Central Peru – on a revitalization movement about 1925-30 led by "Simon Bolivar," which failed and led to a situation worse than before; of theoretical interest.

1242 Zuidema, R. T[om]. "Observaciónes sobre el Taqui Onqoy." *Historia y Cultura* (Lima) 1, no. 1 (1965): 137.
 Suggests that Taqui Onqoy expressed pre-Hispanic messianic beliefs.

Uruguay

Since the population is some 90% European, and there are virtually no Indians, movements of our kind would be confined to the mulattos (only some 50,000) and the black population (about 10,000). There is little literature on these and what there is suggests continuing cultural phenomena, such as dances and festivals, rather than Afro-Uruguayan movements. The three items included are on these themes and therefore somewhat marginal to our main concerns; see M. Bottaro (entry 1243), and I. Pereda Valdés (entries 1247 and 1248).

Umbanda is reported to have begun spreading from Brazil into Uruguay during the early 1970s, and Pentecostalism is present. We may therefore expect to find indigenous forms of these appearing among the nonwhite population in the future.

1243 Bottaro, Marcelino. "Rituals and Candombes." In *Negro*, edited by N. Cunard. London: Nancy Cunard at Wishart & Co., 1931-33, pp. 519-22.
 Negro dramatic dances and rituals.

1244 Carvalho-Neto, Paulo de. "Apuntes críticos sobre algunas fuentes antropológicas afro-uruguayas." *Boletín Bibliográfico de las Cienciais del Hombre* (Montevideo) 1 (1964): 16 pp.
 Lists and discusses studies of the Negro in Uruguay: by a Brazilian anthropologist.

1245 Carvalho-Neto, Paulo de. *El Negro uruguayo: Hasta la abolición*. Quito, Ecuador: Editorial Universitaria, 1965, 345 pp., illus., bib.

Uruguay

A thorough study, historical and anthropological, up to 1960; second part is an anthology.

1246 Moro, America, and Mercedes, Ramirez. *La macumba y otros cultos afro-brasileños en Montevideo*. Montevideo: Ed. de la Banda Oriental, 1981.

1247 Pereda Valdés, Ildefonso. *El Negro en el Uruguay, pasado y presente*. *Revista del Instituto Histórico y Geográfico del Uruguay* (Montevideo) 25, 1965, 301 pp., illus., maps.
    A detailed, well-documented study: pp. 97-104, religious practices of Negroes; pp. 143-48, their folklore; pp. 149-60, their dances (Candombe, etc.).

1248 Pereda Valdés, Ildefonso. "El Negro Rio Platense. Razas y pueblos africanos trasplantados al continente Americano ... costumbres y rituales." In *Les Afro-Américains*. Mémoires de l'Institut Français d'Afrique Noire, 17. Dakar: IFAN, 1952, pp. 257-61.
    Pp. 259-61 on syncretistic cultic practices.

1249 Pereda Valdés, Ildefonso. *El Negro rioplatense y otros ensayos*. Montevideo: Claudio Garcia & Cia, 1937, 138 pp.
    See the essay "Supersticiones africanas del Rio de la Plata," showing the Negro to be no more "superstitious" than other local races.

1250 Villalba, Aglimira M. *Macumba, terapia del pueblo*. Montevideo: Ed. Monte Sexto, 1989.

Particular Movements

Umbanda

In the introduction to the Brazil section we referred to Spiritism in general and also to Macumba and Umbanda; many entries under Brazil contain valuable material on the latter, along with other movements. Items solely on the latter were not included in the Brazil materials because Umbanda might properly be seen to lie beyond the definition of our subject as related to the primal religious forms. These, as represented in the Afro-Brazilian cults, provide one of the main influences in Umbanda, which has been described (U. Fischer, entry 1300, in German, with English summary) as a "polymorphous syncretism" embracing Amerindian, African, Catholic, and European spiritualist (Kardecist) elements. Umbanda operates at all levels of society, and may well be regarded as a new national religion for Brazil, in effect replacing folk Catholicism (see G. N. Howe, entry 1319, in English).

Under Particular Movements we offer a selection of items on Umbanda, as interpreted fairly widely. No attempt is made to be comprehensive, especially for materials available chiefly in Brazil and for those published by Umbandists themselves. This literature is vast, and in Brazilian Portuguese. The following items are largely from expatriate authors, and if not in Portuguese the language is indicated.

Spiritism in General: B. Kloppenburg (entry 1331, German), D. Warren (entry 1390, English), E. Willems (entry 1396, English).

Macumba, Quimbanda: R. W. Brackmann (entry 1260, German), R. Ortiz (entry 1366, French), E. Pressel (entry 1373, English, a very good survey), F. Valente (entry 1388, by a Portuguese anthropologist).

Relation to African Influences: B. Kloppenburg (entry 1329, German).

Umbanda

General: D. Brown (entries 1264, on the middle class; and 1265, English, as national religion), G. M. S. Dann (entry 1277, English, as reform movement), H. H. Figge (entry 1298, German), U. Fischer (entries 1300, German, with English summary, and 1303, German, a good summary), G. N. Howe (entry 1319, English, as more Brazilian than Pentecostalism), H. A. Johnson (entry 1321, English), F. O'Gorman (entry 1361, English, a good brief outline), R. Ortiz (entry 1365, French, as a syncretism become a synthesis), E. Pressel (entries 1373 and 1374, English), J. P. Renshaw (entry 1375, English), E. Willems (entry 1396, English), B. R. Wilson (entry 1397, English).

Beliefs: C. Bandeira (entry 1254, briefly), V. L. P. Pagliuchi (entry 1367, Part 1, French, with English summary), A. Streiff (entry 1385, German, as a new Gnosticism).

Trance, Possession, and Seances: V. L. P. Pagliuchi (entry 1367, Part 2, French, with English summary), E. Pressel (entries 1372 and 1373, English).

Relation to Christianity and Churches: A. Droogers (entries 1282 and 1283, Lutheran), B. Kloppenburg's articles (as the first Catholic priest making a scholarly study), P. Robert (entry 1376, French, attack by a Haitian Catholic bishop), W. Weber (entry 1391, German), L. Weingartner (entry 1393, German), J. P. Wiebe (entry 1050), V. Willeke (entry 1394, German).

1251 Anton, Mari. "Voodoo outside Haiti." *Traveller* 11, no. 2 (1981): 30-31.
    An Indian journalist's description of a ceremony.

1252 *Anuario Espirita*. Expediente Anúario Espírita, órgão do Instituta de Difusão Espírita [IDE], Araras (São Paulo), Brazil, 1964-.
    A good "inside" survey of what is happening in Spiritist circles.

1253 Bandeira, Armando Cavalcanti. *O que é a umbanda: Ensaio histórico doutrinário*. Rio de Janeiro: Editôra Eco, 1970.
    An account from the inside by a member.

1254 Bandeira, [Armando] Cavalcanti. "A teologia da umbanda." In *Macumba: Cultos afro-brasileiros*, edited by C. F. Gomes. São Paulo: Edições Paulinas, 1976, pp. 54-59.

1255 Bandeira, Armando Cavalcanti. *Umbanda – Evolução histórico-religiosa*. Rio de Janeiro, 1961.
    A noteworthy account, by a Umbandist.

1256 Bastide, Roger. "Le spiritisme de umbanda." In *Miscelania de Estudios dedicados el de Fernando Ortiz*. Cuba, 1956.

1257 Bento [de Faria Ferreira Lima], D. *Malunga: Decodificação da Umbanda*. Rio de Janeiro: Civilização Brasileiro, 1979, 241 pp. Summary, pp. 219-41.
A scholarly, comprehensive, systematic account.

1258 Bettiol, Leopoldo. *Do batuque e das origens da umbanda: Simbolismo, ritualismo, interpretação*. Rio de Janeiro: Gráfica Editôra Aurora, 1963, 230 pp.

1259 Blandre, Bernard. "Le vaudou umbanda, est-il lié aux sacrifices humains?" *Mouvements Religieux* (Sarreguemines, France), no. 36 (April 1983).

1260 Brackmann, Richard Willy. "Quimbanda-Kulte." *Staden-Jahrbuch* (São Paulo) 9-10 (1961-62): 89-102.

1261 Brackmann, Richard W[illy]. "Der Umbanda-Kult in Brasilien." *Staden-Jahrbuch* (São Paulo) 7-8 (1959-60): 157-73. Summary in *Anthropos* 56 (1961): 292.

1262 Braga, Laurenco. *Umbanda e quimbanda*. Rio de Janeiro, 1948. Reprint. 1951, 1956.

1263 Braga, Laurenco. *Umbanda magia branca, quimbanda magia negra*. Rio de Janeiro: Ed. Borsoi, 1956.

1264 Brown, Diana de G. "O papel histórico da classe média na umbanda (1)." *Religião e Sociedade* (São Paulo) 1, no. 1 (1977): 31-42.
A study of middle-class Umbandists in São Paulo, Pôrto Alegre, and Belém.

1265 Brown, Diana [de G.]. "Umbanda and class relations in Brazil." In *Brazil, anthropological perspectives: Essays in honour of Charles Wagley*, edited by M. L. Margolis and W. E. Carter. New York: Columbia University Press, 1979, pp. 270-304.
Umbanda as the only truly national Brazilian religion, providing symbols of Brazilian identity, with the potentiality of becoming a "world religion," and appealing to those most dependent on patron-client relations – middle management, small commerce, and civil service among the middle class, and small shops and the self-employed among the lower classes.

Umbanda

1266 Brown, Diana [de G.]. "Uno história da umbanda no Rio." In *Umbanda e política*, edited by D. Brown. Cuadernos do ISER, 18. Rio de Janeiro: Ed. Marco Zero, 1985.

1267 Brown, Diana de G., and Bick, Mario. "Religions, class, and context: Continuities and discontinuities in Brazilian Umbanda." *American Ethnologist* 14 (February 1987): 73-93.

1268 Bruneau, Thomas Charles. *The political transformation of the Brazilian Catholic Church*. Perspectives in Development, 2. Cambridge: Cambridge University Press, 1974, xv + 270 pp., map.
Pp. 62-63, Spiritism (Kardecist and Umbanda) from a statistical viewpoint, in Salvador, the state of Bahia, and Brazil.

1269 Camargo, Cândido Procópio Ferreira de. *Aspectos sociológicos del espiritismo en São Paulo*. Con una introd. histórica del Dr. Fray Buenaventura Kloppenburg y una introd. sociológica de Jean Labbens. Fribourg, Switzerland: Oficina Internacional de Investigaciones Sociales de FERES, 1961. 125 pp., illus. Also in *Estudios Sociológicos Latino-Americanos* (Bogotá) 17 (1961).

1270 Camargo, C[ândido] P[rocópio] F[erreira] de. *Kardecismo e umbanda: Uma interpretação sociológica*. Biblioteca Pioneira de Ciências Socias. Sociologia. São Paulo: Livraria Pioneira Editôra, 1961, 176 pp.

1271 Camargo, C[ândido] P[rocópio] F[erreira] de, and Labens, J. "Aspecto socio-culturelles du spiritisme au Brésil." *Social Compass* 7 (1960): 407-30.

1272 Camargo, Onelia Maria. "Confirmação do casamento no ritual umbandista." *Revista Brasileira do Folclore* (Rio de Janeiro), no. 25 (September 1969).

1273 Carneiro, Edison [de Souza]. *Candombles da Bahia*. Publicações de Museo do Estado, 8. Bahia: Museo do Estado, 1948, 140 pp., illus. Enl. 2d. ed. Rio de Janeiro: Editorial Andes, 1954, 239 pp., illus. 3d ed. Rio de Janeiro: Conquista, 1961, has appendix on Umbanda (pp. 163-68). Reprinted in *Ladinos e crioulos*. Rio de Janeiro: Editora Civilização Brasileira, 1964, pp. 163-68. Reprinted in *MEC* (Rio de Janeiro), September-December 1960, pp. 18-22.

1274 Castellan, Yvonne. *O espiritismo*. São Paulo: Difusão Europeia do Livre, 1955. Translated into Portuguese from the French original.

Spanish translation. *El espiritismo.* Buenos Aires: Los Libros de Mirasol, 1962, 157 pp.
A valuable study.

1275 Cruz Costa, João. *Contribução a historía das idéias no Brasil.* Coleção Documentos Brasileiros, 86. Rio de Janeiro: José Olympio, 1956, 484 pp., bib. 2d ed. Rio de Janeiro: Civilização Brasileira, 1967. English translation. *A history of ideas in Brazil: The development of philosophy in Brazil and the evolution of national history.* Berkeley: University of California Press, 1964, x + 421 pp., bib.
Chap. 3, "The advent of positivism," as a religious influence in Brazil; chap. 4, its decline.

1276 Dammann, Ernst. *Grundriss der Religionsgeschichte.* Theologische Wissenschaft: Sammelwerk für Studien und Beruf, 17. Stuttgart: Verlag W. Kohlhammer, 1972, 127 pp.
Pp. 114-17, Umbanda, by a historian of religions.

1277 Dann, Graham M. S. "Religion and cultural identity: The case of Umbanda." *Sociological Analysis* 40 (Fall 1979): 208-25.
The unique indigenous nature of Umbanda in its combination of Indian, African, European Christian, and Kardecist elements; its nature as a reform movement.

1278 D'Anna, Andrea. "Per chi suonano i tamburi dell' umbanda." *Nigrizia* (Verona) 88, no. 5 (July-August 1970): 26-30, illus.

1279 D'Anna, Andrea. "Questa sera si va all' umbanda." *Nigrizia* (Verona) 88, no. 3 (June 1970): 30-34, illus.

1280 Decelso (pseud.). *Umbanda da caboclos: Estudo sócio-religioso.* Rio de Janeiro: Editôra Eco, 1972, 188 pp.
A Umbandist publication.

1281 Diniz, Edson S. "Um 'Terreiro' de umbanda em Belém do Pará." *Revista Instituto Estudios Brasileiros,* no. 17 (1975), pp. 7-17.

1282 Droogers, André, et al. "Desafio para a Igreja." *Revista do CEM* 6, no. 1 (1983): 21-35, illus.
A report from the Centro de Elaboração de Material da Igreja Evangélica de Confissão Luterana do Brazil, prepared by a group of Lutheran seminary students and two professors in a seminar on Mediums in Brazil and the Bible.

Umbanda

1283 Droogers, André. *E a umbanda?* Série Religiões, 1. São Leopoldo: Editora Sinodal, 1985, 87 pp.
An overview for pastors and others, especially in the Lutheran Church, by a Dutch anthropologist.

1284 Duarte, Isidoro Santos. *O espiritismo no Brasil.* Ecos de uma Viagem. Rio de Janeiro: J. Ozon Editor, 1960.

1285 Dulle, A. "Umbanda do Brasil: Sociokultureller Hintergrund einer Religion." In *Lateinamerika Studien* (Universität Erlangen-Nürnberg), edited by T. Heydenrich, et al., 9 (1979): 301-14.

1286 Estermann, Ch[arles]. "Zum *Umbanda*-Kult in Brasilien." *Anthropos* 59, nos. 5-6 (1964): 935.
A note on the relation of the term Umbanda to Bantu (southern Angola) language, and ancestor cults.

1287 Fancello, Mauro. "Umbanda: Nuova religione per il Brasile?" *Mission Consolata* (Turin), no. 23 (1-15 December 1973), pp. 53-58.
By an Italian Catholic priest.

1288 Félix, Cândido Emanuel. *A cartilha da umbanda.* Rio de Janeiro: Editôra Eco, 1965, 114 pp.

1289 Félix, Cândido Emanuel. *Evangelho umbandista.* Rio de Janeiro: Edições Eco, [1965?], 131 pp.
Umbanda cult – origins, description, rituals, prayers, charms, proverbs, etc.

1290 Fernandez, Gonçalves. "Vergöttlichter Sexus: Eine Untersuchung zur Sexualtheologie der Umbanda-religion." *Estudos Teológicos* (São Leopoldo) 6 (1966): 115-30.

1291 Figge, Horst H. *Beiträge zur Kulturgeschichte Brasiliens unter besonderer Berucksichtigung der Umbanda Religion und der westafrikanischen Ewe-Sprache.* Beiträge zur Kulturanthropologie. Berlin: D. Reimer Verlag, 1980, 144 pp., illus.

1292 Figge, Horst H. "'Besessenheit' als Therapie: Zur Wirkung der 'Geisterbeschwörung' auf 'Inkorporationsmedien' in der Umbanda." *Zeitschrift für Parapsychologie und Grenzgebiete der Psychologie* (Freiburg im Breslau) 12, no. 4 (1970): 207-25.

1293 Figge, Horst H. "Funktionen der Therapieversuche in der Brasilianischem Umbanda." *Curare* (Brunswick) 3, no. 3 (1980): 159-64.

1294 Figge, Horst H. "Heilpraktiker und Kurpfuscher 'aus dem Jenseits,' therapeutische Behandlungsmethoden in Rahmen der brasilianischen Umbanda." *Therapie der Gegenwart* ... *Praktischen Medizin* (Berlin) 111, no. 1 (1972): 96-112.

1295 Figge, Horst H. "Schriftverkehr mit Geistern, eine Untersuchung von Umbanda-Zetteln." *Staden-Jahrbuch* (São Paulo) 20 (1972): 91-102.

1296 Figge, Horst H. "Spirit-possession and healing cult among the Brazilian umbanda." In *What is Psychotherapy? Proceedings, 9th International Congress of Psychotherapists, Oslo, 1973.* 1975, pp. 246-50.

1297 Figge, Horst H. "Trance-Mediumismus als Gruppentherapie, ein Aspeckt der brasilianische Umbanda." *Zeitschrift für Psychotherapie und Medizinische Psychologie* (Stuttgart) 22, no. 4 (1972): 149-56.

1298 Figge, Horst H. "Umbanda – eine brasilianische Religion." *Numen* 20, no. 2 (1973): 81-103.

1299 Figge, Horst H. "Zur psychohygienischen Bedeutung der Dämonen, Gründe für den Exukult in Rahmen der brasilianischen Umbanda." *Zeitschrift für Parapsychologie und Grenzgebiete der Psychologie* (Freiburg im Breslau) 13, no. 4 (1971): 230-41.

1300 Fischer, Ulrich. "Erfüllte Sehnsucht: Umbanda, die jüngste und die älteste Religion der Welt." *Evangelische Missionszeitschrift* (Stuttgart), n.s. 22 (1965): 116-30. English summary in *Mundus* 2, no. 2 (1966): 107.
A "polymorphous syncretism."

1301 Fischer, Ulrich. "Getraut in Namen des grossen Vaters Zambi." *Estudos Teológicos* (São Leopoldo) 8, no. 2 (1968): 72-111.
Research into the official activities of the "syncretistic new religion of Umbanda."

1302 Fischer, Ulrich. "Religion ohne Wenn und Aber: Das Amtsverständnis in der synkretischen Neureligion brasiliens." In *Lateinamerika Studien* (Universität Erlangen-Nuremberg), edited by T. Heydenrich, et al., 9 (1982): 312-36.

Umbanda

1303 Fischer, Ulrich. "Umbanda: Auf dem Weg zur Volksreligion." *Evangelische Missionszeitschrift* (Stuttgart), n.s. 30, no. 4 (1973): 193-201.

The increasing organization, growth, unity, discipline, orthodoxy, and priest-training as this religion becomes the popular religion of Brazil.

1304 Fischer, Ulrich. *Zur liturgie des Umbandakulte.* Leiden: E. J. Brill, 1970.

1305 Freitas, Byron Torres de. *O jogo dos buzios.* Rio de Janeiro: Ed. Espiritista, 1966.

On Umbanda, and the forms of divination by *buzios* (small seashells) tracing back to Yoruba *ifa* divination.

1306 Freitas, Byron Torres de, and Pinto, Tancredo da Silva. *As impressionantes ceremônias da umbanda.* Rio de Janeiro, 1955.

Officially approved by two Umbanda federations and by the Union of Afro-Brazilian Cults.

1307 Freitas, Byron Torres de, and Pinto, Tancredo da Silva. *Camba de umbanda.* Rio de Janeiro: Aurora, 1955. Reprint. 1957.

By Umbandists.

1308 Freitas, Byron Torres de, and Pinto, Tancredo da Silva. *Fundamentos da umbanda.* Rio de Janeiro: Editôra Souza, 1956, 96 pp.

1309 Freitas, Byron Torres de, and Freitas, Vladimir Cardoso de. *Na gira da umbanda.* Rio de Janeiro: Editôra Eco, 1965, 116 pp.

1310 Frigerio, Alejandro. "Umbanda y africanismo en Buenos Aires." *Revista del Instituto de Religion* (Rio de Janeiro), 1989.

1311 Fry, Peter [H.]. "Reflexões sobre o crescimento da conversão à umbanda." *Cadernos do Instituto Superior de Estudos da Religião* (São Paulo), no. 1 (1974), pp. 29-40.

A sociological explanation in terms of the decline of Catholic ritualism since the Second Vatican Council.

1312 Fry, Peter [H.]. "Two religious movements: Protestantism and Umbanda." In *Manchester and São Paulo. Problems of rapid urban growth,* edited by J. D. Wirth and R. L. Jones. Stanford: Stanford University Press, 1978, pp. 177-202.

With appendix: comparison of Umbanda and Methodism.

1313 Fry, Peter H., and Howe, Gary N[igel]. "Duas respòstas a aflição: Umbanda e pentecostalismo." *Debate & Crítica* (São Paulo), no. 6 (July 1975), pp. 75-94.
See Howe's item (entry 1319) for similar argument.

1314 Fülling, Erich. "Umbanda: Eine brasilianische Mischreligion bedroht die christliche Kirche." *Hermannsburger Missionshlatt* 101 (June 1961): 66ff.

1315 Gabriel, Chester E. "Communications of the spirits: Umbanda, regional cults in Manaus and the dynamics of mediumistic trance." Ph.D. dissertation (cultural anthropology), McGill University, 1981.

1316 Harms-Wiebe, Raymond Peter. "A Pauline power encounter response to Umbanda." *Mission Focus* (Elkhart, Ind.) 15, no. 1 (1987): 6-10.
The history, beliefs, conversion process and growth factors of Umbanda; table of comparisons between Umbanda, Pauline, and Western Christianity; missiological and pastoral policy. By a Mennonite missionary.

1317 Hoepeps, M. "Nosso combats ao espiritismo." *Revista Eclesiástica Brasileira* 12 (1952): 891-93.

1318 Höltker, Georg. "Umbanda als neue afrobrasilianische 'Religion.'" *Neue Zeitschrift für Missionswissenschaft* 20, no. 4 (1964): 285.
Comments on V. Willeke (entry 1394) and R. W. Brackmann (entry 1261).

1319 Howe, Gary Nigel. "Capitalism and religion at the periphery: Pentecostalism and Umbanda in Brazil." In *Perspectives on Pentecostalism*, edited by S. D. Glazier. Washington, D.C.: University Press of America, 1980, pp. 125-41.
Umbanda as opposite of Pentecostalism in its cosmology, and more responsive to conditions in Brazil.

1320 Howe, Gary Nigel. "Pentecostalism, Umbanda and the Brazilian socio-economic order from 1945 to the present day." Ph.D. dissertation, University of London (London School of Economics and Political Science), 1978, 409 pp.
Based on study of Campinas: two Pentecostal groups (an independent Pentecostal and a Foursquare Gospel congregation) and Umbanda.

Umbanda

1321 Johnson, Harmon A. "Umbanda: A modern Brazilian religion." In *Dynamic religious movements*, edited by J. D. Hesselgrave. Grand Rapids: Baker Book House, 1978, pp. 247-69.

1322 Kalverkamp, Desidéro. "Os espíritas em face do Direito Canônico." *Revista Eclesiástica Brasileira* (Petrópolis) 13 (1953): 853-89.

1323 Kalverkamp, Desidéro. "Frequentar sessões espíritas?" *Revista Eclesiástica Brasileira* (Petrópolis) 16 (1956): 156-58.

1324 Kardec, Allan [Rivail, Léon Hippolyte Denisart]. *O evangelho segundo o espiritismo*. Translated into Portuguese from the French original. São Paulo, 1958.
       By the prolific French philosophical spiritualist (1804-69) who remains a major influence on Brazilian Spiritism.

1325 Kardec, Allan [Rivail, Léon Hippolyte Denisart]. *Le livre des esprits contenant les principes de la doctrine spirite*. Paris: Didier, 1857. Many editions and translations, including the following: Spanish translation. *El libro de los espíritus*. Mexico, 1951. English translation. *The spirits' book*. Boston: Colby & Rich, 1875, 438 pp.; São Paulo, n.d. Portuguese translation from 22d ed. of French original. *O livro dos espíritos*. São Paulo, n.d.

1326 Kardec, Allan [Rivail, Léon Hippolyte Denisart]. *Le spiritisme à sa plus simple expression*. Paris, 1864.

1327 Kautzmann, A. "A umbanda." *Iglu* 23 (1962): 121-33.

1328 Klein, Herbert [Sanford]. "L'umbanda au Brésil." In *Devant les sectes non-chrétiens*. Louvain: Desclée de Brouwer, [1962], pp. 253-67.

1329 Kloppenburg, Boaventura. "Die Afro-Brasilianer und die Umbanda." *Ordensnachrichten* (Vienna) 20, no. 5 (1981): 367-80.

1330 Kloppenburg, Boaventura. "Ainda o exemplo de Haiti na reação contra a umbanda." *Revista Eclesiástica Brasileira* (Petrópolis) 16 (1956): 122-25.

1331 Kloppenburg, Boaventura. "Der brazilianische Spiritismus als religiöse Gefahr." *Social Compass* 5, nos. 5-6 (1957-58): 237-55.

1332 Kloppenburg, Boaventura. "Chronik: Contra o abuso des imagens nos terreiros de umbanda." *Revista Eclesiástica Brasileira* (Petrópolis) 17 (1957): 822.

1333 Kloppenburg, Boaventura. "Chronik: Espiritismo de umbanda no Rio Grande do Sul." *Revista Eclesiástica Brasileira* (Petrópolis) 17 (1957): 1-66.
On the 300 Umbandist groups in Rio Grande do Sul, with the professional classes to be found among them.

1334 Kloppenburg, Boaventura. "Le démon dans l'umbanda." In *Catholicisme et vaudou*, edited by R. Paul. Collection Sondeos, 82. Cuernavaca, Mexico: Edition du CIDOC, 1971, section 7, pp. 24-37.

1335 Kloppenburg, Boaventura. "Ensaio de uma nova posição pastoral perante a umbanda." *Revista Eclesiástica Brasileira* (Petrópolis), 1968, pp. 404-17.
On the application to Umbanda of the missionary principles enunciated by the Second Vatican Council.

1336 Kloppenburg, Boaventura. "O espiritismo de umbando." *Revista Eclesiástica Brasileira* (Petrópolis) 14 (1954): 305-27.

1337 Kloppenburg, Boaventura. *O espiritismo no Brasil: Orientação para os católicos.* Vozes em Defesa da Fé, Estudo 1. Petrópolis: Editôra Vozes, 1960, 455 pp. 2d ed. 1964.
The first of a four-volume criticism of Spiritism; deals with Kardec and his teachings.

1338 Kloppenburg, Boaventura. "Origens e tendências na umbanda." *Revista Eclesiástica Brasileira* (Petrópolis) 20 (1960): 900-18.

1339 Kloppenburg, Boaventura. *Posição católica perante a umbanda.* Petrópolis, 1954.

1340 Kloppenburg, Boaventura. "A umbanda marcou um grupo de padres." *Revista Eclesiástica Brasileira* (Petrópolis) 20 (1960): 118-23.

1341 Kloppenburg, Boaventura. *A umbando no Brasil: Orientação para os católicos.* Vozes em Defesa da Fé, Estudos 2. Petrópolis: Editôra Vozes, 1961, 263 pp., illus. 2d ed. 1964.
The most complete study of Spiritism to date, from a pre-Vatican II viewpoint.

Umbanda

1342 Kloppenburg, Boaventura. "Versuch einer neuen pastoralen Stellungnahme gegenüber der Umbanda." *Anthropologie und Evangelisierung* (CELEM Botatá), 1969, p. 263f.

1343 Lanczowski, G. "Umbanda." In *Die neuen Religionen*. Frankfurt am Main, 1974, pp. 167-71.

1344 Lerch, Patricia [Jane Barker]. "An explanation for the predominance of women in Umbanda cults of Porto Alegre, Brazil." *Urban Anthropology* 11, no. 2 (1982): 237-61.

1345 Lerch, Patricia [Jane Barker]. "The role of women in possession-trance cults in Brazil." M.A. thesis, Ohio State University, 1972.
Umbanda spirits are regarded as "representative" of the modern social structure in a developing nation.

1346 Lerch, Patricia [Jane Barker]. "Spirit mediums in Umbanda evangelizada of Porto Alegre, Brasil." In *A world of women: Anthropological studies of women in the societies of the world*, edited by E. Bourguignon. New York: Praeger, 1980, 364 pp.

1347 Lerch, Patricia Jane Barker. "Warriors of justice: A study of women's roles in Umbanda in Porto Alegre, Brazil." Ph.D. dissertation (cultural anthropology), Ohio State University, 1978, 357 pp.
Spirit-mediumship offers women authority and power not available elsewhere; "evangelized Umbanda" is one variation on Umbanda that is influenced by Catholicism, Batuque (which preceded it), etc.

1348 Levy, Maria S. "The umbanda is for all of us." M.A. dissertation, University of Wisconsin, Madison, 1968.
Includes estimate of 4,000 *terreiros* in São Paulo in 1968.

1349 Lins, Ivan [Monteiro de Barros]. *História do positivismo no Brasil*. Brasiliana, vol. 322. São Paulo: Editôra Nacional, 1964, 661 pp. 2d ed., rev. and enl. 1967, 707 pp.
As background to Umbanda. By Brazil's leading positivist, but not a member of the Positivist church which he has recorded here with very full documentation – now the definitive history.

1350 "Macumba: Brazil's devil worshippers." *Our Sunday Visitor* (Huntingdon, Ind.), 12 March 1972, pp. 8-9.
A popular Catholic account – the image created in the West.

1351 Menezes, Heraldo. *Caboclos na Umbanda*. Rio de Janeiro: Coleção Afro-Brasileira, 1958. Reprint. 1960.

1352 Mombelli, Savino. "De origine, progressione et sensu vulgaris illius brasilicae religiones quae Umbanda dicitur" [Concerning the origin, progress, and popular meaning of the Brazilian religion known as Umbanda]. Doctoral dissertation (religion), Pontificia Universitas Urbaniana, 1972.

In Latin. For digest in Latin, see *Dissertation Abstracts International*, C, 37, no. 3 (1977): 482, # 1/3305c.

1353 Mombelli, Savino. "Umbanda: Origini, sviluppi e significati di una religione popolare brasiliana." *Fede e Civiltà* (Parma) 9-10 (1971): 1-112. Also published as a book. Milan: PIME, 1971.

Umbanda as a new national religion in protest against current Catholic reforms (e.g., the pastoral movement) that represent Europeanization and modernization as against traditional Brazilian Catholicism in its "colonial" forms.

1354 Montero, Paulo, and Ortiz, Renato. "Contribuição para um estudo quantitativo da religião umbandista." *Ciência & Cultura* (São Paulo) 28, no. 4 (1976): 407-16.

Profile of the movement based on 590 participants; deals with Umbanda trances, recruitment, and education.

1355 Morell, André. *La vie et l'oeuvre d'Allan Kardec*. Paris: Éditions Sperar, 1961.

On the influential French nineteenth-century philosophic spiritualist, well known still in Brazil.

1356 Moritzen, Niels-Peter. "Neue Tendenzen in der Entwicklung der Umbanda-Religion." *Evangelische Missions Zeitschrift* (Stuttgart), n.s. 26, no. 4 (1969): 208-11.

1357 Mott, Toshisko Tanabe. "Caridade e demanda: Um estudo de accusação e conflito na umbanda em Marilia (S.P.)." M.A. thesis (social anthropology), State University of Campinas (Campinas, São Paulo), 1976.

Umbanda *terreiros* and leaders in the city of Marilia since their beginning in 1957; the rivalries and power struggles led to fission, and hence to groups being kept small and also to expansion of Umbanda as a whole.

Umbanda

1358 Nembro, M. da. "Umbanda: Una religione popolare nel Brasile." *Laurentianum* (Rome, Capuchin Order) 13, no. 3 (1972): 365-82.

1359 Nunes, Atila, Filho. *Antologia da umbanda.* Rio de Janeiro: Editôra Eco, 1961. Reprint. 1965, 181 pp., illus. Rev. and enl. ed. 1966, 320 pp.

1360 Nunes, José de Arimatéia. *Orações de umbanda.* Preface by Prof. José Ribeiro de Souza. Rio de Janeiro: Editôra Eco. 3d ed. 1967, 78 pp.

1361 O'Gorman, Frances. *Aluanda – A look at Afro-Brazilian cults.* Rio de Janeiro: Livraria Francisco Alves Editora, 1977, 108 pp.
      Pp. 92-98, "Umbanda: A Brazilian religious ideology" – a good brief outline.

1362 Ortiz, Renato. "La mort blanche du sorcier noir. Umbanda: Intégration d'une religion dans une société de classes." Thèse de 3e cycle, University of Paris, École des Hautes Études en Sciences Sociales, 1975.
      For published form in Portuguese, see entry 1364. Excellent bibliography.

1363 Ortiz, Renato. "A morte branca do feiticeiro negro." *Religião e Sociedade* 1, no. 1 (1977): 43-50.

1364 Ortiz, Renato. *A morte branca do feiticeiro negro umbanda: Integraçao de uma religião numa sociedade de classes.* Petrópolis: Editoria Vozes, 1978, 205 pp., bib.
      Systematic survey by a sociologist.

1365 Ortiz, Renato. "Du syncrétisme à la synthèse: Umbanda, une religion brésilienne." *Archives de Sciences Sociales des Religions,* no. 40 [20, no. 2] (1975): 89-97.
      Afro-Catholic syncretism as exemplified in the origins, development, and current religious and social characteristics of Umbanda, which represents the point where the Afro-Brazilian becomes the Brazilian Negro; discusses Bastide's theory of syncretism, and the relations among Candomble, Macumba, and Umbanda at various stages of its development into a new national religion.

1366 Ortiz, Renato. "Umbanda, magie blanche; quimbanda, magie noire." *Archives de Sciences Sociales des Religions,* no. 47 [24, no. 1] (1979): 135-146.

Umbanda

The two principles of Umbanda religion – Good (Umbanda) and Evil (Quimbanda); their functions, rites and symbols. P. 136 on origin of term *umbanda* from an African word, *kimbundo*.

1367 Pagliuchi, V. L. P. "Le spiritisme d'umbanda. 1: Analyse structurale de la doctrine. 2: Analyse structurale d'une séance." *Psychopathologie Africaine* (Dakar) 10, no. 2 (1974): 381-422; English summary.

1368 Pallavicino, Maria I. *Umbanda: Investigacion sobre religiosidad afro-brasileña en Montevideo*. Montevideo, 1986.

1369 Pechman, Tema. "Umbanda e politica no Rio de Janeiro." *Religião e Sociedade* (Brasil) 8 (July 1982): 37-44.

1370 Pessôa, José Alvares. *Umbanda, religião do Brasil*. Rio de Janeiro, 1960.

1371 Pinto, Altair, ed., *Dicionário da umbanda. Contendo o major número de palavras, usadas na umbanda no candomblé e nos cultos afro-brasileiros*. Rio de Janeiro: Editôra Eco, 1971. 2d ed. 1975, 227 pp.
   With appendix – Yoruba vocabulary, pp. 215-27.

1372 Pressel, Esther [Joan]. "Negative spirit possession in experienced Brazilian Umbanda spirit mediums." In *Case studies in spirit possession*, edited by V. Crapanzano and V. Garrison. New York: John Wiley & Sons, 1977, pp. 333-64.

1373 Pressel, E[sther Joan]. "Umbanda in the Brazilian religious milieu." In *Trance, healing, and hallucination*, edited by F. D. Goodman, et al. New York: John Wiley & Sons, 1974, pp. 121-47.
   A good survey, with relations to Macumba, Quimbanda, Pentecostalism, etc.

1374 Pressel, Esther [Joan]. "Umbanda in São Paulo: Religious innovation in a developing society." In *Religion, altered states of consciousness, and social change*, edited by E. Bourguignon. Columbus: Ohio State University Press, 1973, pp. 264-318, illus., bib.
   Deals with personal problems and social stresses.

1375 Renshaw, Jarrett Parke. "A new religion for Brazilians." *Practical Anthropology* 13, no. 4 (1966): 126-32.
   On Umbanda or Spiritism.

Umbanda

1376 Robert, Paul. "L'Église en face du paganisme de l'umbanda." In *Catholicisme et vaudou*. Collection Sondeos, 82. Cuernavaca, Mexico: CIDOC, 1972, section 4, pp. 4/40-4/49.
By a Haitian Catholic bishop who also attacked Vodou.

1377 Rosa, Celso. *Babalaôs e Ialorixás*. Rio de Janeiro: Editôra Eco, 1967, 159 pp.
Handbook of Umbanda rituals–calendar of festivals, prayers, chants, songs, folk medicine; traces African origins of the Umbanda cult syncretism.

1378 Scarpa, Antonio. *Bagni medicamentosi e a scopo magico-religioso nei riti umbanda e negli usi popolari nei Brasile odierno*. Castalia, 1961.

1379 Seiblitz, Zeila. "Umbanda e 'potencial contestador' da religião." *América Indígena* 45, no. 4 (1985): 669-90; English summary.

1380 Silva, Woodrow Wilson da Matta e. *Lições de umbanda (e quimbanda). Na palavra de umu "prêto-velho."* Rio de Janeiro and São Paulo: Livraria Freitas Bastos, 1961, 170 pp.

1381 Silva, Woodrow Wilson da Matta e. *Mistérios e práticas da lei de umbanda*. Rio de Janeiro and São Paulo: Livraria Freitas Bastos, 1962, 210 pp.

1382 Silva, Woodrow Wilson da Matta e. *Umbanda do Brasil*. Rio de Janeiro: Livraria Freitas Bastos, 1969, 366 pp., illus., bib.
A Umbandist author's popular manual containing history, ritual, beliefs, etc.

1383 Soares, Luiz Eduardo. "O autor e seu duplo: A psychografia e as proezas do simulacro." *Religião e Sociedade* 4 (1979): 121-41.
The prestige of conveying truth from a "high order" (i.e., Kardecism and its developments) and seen in the popular books of Francisco Xavier; the effects on Brazilian society.

1384 Soboll, Walter. "Umbanda: Apresentação de sua doutrina e ritual." *Estudos Teológicos* (São Leopoldo), 1961, pp. 38-52.

1385 Streiff, Andres. "Eine neue Gnosis: Der brasilianische Spiritismus." *Reformatio* (Zurich) 10 (1960): 567-70.
Spiritism interpreted as a new Gnosticism.

1386 Subirats, Jean. "Remarques sur l'état présent de l'umbanda." *Travaux de l'Institut d'Études Latino-Américaines de l'Université de Strasbourg. TILAS 9* [ca. 1968?], pp. 565-76.

1387 *Umbanda e quimbanda (magie blanche et magie noire)*. Rio de Janeiro, 1942.
Seeks to formulate the positions of the growing black "spiritism" as against white spiritism. By black spiritist groups.

1388 Valente, Francisco. "Feiticeiro ou quimbanda?" *Ultramar* (Lisbon), no. 39 [10] (1970): 97-112.

1389 Vanackere, H., ed. "The future of religion in Latin America: Divergencies in Brazil." *Pro Mundi Vita Bulletin* 90 (July 1982): 26 pp.
P. 5, the growth of Spiritism-cum-Umbanda.

1390 Warren, Donald, Jr. "Spiritism in Brazil." *Journal of Inter-American Studies* (Coral Gables, Fla.) 10, no. 3 (1968): 393-405.

1391 Weber, Wilfried. "Der Umbandakult in Brasilien als ausserchristliche Erneurungsbewegung." *Zeitschrift für Missions- und Religionswissenschaft* 60, no. 2 (1976): 91-109.
History and features of Umbanda; the past failures of the Catholic church and ignorance and condemnation of Umbanda; the possibility of the Catholic charismatic movement as a Christian response to Brazil's new religions.

1392 Weingartner, Lindolfo. "Umbanda – die 'vierte Offenbarung.'" *Dynamis*, no. 4 (February 1969), 6.

1393 Weingartner, Lindolfo. *Umbanda: Synkretistische Kulte in Brasilien. Eine Herausforderung für die christliche Kirche.* Erlanger Taschenbücher, Band 8. Erlangen: Verlag der Evangelisch-Lutherischen Mission, 1969, 230 pp. + glossary.

1394 Willeke, Venantius. "Umbanda und Christentum in Brasilien." *Zeitschrift für Missionswissenschaft und Religionswissenschaft* 44, no. 2 (1960): 107-14.

1395 Willems, Emílio. "Religiöser Pluralismus und Klassenstruktur in Brasilien und Chile." In *Internationales Jahrbuch für Religionssoziologie*. Vol. 1. Cologne: Westdeutscher Verlag, 1965, pp. 189-209; English summary (pp. 210-11).

Umbanda

Includes Pentecostalism, Umbanda, and Spiritualism.

1396 Willems, Emílio. "Religious mass movements and social change in Brazil." In *New perspectives on Brazil*, edited by E. N. Baklanoff. Nashville: Vanderbilt University Press, 1966, pp. 205-31.
Places Umbanda in the context of Spiritism in general, Pentecostalism, and the churches.

1397 Wilson, Bryan R[onald]. *Magic and the millennium: A sociological study of religious movements of protest among tribal and third-world peoples.* London: Heinemann Educational Books; New York: Harper & Row, 1973, 540 pp. Reprint. Frogmore, St. Albans: Granada Publishing, Paladin Books, 1975.
Pp. 112-20, syncretic Spiritualism, urban magic, and intellectual Spiritualism.

1398 Xavier, Francisco Candido. *Brasil, coração do mundo, pátria do evangelho, pelo espírito de Humberto de Campos.* Rio de Janeiro: Federação Espírita Brasileira, 1938. 7th ed., 1965.
A Brazilian medium known as "Chico" interpreting Spiritualism in Brazilian terms. Has about a dozen books for all age levels, all with a moral, "be good." This work is a melodramatic account of the direction of the destiny of Brazil by the spirit Ismael over the past 450 years – and thus has increasing public appeal.

1399 Xavier, Francisco Candido. *Jovens no além.* São Bernardo do Campo, Brazil: Grupo Espírita Emmanuel, 1975, 223 pp.
Experiences of a medium.

1400 Xavier, Francisco Candido, and Vieira, Waldo. *The world of the spirits.* Translated from the Portugese original by R. Baldwin and W. Leal. New York: Philosophical Library, 1966, 103 pp.
Messages received in Portuguese and English, by "inspirational automatic writing."

1401 Zespo, Emmanuel. *Codificação da lei de umbanda.* Rio de Janeiro: Editôra Espiritualista, 1951. 2d ed. 1960.

1402 Zespo, Emmanuel. *Pai José: Romance umbandista do prêto velho sôbre os mistérios da reencarnação.* Rio de Janeiro: Editôra Espiritualista Brasileira, 1954, 78 pp.

Umbanda

1403 Zespo, Emmanuel, ed. *Pantos cantados e riscados da umbanda com vocabulário dos têrmos mais usados*. Rio de Janeiro, 1951. Reprint. 1953, 152 pp., illus.
   A guide to Umbanda cult groups in the Rio de Janeiro area.

Glossary

The following are the anglicized forms of the most common terms among a great variety used for movements and religious forms and for ethnic origins, primarily but not exclusively in Brazil. Usage is somewhat fluid and varies from one region to another within Brazil, as well as within the literature itself. This glossary is therefore a working or preliminary list rather than a definitive guide.

Religious Movements, Cults, or Forms

Afro-Brazilian: The most general term, not excluding Amerindian and other elements, but less applicable at the more sophisticated or elite end of the spectrum.

Babacue: A general term in Amazonia for Afro-Brazilian cults.

Batuque (from a kind of drum): Used mainly in Rio Grande do Sul and Amazonia, and especially in Belem, for what is more generally called *Candomble*.

Candomble: Used especially in Bahia (the most African area of Brazil), but also widely for the most African in rituals and language of the spectrum of cults.

Candomble do Caboclo: Candomble featuring communication with the spirits of Amerindians and Africans (especially with "pretos velhos," or "old blacks" who were "elders" in their slave communities, and also with nature spirits). See also *Caboclo* below.

211

Catimbo (from a shaman's pipe): Afro-Brazilian cults in the northeast, with major Amerindian influences.

Espiritismo. See *Spiritism*.

Kardecism. See *Spiritualism*.

Kimbanda. See *Quimbanda*.

Macumba: Strong in Rio de Janeiro. Ma-cumba = "the elders," who take dramatic possession of members; magical elements also.

Pajelanca (from *pagé*, "shaman"): Amerindian shamanism in Amazonia and Para.

Para: Afro-Brazilian forms in Rio Grande do Sul.

Quimbanda or *Kimbanda:* African forms focused on witchcraft and magic, with no doctrinal basis or emphasis on spirits, but with secret practice of rituals and sacrifices; strongest in Rio de Janeiro.

Spiritism: A general term for the more folk forms of Candomblé and Macumba, or more widely for the religious situation in Brazil in general, where "spiritism" in some form has been described as "the new national religion."

Spritualism: The more sophisticated forms of Spiritism among the more urban, educated middle and professional classes, deriving from the influence of the 19th-century French philosophical spiritualist Allan Kardec (pseudonym of L. H. D. Rivail), and including much Umbanda.

Umbanda: A varied and complex range of movements concerned with physical (healing), material, and spiritual welfare, showing a mixture of Amerindian, African, Catholic, and European occult influences, with sophisticated organization and varied social and public activities among the middle classes; especially widespread around São Paulo; it is becoming a general term for all forms of Spiritism.

Xango (from the Yoruba *Shango*): A general term in northeast Brazil for Afro-Brazilian cults.

Terms Referring to Peoples and Racial Groups or Origins

Caboclo: (a) "Tame" or civilized Indians, or any rustic person. (b) People of mixed racial descent; Amerindian-Europeans. (c) In religious context, great Amerindian leaders of the past consulted through a medium.

Cafuz (= Spanish *Zambo*): People of mixed racial descent: Amerindian-Negro.

Curiboca or *Mamaluco:* People of mixed racial descent: Amerindian-European.

Gege: Descendents of the Fon people in Dahomey, now Benin.

Mamaluco: See *Curiboca.*

Mestizo or *Mestico:* People of mixed racial descent: Amerindian-European.

Mulatto: People of mixed racial descent: Negro-European.

Nago: A Dahomean term for the Yoruba people.

Quilombo: Communities of escaped Negro slaves.

Sertanejo: A dweller in the Sertão (wooded interior highlands of Brazil); these people are usually also Mestizo.

Tapuya: "Wild Amerindians." (i.e., opposite of *Caboclo* [see above]).

Index of Authors and Sources

Note: References are to entry numbers, not to pages.

215

Dornas, João, 562
Dorsinfang-Smets, A., 289
Doughty, Paul L., 1142
Dowell, M., 563
Doyon, Philippe, 564
Drake, St. Clair, 80-81
Drolet, Patricia L., 285
Droogers, André, 1282-1283
Duarte, Abelardo, 565
Duarte, Isidoro S., 1284
Duarte, Ophir M., 566
Dulle, A., 1285
Dumond, Don E., 196-197
Dussel, Enrique, 8
Duviols, Pierre, 1143-1148
Dyke, Annette J. Van, 82

Ebner, Carl B., 567
Eckert, Georg, 1075-1076
Eco, Umberto, 568
Edmonson, Munro S., 159
Eduardo, Octávio da C., 569-571
Eliade, Mircea, 290
Ertle, Brigitte, 291
Espin, Orlando, 572
Espíndola, Julio C., 1092
Espinoza, Enrique, 1149
Espinoza Soriano, Waldemar, 1150
Estermann, Ch., 1286
Etienne Ignace. *See* Brazil, Etienne I.

Fancello, Mauro, 573, 1287
Félix, Cândido E., 1288-1289
Fernandes, Albino Gonçalves, 574-579
Fernandes, Florestan, 580-581
Fernandes, Trinidade, 755
Fernandez, Gonçalves, 1290
Ferraz, Aydano do C., 513, 582-583
Ferreira, Climério J., 584

Ferreira, José C., 585
Ferretti, Mundicarmo, 586
Fichte, Hubert, 83, 109
Figge, Horst H., 1291-1299
Figueiredo, Napoleão, 587-588
Finkler, Kaja/Kaya, 198-200
Fischer, Ulrich, 1300-1304
Flasche, Rainer, 589-591
Flora, Cornelia B., 1077
Fonseca, Elias, 592
Fontenelle, A., 593
Formiga, Manuel da. *See* Santos, Manuel V. dos
Foster, George M., 9, 25
Franco, José L., 84
Franco, R. di, 315
Frankowska, Maria, 201-202
Frazier, E. Franklin, 594
Freitas, Byron T. de, 1305-1309
Freitas, João de, 595-596
Freitas, Newton, 597
Freitas, Vladimir C. de, 1309
Frey, Hermann, 598
Freyre, Gilberto, 599-602
Frickel, Protásius, 603-604
Friderichs, Edwin (Edvino) A., 605-607
Friede, Juan, 1078
Frigerio, Alejandro, 324-325, 608, 1310
Fry, Peter H., 609-610, 1311-1313
Fuenzalida, Fernando, 1151
Fülling, Erich, 611-619, 1314
Fundação Cultural do Estado de Bahia, 620

Gabriel, Chester E., 621, 1315
Gaçon, Annie, 622
Gade, Daniel W., 1152
Galeano, Eduardo H., 623
Gallardo, Jorge E., 624-625
Galvão, Eduardo E., 626-628
Gamonal-Ataucusi, Ezechiel, 1153

United States Government
Department of the Army,
176, 353, 1010-1011, 1088,
1108
Urbano, Henrique O., 1232-1233
Urquiaga, José, 1234

Valcarcel [Esparza], Carlos D.,
1235
Valente, Francisco, 1388
Valente, Waldemar, 1012-1019
Van Young, Eric, 264
Vanackere, H., 1389
Vanderwood, Paul J., 265
Vargas Ugarte, Rubén, 1236
Varon, Rafael, 1237
Vasallo, Manuel, 1238
Vasconcelos, Salomão de, 1020
Vega, M. Moreno, 1021
Velasco Toro, José, 266
Velásquez, Rafael E., 1109
Velho, Yvonne M. A., 1022. *See
also* Maggie, Yvonne
Ventur, Pierre, 267
Verger, Pierre, 147-148, 439,
1023-1032
Vergolino e Silva, Anaíza, 587-
588, 1033-1034
Vidale, Maria, 1035
Vieira, Waldo, 1400
Villalba, Aglimira M., 1250
Villa Rojas, Alfonso, 268-270
Villela, Lavinia C., 1036
Vogt, Evon Z., 271
Vuoto, P., 342

Wachtel, Nathan, 17, 46, 1239-
1240
Wagley, Charles, 177, 1037-1039
Walker, Sheila S., 149-150, 1040-
1043
Warren, Donald, Jr., 1044-1045,
1390

Wasson, R. Gordon, 272
Waterman, Richard A., 151, 665
Watson, James B., 1046
Watson, Peter, 1047
Weber, Wilfried, 1391
Weingartner, Lindolfo, 1392-1393
Wellington, R. A., 1048
Westra, Allard D. W., 1049
Whitten, Norman E., Jr., 152-153
Wiebe, James P., 1050
Willeke, Venantius, 1051, 1394
Willems, Emílio, 47, 1052-1053,
1395-1396
Williams, Ethel L., 154
Williams, Paul V. A., 1054-1058
Wilson, Bryan R., 312, 343, 1059,
1397
Wilson, Carter, 273
Wilson, John, 281
Winters, Clyde-Ahmad, 1060
Winz, Antônio P., 313, 1061
Wistrand, Lila, 1241
Wittkower, E. D., 155
Wöhlcke, Manfred, 1062-1063
Wolf, Gemmea, 344
Woodward, Ruth E., 1064
Wright, Pablo G., 345-346
Wright, Robin M., 1065
Wulfhorst, Ingo, 1066

X, 1067
Xavier, Francisco C., 1398-1400
Ximénez, Francisco, 178, 274

Yai, Olabiyi B., 1068
Young, Philip D., 288

Zanichelli, Nicola, 1069
Zaretsky, Irving I., 156
Zespo, Emmanuel, 1401-1403
Zimmerman, Ben, 1070
Zimmerman, Charlotte, 275-276
Zuidema, R. T., 1242

Index of Main Movements
and Individuals

The entry numbers of the main or more substantial or significant references are included here (i.e., those mentioned in the titles of the items or in the annotations). The list is therefore not exhaustive as to text references, but is fairly complete as to known named movements, apart from those that are designated only by general area or by dates. Founders, leaders, and other significant individuals appear under their most common names, but alternative spellings and names are also given or cross-referenced.

The materials on the one particular movement placed in a separate section at the end of the volume refer primarily to the movement concerned, Umbanda. Where this movement is treated along with others it may be found through the various other entry numbers also given for Umbanda.

Crusada Cristiana para Naciones, 1223
Culto a la Mercaderia, 317
Cult of the Cross, 170, 220, 249, 268-270, 275-276
Cult of the Cross (Paraguay), 1091
Cuzcat revolt. *See* War of the Castes

Divine Light Mission, 43
Dos Santos, Deoscóredes, 1043

Eglesia Evangelica Unida. *See* Toba Movements
Elias (Father), 198
El Nino Fidencio, 240
El Zapaltar, 323
Espiritualismo Trinitario Mariano, 227-228

Ford, Arnold, 138

Garvey, Marcus, 76
Gauchos movement, 305
Gege, 763-764, 900, 1011
Guarani Millennialism, 290-291, 297-299, 304-312, 344, 351, 354, 393, 468-469, 637, 756, 805-808, 828-830, 869, 884, 896, 962-963, 965-966, 968, 1059, 1089, 1091-1092, 1096, 1102, 1105
Guarayu, 304, 352
Guaycuru, 323
Guiravera, 880, 1096, 1100

Hallejuah, 305
"Hand of Stone." *See* Rumi Maqui
Hare Krishna, 43
Hernandez, J. G., 11
Herrada, José Bernardo, 264

Hommes-dieux, 357, 680, 806, 994, 1096, 1099, 1104, 1108
Huaca cults, 46, 1182, 1199
Huanca cult, 1148

Ica revival, 1190
Iglesia Apostolica de la Fe en Cristo Jesus, 206-208, 211-212
Iglesia de Dios, 279
Iglesia Mexicana Patriacal del Elias. *See* Elias
Independent churches, 66, 78, 109, 206-208, 211-212, 216, 279, 283. *See also* Moskito revival; Toba movements
Inkarri, 1156-1157, 1200, 1207
Islam, 420, 461-462, 471, 492, 504, 577, 603-604, 629, 688, 833, 890, 896, 911, 1014, 1018, 1060
Ismael, 1398
Israelitas del Nuevo Pacto Universal, 1110, 1113-1115, 1120, 1129, 1132, 1134, 1149, 1153-1154, 1159, 1163, 1170-1176, 1202, 1204, 1208, 1210, 1212-1215, 1217-1224, 1230-1231

Jacinto Canek revolt, 253
Jaguaripe, 470. *See also* Santidade
Japanese movements, 578, 650, 825, 960
João Santos, 983
Joaquin (Prophet), 216
Juan de la Cruz, 174, 270
Jump-Up Church, 283

Kamiko, Venanciéo, 1065
Kardecism, 230, 375, 434, 473, 539, 611, 769, 826, 1058,

Index of Main Movements and Individuals

1066, 1269-1270, 1277, 1324-
1326, 1337, 1355, 1383
Keekhwei (Prophetess), 553-554
Ketu (sect of Candomble), 658,
804
King, Walter Serge. *See* Adefunmi
Kraho messianism, 792-793, 966

"Lord-of-the-Earthquake" cult,
1152
Lord of the Miracles, 1229
Loreto messianism, 308
Lucumi, 54, 105
Lundum do Padre, 415
Luz del Mundo, 216

McGregor, Pedro, 769
McGuire, G. A., 73, 110

Macumba, 4, 54, 366, 375, 381,
386, 396, 401, 419, 422, 427,
435, 438, 456, 504, 508, 513,
522, 536, 540, 544, 556, 567,
571, 576, 578, 581, 589, 595,
611-613, 619, 630, 639, 687,
723, 727, 729, 735-736, 767,
787-788, 811, 839, 845, 866,
878, 890, 908, 942-943, 975,
982, 997, 1008, 1047, 1060,
1062, 1250, 1365, 1373
Male. *See* Islam
Mama Chi, 282-283, 286-288
Mammy Water, 118
Manco Inca, 46, 1116
Man-gods. *See* Hommes-dieux
Mantfort, Antonio Diaz, 266
Maria Candelaria. *See* Candelaria,
Maria
Maria Lionza, 83, 109
Mariano, 180
Maroons, 56, 132, 229, 244, 870
Martinez y Luciano, Pedro, 342
Mayan "church," 184

Mayombe, 78
Mazavi, 1093
Mea, Luis, 1073
Miskito revival, 277-278, 280-281
Mixton revolt, 46
Moro Oncoy, 1137
Moscoso (Bishop), 1119
Moskito revival. *See* Miskito
revival
Moures (Prophet), 1003
Muckers, 430
Myallism, 78

Nago, 402, 741, 761, 838, 948, 1028
Nanigo, 78, 323
Napalpi movement, 323
Natochi, 323
Néo-Pitagorismo, 1008
"New Christs," 308, 385, 626, 683,
722, 724, 859, 880
"New Savior" movement, 260
Nossa Senhora de Copacabana,
313, 1061

Obeah, 56, 78, 136, 168
Obera, 305, 307-308, 880, 1101
Ordem Espiritualista Crista, 529,
1066
Order of Damballa Hwedo, 101
"Our Father" cult, 1098
Our Lady of the Rosary of Black
Men, 1044
Oxum, 325, 452
Oyotunji Village, 68, 101, 110, 146

"Pae Martiniano," 369
Page cult, 1094
Pagelanca, 381, 915
Pajelanca. *See* Pagelanca
Palomino, Edwardo C., 1224
Pampa del Indio, 323
Panan, 658
Parma, Guaman, 1201

230